# NOBLESSE OBLIGE

# NOBLESSE OBLIGE

## Charity & Cultural Philanthropy in Chicago, 1849-1929

KATHLEEN D. MCCARTHY



The University of Chicago Press
Chicago & London

KATHLEEN D. MCCARTHY is a Visiting Research Fellow at the Rockefeller Foundation.

The University of Chicago Press, Chicago 60637
The University of Chicago Press, Ltd., London


89 88 87 86 85 84 83 82     5 4 3 2 1

**Library of Congress Cataloging in Publication Data**

McCarthy, Kathleen D.
Noblesse oblige.

Bibliography: p.
Includes index.
1. Chicago (Ill.)—Charities—History—19th century. 2. Chicago (Ill.)—Charities—History—20th century. I. Title.
HV99.C39M35     361.7′09773′11     81-21849
ISBN 0-226-55580-1     AACR2

For
Barry D. Karl

# CONTENTS

# PREFACE

William Butler Ogden was a model civic steward. During the crucial decades between Chicago's inception and the Civil War, he conscientiously volunteered for a welter of public and private positions, personally helping to shape the city's government, economy, charities, and cultural institutions. Nor was his example uncommon. During the antebellum years, men and women unstintingly volunteered their time and talents to deal with the city's changing needs, moved by religious injunctions, the desire to protect their investments, and a sharp sense of noblesse oblige.

Noblesse oblige can take many forms. In the Old World, it represented the duties attendant upon noble birth. But in a country devoid of hereditary aristocracy and the trappings of baronial tradition, it took on new meaning. Transported to American shores with the first settlers, it survived and flourished. Often, it is interpreted as richesse oblige: the duties of the rich to the society which has enriched them. But it has another, equally long-lived interpretation which is often overlooked. Civic stewardship—the notion that successful citizens owe a dual obligation of time and money to the communities in which they have prospered—is a uniquely urban interpretation of this ancient ideal. In a highly mobile society such as ours, it has continually served to graft people's loyalties to their adopted cities, rekindling their commitment to the community ideal, and encouraging them to assume responsibility for the provision of essential social and cultural institutions.

By 1929, men of Ogden's ilk seemed to be a dying breed. Caught up in a whirlwind of fads and amusements, citizens were content to "buy out" of civic responsibility, signing checks while lavishing the fruits of their leisure upon themselves. Harvey Zorbaugh's classic study of *The Gold Coast and the Slum* (1929) painted a vivid picture of elites far more interested in pursuing their own amusement amid the social swim than in serving their community, a portrait mirrored in contemporary literary masterpieces like F. Scott Fitzgerald's *The Great Gatsby*.[1]

To understand the import of this change it is necessary only to look at a newspaper, or examine the legions of jeremiads for our "sick" and "dying" cities which filled the bookshelves of the 1960s. Urbanites no longer seemed to care about the fate of their towns. Pointing an accusing finger, critics argued that those who could afford to fled to the suburbs, leaving the increasingly impoverished central cities to care for the swelling populations of the poor, strangled by a ring of affluent indifference. Americans had turned their backs on *The Other America* cried social critic Michael Harrington, they had blinded themselves to their communities' needs, they had forgotten the poor.[2]

Accordingly, scholars embarked on a witch hunt for the culprits who had inspired this deadening apathy. Big government was a favorite choice. Because municipal and federal agencies oversaw the care of the needy, the schools, and the clinics, citizens no longer felt the need to intervene. The torch of responsibility had been passed.

Did community apathy develop naturally, an insidious concomitant of the welfare state? Or did it antedate the Great Depression? Ironically, although the question of citizen participation in governmental affairs has been vigorously debated for decades, the issue of individual responsibility for the development of nonprofit organizations remains virtually unexplored. The best community-oriented studies, those of W. Lloyd Warner, Sam Bass Warner, Jr., and E. Digby Baltzell, argue that local elites abandoned political responsibility as their interests became nationalized, but say little of their role in maintaining charities, hospitals, or museums.[3] Nor does the voluminous literature on charity and social work provide a satisfactory answer. Most confine their discussions to the exploits of individual pathbreakers[4] and institutions,[5] or minimize the role of the twentieth-century steward in order to chart the professionalization of social work[6] or the rise of the welfare state.[7] Others eschew local issues in order to descry broader, national trends.[8] Even the handful of studies which have attempted to remedy this inadequacy focus on a limited range of institutions, or an abbreviated time frame.[9]

Between the founding of the city's first nonsectarian asylum in 1849 and the final years before the advent of the Great Depression in 1929, hundreds of individual charities and cultural undertakings were founded in Chicago. Some perished, others endured. For the sake of coherence and manageability, I have chosen to focus on three areas of endeavor: family welfare, medical charities, and cultural institutions. Each embodied different imperatives, and each experienced the impact of professionalization at a different rate. Despite their importance, many of these organizations have received little scholarly attention. Only the cultural institutions have been subjected to intensive study, and then only for a limited period bracketed by the temporal framework I have proposed. Because of the magnitude of the available data, only a single city has been surveyed. Mention should also be made of my decision to treat men's and women's organizations separately in the first half of the study but not the second. Ever the Victorians, nineteenth-century Americans scrupulously separated their undertakings by gender, compelling me to do the same.

Admittedly, other organizations might have been included. Each of the city's myriad religious and ethnic agencies has a fascinating history, and each deserves to be chronicled in a separate study of its own. Because they were limited in focus, serving only a specific sector of the population, they did not hold the answers to the questions I have posed. Reform organizations have also been omitted. Many have already been amply documented. More important, their financial records are often impossible to obtain, making them unsuitable for inclusion here. Only city-wide, nonprofit organizations have been included, highlighting the activities of the men and women who created permanent institutions in response to local needs.

Three disparate factors inspired Chicago's civic stewards and ultimately shaped the nature of their responses: social attitudes about private beneficence, the manner in which urban problems were perceived and communicated, and the available opportunities for individual social action. Stated briefly, the first factor deals with the image of the Samaritan in sermons, periodicals, advice and etiquette books, movies and the popular press. Perception focuses on the impact of technology and urban sprawl on the decision-making process, while opportunity deals with the issue of professionalization.

During the eighty-year interim between the founding of the first asylum and the economic collapse of 1929, four generations of Chicagoans matured, came to power, and passed from the scene: the volunteers of the 1850s, Gilded Age plutocrats, progressive iconoclasts, and Jazz Age donors and dilettantes. Although these categories are not necessarily mutually exclusive—the Gilded Age had its donors and the Jazz Age its volunteers—each reflects the pervasive patterns of the era.

Each generation had its own distinctive criteria, composition, and techniques. Antebellum Chicagoans created enduring institutions with little more than native skills, gifts-in-kind, and an urgent desire to succeed. Rather than dealing directly with the poor, Gilded Age stewards fashioned and administered centrally located institutions, where they could mingle with the rest of society on safe and neutral ground. The progressives shifted their gaze to the city's neighborhoods, enlisting the aid of experts in their drive to revitalize the homes and habitats of the poor. By the twenties, a new technocratic elite had wrested much of the decision-making responsibility from native Samaritans, leaving a reform-sated citizenry to pursue their pleasures as donors, fund raisers, and agency liaisons.

Several factors conspired to whittle the role of the civic steward into its final form. As Chicago jumped the confines of the traditional walking city, stretching endlessly outward along rail and transit lines, it transcended the range of individual capabilities and perceptions. At the same time, well-to-do citizens were insulating themselves from the rest of society, turned inward by the strikes, violence, and heterogeneity which earmarked the fin-de-siècle city. Comfortably ensconced in their privatized world of wealth and breeding, many willingly deferred to the claims of middle-class "visitors" who vowed to monitor urban needs on a full-time basis.

Secure in their Gold Coast mansions and verdant suburbs on the north shore, Jazz Age elites increasingly came to measure community needs through abstractions: publicity, lectures, the photographs in annual reports. Communications innovations, like professionalization, separated the twentieth-century donor from the object of his largesse. Even as the city's stewards withdrew from the decision-making arena, professionals conspired to further diminish their role, setting restrictions on gifts and reshaping the prerogatives of boards.

These are some of the trends which hastened the transition from active to monetary beneficence on the eve of the Great Depression. It was a complex transition, not easily reduced to glib formulas or simple explanations. Professionalization, reform nausea, the rise of modern communications technology, urbanization, suburbanization—each played a role. In the process, Chicagoans shifted from a service ethic to a leisure ethic, turning inward upon themselves. The stage had been set for the events of the New Deal.

A book is rarely an individual achievement, and this volume is no exception. My most profound debt is to Barry D. Karl, who oversaw the project from its inception, and whose work has served as a constant source of inspiration. I also owe an enormous debt of gratitude to Stanley N. Katz, who unstintingly gave of his time, assistance, and expertise. Neil Harris's insights constructively challenged my comfortable assumptions, and Perry Duis alerted me to many unusual aspects of Chicago's history which I might otherwise have overlooked. Countless librarians and archivists at the Chicago Historical Society, the University of Chicago, the University of Illinois at Chicago Circle, Hull-House, the Newberry Library, the State Historical Society of Wisconsin, and the Art Institute of Chicago also aided me as the project unfolded, but Archie Motley of the Chicago Historical Society deserves special thanks. Through his humor, skill, and untiring assistance, he transformed what might have been a tedious odyssey into a challenging quest.

Others offered their support and enthusiasm at critical junctures, considerably easing my task. Through their comments, friendship, and well-timed encouragement, Kenneth L. Kusmer, Kathleen N. Conzen, Joel Colton, Lamar Riley, and Malcolm L. Richardson contributed more to this book than they can ever know. As have my parents, and Nan. I thank them all. My final debt, to my husband, Christopher, is too deep to be adequately expressed, for it is impossible to thank someone with mere words for so many years of patience, proofreadings, and love.

# PART ONE
## 1849-1889

*Godey's Lady's Book,* vol. 62 (1861) (frontispiece entitled "1861"). Courtesy of General Research Division, The New York Public Library, Astor, Lenox and Tilden Foundations.

# 1
# BENEVOLENT LADIES

## I

Each generation has interpreted the notion of civic stewardship to fit the special contours of its world. The antebellum era was the heyday of the benevolent volunteer, and personal service the leitmotiv of its ethic. Goaded by pulpit, press, and popular expectations, antebellum urbanites flooded into the side streets of their cities, personally aiding the sinner and the poor, surveying developing needs, and creating new associations to deal with them. Many responded generously, unstintingly, offering time, and often money as well, to the task of civic betterment. Through their offices, the quality of urban life was continually enhanced by the introduction of new ideas and novel solutions to urban ills.

Wealth was inextricably linked to public service from the outset, and if one succeeded in attaining riches he knew that he must also assume the attendant obligations of stewardship. By virtue of their leisure, breeding, education, and success, the rich were deemed ideally suited to minister to their cities' needs, particularly in periods when governmental functions were limited. According to one source, more than half of New York's richest 1% were involved in voluntary organizations prior to the Civil War, donating a major portion of their leisure hours to civic activities. Similarly, upper-crust Philadelphians and Bostonians spent much of their free time creating necessary charitable and cultural amenities themselves.[1]

However, these statistics obscure the inclusive nature of the antebellum ethic and the heterogeneity of the public's response. All classes were expected to participate, each contributing to the public weal in a specific way. While businessmen sparked a range of civic, charitable, and cultural organizations, women ministered directly to select sectors of the poor, visiting them in their homes and creating institutions for their care. The rich donated time and money, while the poor fashioned informal networks of mutual aid. In Chicago, clerks labored shoulder-to-shoulder with employers, dressmakers and milliners mingled with their patrons, and a few evangelical societies even conscripted volunteers from ethnic congregations. Although countless citizens undoubtedly remained aloof, those who did come forward displayed a strong commitment to community welfare, serving in a variety of time-consuming offices to ensure the continued survival of their fledgling ventures. Voluntarism was the social currency which bound antebellum communities together, nurturing a sense of communal spirit and constantly renewing public commitment to community well-being.

Volunteer efforts were shaped and marshaled by a variety of factors. Prevailing notions of stewardship urged men and women, the well-to-do and those of more moderate means, to participate, each in his or her own special way. The periodic religious revivals which swept the nation in the 1820s, and again in the fifties, helped to kindle the voluntaristic spirit, sending the middle classes into the slums to labor in concert with the rich, binding them to their impoverished brethren with ties of familiarity and aid.

Another important factor hinged upon the manner and speed with which news of innovative programs circulated from city to city. Initially, the seaboard cities monopolized the spread of news. Hamlets like Chicago were informational backwaters, informed of movements and trends only by the occasional passing traveler. However, by the 1850s the lines of communication had been extended through the introduction of commercial rail, stage, and lake travel. Churches, correspondence, itinerant lecturers, settlers, and local residents who traveled to the coast with increasing regularity on missions of business and pleasure all helped to spread the latest currents of culture, charity, and reform.

Churches played an absolutely central role in rousing public support for charitable endeavors and formulating ground rules for their development. Clergymen were in an ideal position to assume such a role, apprised of the latest trends by conferences, correspondence, religious journals, and additions to their congregations. Moreover, they had direct access to the consciences and purse strings of the well-to-do, for this was an era in which church membership was a fundamental badge of respectability, those "who did not attend church being anathema."[2]

The clergy were aided in their campaign to touch the consciences of their parishioners by the shape of the city itself. Most mid-nineteenth-century American cities were still "walking cities," compact settlements in which neighborhoods were often mixed, and rich and poor lived cheek-by-jowl in "miserable hovels . . . mixed up with the most beautiful and costly stores and edifices."[3] Most people still walked to work, daily encountering fellow citizens of all economic strata. Casual contact was augmented by the more rigorous examinations of tract distributors, city missionaries, and charity visitors. Armed with impressions garnered at close range, citizens labored to keep pace with geometrically increasing needs, creating new undertakings as each new problem was unearthed.

And problems abounded. Poverty was endemic in the larger American cities after 1800. In the colonial era, the town poor were boarded with families at the public expense, and vagrants "warned out," or sent to the next town, where the process would be repeated. Although these were satisfactory means of dealing with want in small communities, urban growth and anonymity quickly diminished the efficacy of such policies. The first voluntary societies began to appear early in the eighteenth century, proliferating rapidly after the Revolution. Asylums, too, began to dot the urbanscape from the 1820s onward, as scores of private orphanages, reform schools, hospitals, and homes for erring women took their places among publicly sponsored prisons, almshouses, and insane asylums to shelter, discipline, and train the poor. Within institutions and in the slums, volunteers unstintingly ministered to the needs of the deviant and the dispossessed.[4]

Whether drawn to charities or culture, sponsors participated in a very personal way, often amassing paintings and books, caring for inmates, or distributing alms themselves. Antebellum Americans had very little patience with self-proclaimed experts. With the exception of the clergy, most professions were weak, disorganized, or nonexistent. Medicine was torn by sectarianism, as homeopaths, allopaths, and a spate of eclectic iconoclasts like the Thompsonians competed for patients and public regard. Law, too, was atomized, quietly recruiting and training apprentices in hundreds of separate offices throughout the country. Social work was shared between clergy and volunteers. And while a few intrepid souls like New York collector

James Jackson Jarves tried vainly to win apostles to their cultural views, every man deemed himself a qualified judge of art, willingly deferring to no one.[5]

In an era of primitive communications and limited governmental responsibility, voluntarism played a unique role in maintaining stability and community cohesion, forging a personal bond between rich, middle class, and poor. Civic stewardship—noblesse oblige—this was the "social glue" which bound urbanites to their neighbors.

## II

Within this framework, both men and women were allotted specific roles, each with its own distinctive purpose and rationale. While voluntarism was the earmark of Chicago's antebellum civic stewards, asylum work emerged as the special terrain of the feminine volunteer. From a modest beginning in church work and sewing societies, Chicago's benevolent ladies quickly moved to the more compelling task of institution building, founding a variety of Homes between 1849 and 1865. In addition to helping the poor, these activities netted their sponsors a number of personal rewards. For the ambitious, such service offered an opportunity to shape the lives and destinies of others; for the devout, a means of personal salvation; and for the timid, a conservative alternative to abolitionism and the women's movement. Born of necessity, and heartily sanctioned by community and church, feminine beneficence became an increasingly significant factor in the development of Chicago's social welfare schema on the eve of the Civil War.

A New York woman, Isabella Marshall Graham, is generally credited with introducing the idea of feminine benevolent associations to American soil. Modeled on a similar undertaking in London, her Society for the Relief of Poor Widows with Small Children (1797) employed worthy widows, conducted Sabbath schools, and educated impoverished orphans. Women in other cities soon copied her innovation, founding scores of organizations to minister to the poor, the unchurched, and the very young.[6]

As the nation moved westward, feminine charities kept pace. Chicago's first societies dated from the 1830s, when the town consisted of little more than a handful of ill-assorted buildings on the open prairie. In an era when servants were scarce, and ready-made household goods even more elusive, charity and churchwork provided a brief respite from the drudgery of frontier life. Ostensibly devised to sew for the poor, or raise funds for the church, many of these groups were quite informal, initiating ambitious programs during times of need but settling back into the comfortable routine of the sewing society when the crisis had passed. Under the rubric of charity, ladies of the Dorcas Society (1835) and the Ladies Benevolent Association (1843) gathered in each other's homes to chat and share the warmth of human companionship. After the last garment was finished and set aside, husbands and beaux were called in to supper, underscoring the social nature of their meetings.

Their maiden venture into the realm of institutional work was the city's first nonsectarian Home, the Chicago Orphan Asylum (COA), founded in 1849. Prior to 1825, orphanages had been confined primarily to the eastern and southern seacoast cities, ports of entry for European innovations like August Hermann Francke's ragged school, which served as a model for some. The diffusion of the asylum paralleled the growth of the nation's transportation network. Utica, Albany, Troy, and Buffalo built Homes shortly after the opening of the Erie Canal in 1825, and frontier towns like Chicago followed suit in the late 1840s and 1850s, after the completion of the Illinois and Michigan Canal (1848) and the introduction of rail service.

Men and mails plied their way over these routes, spreading news of eastern humanitarian undertakings. Travel generated new needs, even as it served to disseminate models for asylum development. Epidemics regularly stalked the nation's highways and waterways. Carried from town to town by travelers, cholera and smallpox left a legacy of invalidism and dependency wherever they passed. Some parents died, others abandoned unwanted children on public conveyances, leaving them to fend for themselves or be cared for by public authorities. As western towns urbanized, they began to experience all of the social ills of their sister cities in the east.

By the mid-1850s, hundreds of homeless children, many of them orphaned or abandoned by westward-bound families, roamed Chicago's streets. One source hysterically estimated their number in the thousands. Growing up beyond the sphere of parental discipline, startlingly profane, adept at the arts of begging and petty theft, content to live in filthy alleyways, under bridges, and in packing crates, they were regarded by some as "little two-legged brutes with no more correct moral sense than so many pigs whose habits they imitate(d)."[7] Unattached women presented another problem. Separated from kith and kin by migration, many arrived destitute and alone. Some found work in reputable households and firms, some spent weeks fruitlessly searching for work as their tiny cash reserves dwindled, and some were lured into prostitution by sharp-eyed madames and panderers who played on their confusion and need. Desperate, unskilled, impoverished, many were forced to choose between the brothel and the street. By 1865, there were an estimated five thousand prostitutes operating both in and out of the city's hundreds of houses of ill fame.[8]

The plight of the children was particularly compelling. Chicagoans had always felt a great deal of uneasiness about the practice of consigning impoverished youngsters to the public almshouse, with its dilapidated buildings, fetid miasmas, and unsavory population. The issue came to a head during the cholera epidemic of 1849. By midsummer, the poorhouse was so badly overcrowded that cholera victims and their children were being turned away. The city's Protestant churches appealed to families to take the children in as apprentices, but with little result. On August 3, designated a day of fasting and prayer by President Tyler in response to the emergency, Chicagoans met in the First Baptist Church to consider the fate of the orphans. It was quickly decided that an asylum must be built to accommodate them. Four hundred dollars was raised by passing the hat, a board of directresses appointed ten days later, and on September 11 three children were admitted to the Home. The era of the asylum had begun.

In a pattern common to all of the city's Homes, feminine volunteers controlled "every aspect of the Asylum and the head employee merely followed their directions."[9] The Chicago Orphan Asylum (COA) suffered a high turnover rate among its matrons, a problem shared by all of Chicago's early asylums. Between 1849 and 1868, ten women were hired, stayed briefly, then left. In order to sustain the continuity of day-to-day operations, board members made the clothes and bedding themselves, purchased supplies, investigated and admitted inmates, hired and fired the staff, nursed the children, placed them, taught them, mothered them, and when necessary buried them as well. Funding was a constant problem. After opening in a rented frame bungalow, the asylum lived a peripatetic, hand-to-mouth existence, moving through a succession of rented cottages before finally coming to rest in a permanent institution in 1854. The agency remained unendowed through the fifties, its requests for municipal subsidies repeatedly denied. Directresses districted the city and canvassed relentlessly to raise the necessary funds to keep the Home open, staging fairs and benefits as well, often doing "the actual drudgery of the entertainments" themselves.[10]

Board members rendered extraordinary service during these precarious first years, visiting the institution daily, ministering to the children's needs, and occasionally adopting inmates into their own families. Some even tarried in the city during the cholera-ridden summers of the early fifties to ensure the children's proper care.[11]

Their rule was strict but benign. The board placed a high premium on obedience, in order to facilitate "the proper maintenance and education of the future citizens of our commonwealth."[12] Youngsters were expected to help with the daily chores, memorize Scripture, hymns and prayers, and conscientiously attend classes at the nearby public school. Yet rules were few and punishments mild. Whips and solitary confinement were not part of the daily fare at the COA.[13]

Nevertheless, the directresses wielded a tremendous amount of discretionary power over the lives of the orphans, half-orphans, street children and boarders entrusted to their care. Between 1852 and 1861, 48.9% of the inmates were committed by their parents, 44.3% by city officials, and 6.8% by friends and kin.[14] Directresses considered the merits of each individual case themselves. The city could commit youngsters on a variety of pretexts, a prerogative which was later extended to other asylums as well. Children of dead, imprisoned, or abusive parents, as well as the offspring of prostitutes and habitual drunkards, all faced the possibility of being arrested and placed in the COA. Eventually, these youths were sent out to farms in Illinois and other states, often on the flimsiest of reasons. People desiring a child would simply write in, specifying their preference, and the inmate best fitting that description would be trundled off to the train and sent to them. In return, the new family was required to sign an agreement to provide religious instruction, clothe and feed the child, treat him kindly, and give him a new suit of ordinary wearing apparel, a Bible, and $20 when he reached sixteen. In the process, the farmer obtained an inexpensive laborer, the city was rid of another potential vagrant, and the institution frequently received much needed donations of fresh produce and fuel. Only the child netted dubious gains.[15]

Later asylums emulated the patterns, policies, and standards set by the COA. Housed in a vacant west-side tavern, the Chicago Home for the Friendless (CHFF) opened on August 8, 1858. A catchall institution, it opened its doors to all women and children who applied. Neither toddlers nor grandmothers were turned away, for, as the directresses proudly explained, "No person is too poor, too old, too young, or tried by too great a variety of complications, as to forbid her admission here. Red tape is not in vogue at the Home for the Friendless."[16]

Like the Erring Woman's Refuge founded a few years later, the

Home made do "with nothing but what was begged or borrowed."[17] Although little information survives about the original furnishings, it was probably decorated in the same manner as the COA, filled with cast-off chairs and beds donated by sympathetic citizens. Accommodations were far from luxurious, and the emphasis was on temporary care. Homeless and neglected children passing through its portals were quickly transferred to rural homes. Destitute girls were taught domestic skills and placed with reputable families, while adult women were sheltered only until they found jobs and suitable lodgings elsewhere. Internal management was informal, the rules simple and few. Inmates were expected to help with chores, attend school, rise and retire at stated hours, and keep presentably neat.

"Owing to the difficulty of obtaining suitable persons for holding official positions in the Home, such persons being then not as readily obtained," the directresses did much of the work themselves.[18] The supply committee solicited funds and provisions, the reception committee admitted and placed inmates, the reference committee investigated applicants, and individual directresses volunteered to nurse the inmates themselves. In many instances, the latter task was more dangerous than they realized, for until the eve of the twentieth century most asylums were little better than pestholes. Cholera, scarlet fever, whooping cough, smallpox, and hospital gangrene afflicted the inmates with appalling regularity. In one particularly chilling instance, the CHFF's physician recorded the outbreak of "gangrenous sore mouth of the most rapid and fatal kind . . . . A child one day might be affected with dullness and evident stupor, and on examination, were slight redness and soreness of the gums. These precursory symptoms, if not promptly and effectually counteracted, might on the following day have developed a gangrene that presaged death."[19] Nevertheless, women like board president Jane Hoge made daily visits to the Home, nursing the inmates and laying out those who had died.

"To be a manager in those early days meant work in season and out of season, not only at the Home but in many of the out of the way places of the city and the adjacent country."[20] The investigating committee ventured into some of the city's worst rookeries, including the notorious Sands, a vicious assemblage of shanties, saloons, gambling dens and brothels. As one veteran pointed out, "Many a lady took her life in her hand as she frequented the squalor and wretchedness of the then rapidly growing city."[21] "One could never forget the homes we sometimes visited," shuddered another.[22]

Funding presented an ongoing source of anxiety. One directress later recalled exhausting soliciting campaigns which had taken her "from store to store to feed those hungry children."[23] When cash was tight, inmates dined on leftovers from the Tremont Hotel. In 1860, the board began to publish *The Home Visitor,* to generate public interest in their cause. Although the editors hoped to one day make it "equal in interest and circulation [to] the organ of its sister institution in New York, the *Advocate and Guardian,*" their "ability to make it larger and better was circumscribed by their poverty."[24] The Home's financial distress was briefly alleviated by a $10,000 grant from banker Jonathan Burr, which underwrote the construction of a permanent building in 1860. Nevertheless, the directresses still faced many "dark days when the provision(s) and fuel were getting low with little prospect of replenishment."[25] By 1861, the infant organization was once again in precarious financial straights as the board "voted that no more applicants for admission be received until our treasury be replenished."[26]

The pattern of limited funds, informal organization, and intense personal involvement by feminine board members was repeated in the city's other private asylums: the Chicago Nursery and Half-Orphan Asylum (CNHOA, 1860), the Home for Aged and Indigent Females (1861), and the Erring Woman's Refuge, founded in 1863 to rehabilitate young women "urged into a life of vice by orphanage, poverty, and deception, at a period when the young heart is confiding and unsuspecting."[27] Women did whatever was necessary to ensure the management of day-to-day operations: sewing clothing and bedding, raising funds, investigating applicants, sometimes even cooking the inmates' meals in their own kitchens.[28]

Who were these extraordinary women, and why did they participate so enthusiastically? Unfortunately, little biographical information survives for them. The majority were drawn from the city's Protestant congregations. Each church was accorded a requisite number of places to fill on the various boards. Because they were chosen to represent congregations of varying economic status, asylum boards included professional, white-collar, and a limited number of blue-collar wives. The officers, however, were generally wed to businessmen and professionals. With few exceptions they were married, and some still had toddlers at home. A composite portrait (see table 1), drawn from the small number listed in the 1850 manuscript census report, reveals a woman born in New England or New York, with three children and a small (1.4) staff of household servants.[29]

Asylums also had corollary boards of male trustees who oversaw the

**Table 1**
**Characteristics of Asylum Directresses Listed in 1850 Census**

| Age in 1850 | Place of Birth | Number Children | Ages of Children | Number Servants | Husband's Occupation | Property |
|---|---|---|---|---|---|---|
| Under 25 (1) | New England (8) | 0 (2) | Less than 1 (3) | 0 (4) | Businessman (10) | Not listed (13) |
| 25–30 (3) | Mid Atlantic (5) | 1 (2) | 1–3 (8) | 1 (6) | Physician (2) | $5,000–$9,999 (1) |
| 31–35 (3) | Midwest (1) | 2 (2) | 4–6 (7) | 2 (3) | Lawyer (1) | $10,000–$20,000 (2) |
| 36–40 (4) | Europe (1) | 3 (4) | 7–10 (11) | 3 (1) | Bookkeeper (1) | |
| 41–45 (4) | Not listed (1) | 4 (2) | 11–14 (11) | 4 (1) | Gov. agent (1) | |
| 46–50 (1) | | 5 (2) | 15–18 (4) | 5 (1) | Widow (1) | |
| | | 6 (2) | 19 and above (3) | | | |

NOTE: Numerals in parentheses = number of women in category.

management of legal and fiscal details. Unlike the women's boards, the trustees were almost uniformly drawn from among the landholding businessmen and attorneys who had arrived in Chicago in the 1830s and early 1840s, when land was cheap and opportunities plentiful. The cumbersome system of dual trusteeship may seem incongruous at first glance, but it must be remembered that women had little legal authority in this period, particularly where financial matters were involved. Until 1840, Massachusetts law forbade them to serve as treasurers, even of their own sewing societies, unless a man assumed responsibility for them. In Illinois, the Married Woman's Property Act was not passed until 1861. A separate board of male trustees, particularly if they were prominent citizens, helped to inspire public confidence while sidestepping any legal problems.

Churches played a particularly important role in funneling both men and women into charitable endeavors. Ladies comprised a growing share of the nation's congregations after 1800, and as American religion became increasingly "feminized," ministers tirelessly exhorted their swelling flocks of lady parishioners to join forces in the service of the Lord. "This holy vocation of charity has been committed to her," exclaimed Reverend Young of Boston. "It is her task, her lot, her ministry, her special destination; and it constitutes one of her highest claims to our gratitude and admiration."[30] Chicago ministers agreed. As Reverend W. W. Everts admiringly noted, "It is while thus engaged man sees her his highest ideal of 'the beautiful, the true, and the good.'"[31]

Ministers and national benevolent associations helped to spread the asylum movement to new cities at the edge of the frontier. The religious press also regularly published accounts of American and European charities. As Timothy L. Smith points out, "Religious newspapers reviewed English books and pointed to European examples in their efforts to quicken humanitarian impulses."[32]

National organizations like the American Female Guardian Society provided a second important source of inspiration. Founded in 1834, this feminine antivice group developed a host of auxiliaries stretching from New York to Chicago by 1840. The society's far-flung empire was held intact through letters, annual meetings, and its journal, the *Advocate for Moral Reform.* Launched "to afford a channel of communication, in which the thoughts and feelings of females throughout the country may more freely mingle," the *Advocate* kept its 20,000 subscribers up-to-date on the workings of the agency's Magdelen home and Home for the Friendless.[33] Almost a decade before the founding of its "sister institution" in Chicago, Homes for the Friendless began to appear in affiliate cities like Poughkeepsie (1847), Rochester (1849), and Albany (1852). Educated on the boards of eastern Homes such as these, pioneer women implemented the gospel of the asylum as they settled along the borders of the moving frontier.[34]

The scores of biographies which poured from the pens of ministers and benevolent agency presses were also designed to kindle feminine beneficence. Particularly charitable ladies were celebrated, and their lives held up to public scrutiny with the expressed design of stimulating imitation. "I wish to be an example to wives," city missionary Margaret Prior is quoted as saying in one such work. In an era when few other role models were available to women, these histories must have had tremendous impact.[35]

Biographies offered not only inspiration but practical advice as well. One particularly thorny problem was the proper apportionment of time. Women were urged to be charitable but cautioned not to neglect their domestic duties in the process. As one cleric sympathetically commented, "Many a Christian matron has stood tearfully between these two and cried, 'Lord help me.'"[36] Biographies gave their readers hints on how to balance the two, while offering reassurance that their dilemma was shared by even the most efficient Samaritans. "How difficult, how hopeless is the task of pleasing everybody!" one exasperated protagonist whined.[37]

This issue seems to have piqued the consciences of most women involved in public activities. Thus, Chicagoan Mary Livermore felt constrained to pause amid her description of Sanitary Commission work to pay lip service to the joys of the ménage: "Its pleasant order and quiet, its welcome rest, its cheerful companionship, its gayety, which comes from the prattle and merriment of children—all seem strange and unnatural after the experiences of the day. It is as if I had left the world for a time, to refresh myself in a suburb of heaven."[38] Biographies demonstrated that the two spheres were not incompatible, if carefully managed. Margaret Prior found time for both by shunning unnecessary visiting, idle gossip, and a full night's sleep. Thrift and fastidious accounting of household expenses also helped her to set aside her mite for the poor, a technique encouraged in Catharine Beecher's *A Treatise on Domestic Economy,* since, as Beecher explained, few housewives "have the control of an income, so as not to be bound by the wishes of a parent or husband."[39] By demonstrating that "although called to so many public duties" the model Samaritan's "home order and comfort were never neglected," biographers reassured their readers that charitable work need not clash with the imperatives of their domestic sphere.[40]

Many pious ladies, like Margaret Everts, conscientiously followed their injunctions, immersing themselves in charitable endeavors. Born of a prominent Philadelphia family in 1817, Margaret was a lively girl who loved dancing and had a voracious appetite for learning. Her conversion in 1831 marked the beginning of a life of self-denial and good works. After attending a four-day meeting at a local Presbyterian church, she experienced a profound conviction of personal guilt, which prompted her to embrace her mother's Baptist faith. On a frigid November morning, Margaret, now fourteen, went down to the Delaware River "where they had opened a place in the ice" and was baptized.[41] Returning home, she laid aside her jewelry and fashionable wardrobe, renouncing forever the dancing which she loved so much, and began to hoard money for the poor. When her career at the Collegiate Institute for Young Ladies was cut short in the first year by her mother's death, Margaret obediently abandoned her studies to take her mother's place in the household. What free time she had was devoted to the Dorcas Society, the Philadelphia Female Tract Society, her Sunday school classes, visits to the poor, and the class for working girls which she established in her father's factory. After her marriage to W. W. Everts, a Baptist minister, in 1843, she joined similar activities in his parishes in New York City, upstate New York, Louisville, and Chicago, where she sat on the boards of the COA, the CHFF, and the Erring Woman's Refuge.

Her dedication was extraordinary, particularly in the case of the Magdelen home, which she had helped to found. As her husband explained, "She had no sympathy with the cold public sentiment . . . that would allow classes of the unfortunate and wretched to perish without attempted relief."[42] While her family left the city during the sweltering summer months, Margaret remained behind, devoting herself to the task of raising funds. Drafting resolutions and petitions to the Common Council, doggedly writing and calling upon prominent citizens, and then canvassing the city for building materials, she literally built the asylum herself, and ultimately convinced the city to underwrite it with brothel fines. Her "life-long habit to sacrifice personal ease for a worthy cause" undoubtedly contributed to her early demise.[43] While ministering to the sick, she contracted a fever which lingered for four weeks. Undeterred, she rose from her sickbed to solicit goods for the asylum. A few days later she died at the age of forty-nine.

Women like Everts were drawn to religion for a variety of reasons. Harriet Martineau suggested that they were "driven back upon religion as a resource against vacuity."[44] Certainly, religious activities helped to give meaning and focus to their lives, providing socially approved avenues of self-expression as well as causes for which to struggle, all backed by the unimpeachable authority of Divine righteousness. It took them out of the home and welded them into a community bound by shared beliefs and passions.[45]

Moreover, in an era of jarringly high mortality rates, the attractiveness of religion was doubtless enhanced by the comfort and solace which it offered to the recently bereaved. This, in turn, could be translated into a need to help others. In one poignantly revealing passage, one woman discussed the interrelationships of grief and religion. Shortly after the death of her parents and a close friend, she wrote, "Now, when laboring with grief, and at times ready to sink, the precious truths of the gospel are sometimes sent to my mind, for my relief, with an efficacy altogether superior to any other sources of consolation." The passage continues: "Constituted as I am, with strong feelings, susceptible nerves, and a heart prone to forbode evil, what should I do without religion? This, I often feel, is the only anchor that holds me from drifting into the gulph [*sic*] of despair. Oh! if the religion of Christ were false, as the infidel tries to make us think, what would become of me?"[46] Religion helped women like this to deal with the harsh realities of antebellum life, the sudden losses and frequent bereavements which typified their lot. Desperately embracing Christianity, they were driven to make others believe as well. Widowhood, the "empty crib," the lost friend—all helped to stoke the fires of feminine charity and evangelicalism.

Revivalism also played a major role in marshaling the forces of feminine benevolence. Like Everts, the "reborn" were stricken with an acute awareness of their own transgressions and an intense loathing of the sinfulness from which they had so narrowly escaped. This in turn led to an intense desire to save others from their erring ways and to succor the victims of sin and lust: prostitutes, women abandoned or mistreated by intemperate spouses, children growing up in the haunts of vice and crime. Revivalism not only inspired them to good works; it made charity both a duty and a right.

Domestic publicists seconded ministerial injunctions, urging their readers to participate on patriotic as well as religious grounds. Many critics feared that the nation was dissolving into a frenzy of anarchistic democracy. Hotly contested, sometimes violent political campaigns were the order of the day. Urban rioting, muted after the Revolution, was once again recurring with alarming frequency. The Astor Place Riot, Chicago's Lager Beer Riot of 1855, and the outbreak of vigilantism in San Francisco were among the many disturbances which punctuated the final decades before the Civil War. Emotional issues like abolitionism and nativism also fed the fires of unrest. Individualism, materialism, and dissent seemed to be growing like cancers on the body politic.

Against this backdrop motherhood, home, and family were spiritualized, sentimentalized, and ultimately regarded as the antidote for disorder. In contrast to the aggressive male, the gentle, pure, and virtuous wife was deemed the embodiment of moral sentiment, stability, and human compassion. Under her supervision, the home was to be a refuge from the competitive world outside, a shelter to which the tired father could return after the day's struggles to be rehumanized in an atmosphere of tenderness and love. Domestic tranquility was to be the guardian of society against the competitiveness of a male-dominated world.

Feminine charity projected this civilizing influence onto the larger society. "Woman's great mission is to train immature, weak, and ignorant creatures, to obey the laws of God," firmly noted educator Catharine Beecher, "first in the family, then in the school, then in the neighborhood, then in the world—that great family of God whom the Master came to teach and to save."[47] Sarah Josepha Hale, editor of the popular *Godey's Lady's Book* concurred. Carefully reassuring her readers that "we do not desire to change the station of the sexes, or give to women the work of men," Hale asserted:

> We only want our sex to become fitted for their own sphere. But we believe this comprises, besides all household care and domestic duties, THREE IMPORTANT VOCATIONS... [in addition to teaching], WOMEN ARE THE PRESERVERS—they should be instructed in medical science and become physicians for their own sex and for children. WOMEN ARE THE HELPERS—they should be intrusted with the management of all charities where their own sex and children are concerned.[48]

It was their intuitive right. Women were fitted for such work, not by formal training, but by the instinctive, biological prerogatives of motherhood. Mere contact with a lady, and thus the civilizing influence of hearth and home, was deemed capable of reforming the most hardened offender, the most cunning street Arab. "One tone like a mother's voice might have wholly changed his earthly destiny," mused Lydia Maria Child after encountering a tough New York newsboy: "One kind word of friendly counsel might have saved him—as if an angel, standing in the genial sunlight, had thrown to him one end of a garland, and gently diminishing the distance between them, had drawn him safely out of the deep and tangled labyrinth, where false echoes and winding paths conspired to make him lose his way."[49] Only "let her voice fall in tones of kindness and love on the ears of even the wayward and vicious and... there is still hope of reformation."[50]

Under the banner of family and religion, women were encouraged to venture into even the most unsavory places, although few were completely sanguine about the risks entailed. "You fear personal abuse, it may be, and even violence," commiserated the author of *The Gift Book for Young Ladies*, "but I do not think it need be so. Females generally pursue their errand by daylight, when rogues are apt to be cowardly. Besides, there is not one man in a thousand who will have the hardihood to insult an honest and straightforward missionary, of any age or of either sex."[51]

The homes of the poor could occasionally test the visitor's fortitude. As one writer warned, "Instead of the woodbine-wreathed cottage, with its neat and rosy tenants, grateful and good... you may find, in the abodes of poverty, much to disgust a refined taste; in the gross manners and vulgar ignorance of their inmates, some things to alarm your scrupulous delicacy."[52] Despite the obvious drawbacks, women were expected to personally visit the poor, comfort the sick and dying, cheer the aged, teach Sunday schools, and manage benevolent institutions. "You have discharged but a small part of the duty of benevolence to the poor, by bestowing money," warned popular authoress Louisa Tuthill.[53]

Advice books continually emphasized the need for personal service. Acting in accordance with society's expectations, charitable ladies gained first-hand knowledge of urban problems which was an invaluable aid in their quest for an enlarged share of civic responsibility. Charitable work imbued the domestic circle with meaning and influence that transcended the confines of hearth and home. Adherents to the cult of domesticity, like Catharine Beecher, helped to accord women a central place in American society by equating womanly self-fulfillment with self-sacrifice, and self-sacrifice with national well-being.[54]

The call to personal service was given added immediacy by

Chicago's dismal economic situation. Almost all of the city's benevolent undertakings were plagued by fiscal problems from the moment of their inception. Few received sizable endowments before the Civil War. Only theological seminaries drew consistently large gifts, and even these generally consisted of real estate, leaving them well endowed but land poor. The Garrett Biblical Institute (1855) is a case in point. The founder was Eliza Clark Garrett, the widow of the mayor Augustus Garrett, a wealthy auctioneer who died in 1848. No longer young, with no close heirs (both of her children died in infancy), Mrs. Garrett resolved to found a theological seminary in memory of her husband, an undertaking which appealed to her deeply religious nature. Unfortunately, the bulk of her $100,000 gift consisted of unproductive land. The trustees managed to collect ground rents on it until the panic of 1857, when the tenants began to relinquish their leases. Three years later the Wigwam convention hall was built on the site, but when it burned in 1871 the institute was left with $92,000 in debts. Basing new institutions on gifts of land could be an extremely risky business.[55]

Many Chicagoans, rich on paper, were land poor. Although the 1860 census lists ample wealth, including five millionaires and 266 citizens worth over $100,000 (figures which compare favorably with eastern cities in the 1840s), many of these fortunes were based on real estate holdings rather than liquid assets. Surplus cash was so scarce in the 1850s that local merchants still accepted "country pay" (payment-in-kind). Like their colonial ancestors a century before, Chicagoans forwarded most of their available specie to creditors in the east. Western states had the smallest amount of banking power in the country. After the fall of the Second Bank of the United States in 1837, the area was inundated with unstandardized, unreliable media of exchange: foreign coins, IOUs, scrip, stump-tail and wild-cat currencies (so named because they were said to be issued "in the deep woods where wildcats might more easily find their way than bank note holders"),[56] and state bank bills which "would not buy a dinner across the state line."[57]

With the advent of the financial depression of 1857, "most of the subscriptions, given in good faith, became worthless."[58] Money was so slowly and painfully acquired that some institutions, like St. James Hospital, were forced to close their doors. Universities desperately sought aid from eastern philanthropists "in much the same way that the colonial colleges had sought help from England," while the trustees of Northwestern University managed to raise some badly needed cash through the sale of $100 perpetual scholarships, entitling the bearer and his descendants to complete tuition benefits.[59]

Crimped budgets enhanced the value of even the most modest gifts. Institutions were built upon the offerings of hundreds of small donors rather than the beneficence of the few. Gifts-in-kind, like the cakes and pies housewives brought to asylums, were quite common. Because funds were limited and salaried staffs minimal, volunteer skills were particularly important. Although wives could neither own nor alienate money before the passage of the Married Woman's Property Act in 1861, their household skills—sewing, shopping, and nursing—were of inestimable value in shaping the city's fledgling institutions.

Only one asylum, the publicly subsidized Chicago Reform School (1854) was wealthy enough to implement elaborate programs. Initially devised as a congregate institution, the school became one of the city's showplaces under the guidance of the superintendent G. W. Perkins and prominent attorney Mark Skinner. After visiting several eastern reformatories and pouring endlessly over the publications of European reform schools, Skinner concluded that the asylum must be reorganized on the cottage plan. The end result was a masterpiece of organizational ingenuity. Inmates were divided into graded families according to merit. Each sported uniforms of a different color, ranging in hue from prison gray to resplendent shades of purple. Each "family" marched to recreational and devotional exercises, work, and meals to the tempo of drumrolls, "a brown coat appearing side by side with a gray, a blue coat with a purple." Thus, the superintendent facetiously explained, "They meet in work, in school, and at play, the same temptations, and the same life as village boys."[60] Access to the public till enabled authorities to hire the large numbers of employees necessary to choreograph such an elaborate undertaking. To their care were entrusted confirmed delinquents and the potentially antisocial progeny of "parents who make themselves poor and wretched by drink, who are dishonest, who are daily distracted by family quarrels, who are indolent and filthy."[61] Discipline was sometimes harsh, and strictly paternal. As the superintendent explained, "We have made it our aim to fill a father's place to these unfortunate youth(s)."[62]

Spokesmen for the private asylums were resentfully aware of the contrast between their own modest undertakings and the reform school. "One institution in this city which I COULD name, has the advantage of us in the systematic training it affords its inmates," carped the matron of the CHFF.[63] The distinction between the city's public and private charities was sharpened by funding practices. Sustained by donations alone, organizations like the COA and the CHFF could ill afford the sizable staffs necessary to oversee elaborate programs like that of the reform school. Since even good matrons were hard to find, and harder to hold, many of the tasks of daily management fell to the directresses themselves.

Nevertheless, within their tiny fiefdoms directresses wielded a considerable amount of power. "Her executive ability was a wonder to every one," a colleague admiringly noted of CHFF president Jane Hoge. "No matter how complicated and gigantic the undertaking, she quickly systematized the work, appointed committees for the various departments, and maintained a hopeful and inspiring superintendence of the whole, compelling success." Plain, plump, stolid, and stoic (she gave birth to thirteen children, of whom eight survived to maturity), Hoge could be a formidable enemy when the interests of the asylum were at stake. In one celebrated encounter, she bested a lawyer retained by a dissolute father when his children received a small inheritance. After several futile clashes, the exasperated lawyer screamed, "Are there no MEN connected with this institution, no FATHERS who have sense and authority?" Hoge snapped in reply, "Women are in authority in this house, sir, and they will excuse your presence, now and forever."[64]

Like Hoge, many directresses may have been seeking enlarged outlets for their considerable energies and talents. On the whole, they were a well-educated, ambitious, interesting group. Several, including Hoge, were alumnae of female seminaries, and many managed to excel in a variety of enterprises beyond their allotted domestic sphere. Juliette Kinzie, the first president of the COA, was a descendant of Connecticut's aristocratic Wolcott clan. Educated at Emma Willard's celebrated school at Troy, New York, she was an accomplished linguist and a successful author whose published works included the popular *Wau-Bun* (an account of her experiences on the Wisconsin frontier), and two romantic novels, *Walter Ogilvie* and *Mark Logan.* Mrs. C. V. Dyer assumed a leading role in Chicago's underground railroad; Elizabeth Atwater, for whom a new species of American flower was named, was a renowned amateur botanist; Mary Livermore and Jane Hoge were decorated by Lincoln for their Sanitary Commission work during the Civil War. As Livermore candidly confessed, "I have never found much pleasure in either needle-work or cooking, and have developed considerable ingenuity in devising means by which I could honorably escape from these pursuits."[65]

Mary Livermore was one of several former teachers. Teaching was one of the few respectable professions open to women in the antebellum era. A semipublic occupation, it afforded an ideal training ground for public life, offering a modicum of autonomy and self-reliance, while enabling them to cultivate their leadership capabilities. It also provided a clearly defined set of grievances, reflecting the "separate but unequal" philosophy of the time. While men forged ahead politically and economically, female teachers remained underpaid, overworked, and with little hope for advancement.[66]

An alumna of Miss Martha Whiting's Female Seminary in Charlestown, Massachusetts, Livermore briefly taught in her home state before accepting a position as a tutor on a Virginia plantation. This career ended with her marriage to Daniel Livermore, a Universalist minister, after which she devoted herself primarily to charity and moral reform. "I was untiring in my labors for the Chicago Home of the Friendless," she recalled, and these duties introduced her to her lifelong friend, Jane Hoge.[67] Both became national heroines during the Civil War, visiting the front, conscripting nurses, rationalizing the system of relief distribution, and creating the Sanitary Fair to raise funds for the Union Army. Afterward, Livermore became an adamant feminist, stumping the lecture circuit to promote the suffragist's cause. As editor of the *Agitator* (1869) and the *Woman's Journal* (1870), and later as president of the American Woman Suffrage Association and the Association for the Advancement of Women, Mary Livermore remained a feminist crusader until her death in 1905.

Like many of her peers, Livermore was keenly aware that the rhetoric of Jacksonian equality had little relevance for women, whether married or employed. During the antebellum era, feminine labor was markedly devalued and circumscribed, with women workers shunted into a narrow range of low-status, low-paying occupations like teaching and domestic service. Household industries, formerly the housewife's special province, were increasingly co-opted by the factory and mill. Public schools assumed a growing measure of responsibility for the education of their children. Under the doctrine of *femme couverte*, wives were legally denied the right to personal economic security, controlling neither their dowries nor their pay. Dissolute spouses could squander their dowries, mortgage their possessions (including jewelry and clothes) to pay debts, and render them completely indigent if they so chose. Politically disfranchised, denied many legal rights as well, women came to occupy a decidedly inferior place in the social schema.[68]

These trends were mitigated somewhat on the frontier, where the primitive nature of life and the importance of establishing viable households made pioneer women genuine partners with their husbands in the arduous task of settlement. Some, like Kinzie, had eagerly renounced the comforts of eastern society for the challenges of the open prairie.

But, by 1850, Chicago was on the cusp of change from a pioneer society to an established community. As settlers began to pour into the city after the economic depression of the late thirties and early forties, men turned their attention to the exhilarating tasks of establishing a viable economy, forging markets, and creating transportation links—pursuits from which women were excluded. Newly created schools, factories, mercantile establishments, and the increasing availability of servants simultaneously divested housewives of their former duties, changing them almost overnight from producers to consumers.

For ambitious and talented women, this prospect must have been stultifying. Significantly, they turned to asylum work precisely as their traditional social and economic roles began to narrow. Institution building afforded a sense of purpose and identity, increased their mobility, and won a good deal of public approval. It allowed them to escape the narrow confines of the home without openly challenging the dictates of the cult of domesticity.

It also gave them a platform from which to criticize the masculine world which had excluded them. While men dealt with incorrigibles and criminals who had erred to their own volition, women assumed responsibility for society's flotsam: orphans, abused and forsaken wives, widows, "ruined" girls, and aged mothers abandoned by their children. By celebrating and sentimentalizing the virtues of their inmates—meekness, piety, gentleness, and love—they also celebrated themselves. By publicizing the plight of their charges, directresses castigated a world which demanded frailty and passivity but did not honor it. Charity gave them power in a society intent upon rendering them powerless.

Unlike the stereotypic "Lady Bountiful," Chicago's benevolent ladies were a dedicated band of semiprofessional humanitarians. As a group, they defy easy categorization. Some were feminists, some bluestockings, while some were sincerely pious women who had dedicated their lives to furthering Christian aims. Legally barred from

donning the mantle of the patroness, financially constricted by the city's adolescent economy as well, they applied their domestic expertise to the solution of Chicago's growing list of social ills. Under their supervision, the city's asylums became the "homes" which their rhetoric implied.

In return, women netted enhanced mobility, a suitable arena in which to test their executive capabilities, an outlet for their religious zeal, and a healthy share of public approbation. Antebellum women were expected to participate, not as donors but as volunteers. Sanctioned by ministers and leading proponents of the cult of domesticity, charitable service became their religious imperative, their patriotic duty, and their personal right. In the decades after the Civil War, they would begin to expand these prerogatives beyond the narrow universe of hearth and Home.

Anders L. Zorn, portrait of Mrs. Potter Palmer (1893). Courtesy of the Art Institute of Chicago.

# 2
# MANAGERS & PATRONESSES

## I

A new generation of feminine stewards came forward to demand an increased measure of civic and social responsibility in the 1870s and 1880s. Well-to-do managers and patronesses rather than self-abnegating servants of the poor, Chicago's Gilded Age ladies bountiful rapidly moved beyond the limited range of alternatives which shaped their mothers' activities, creating a welter of new ventures to parallel the efforts of their spouses, sires, and sons. Increasing wealth, legal reforms, travel, clubwork, changing urban conditions, new behavioral norms—each in turn drew Chicago's Gilded Age feminine stewards further from the democratic service ethic of their antebellum peers.

Postwar Chicago was more heterogeneous and far more distended than the settlement their mothers had known. By 1890, the number of Chicagoans born of foreign parentage had risen 77.9%. Industrialization acted as a magnet, creating new jobs, drawing immigrants and American ruralites over improved transportation routes, and growing fat on the new markets which their presence opened. The introduction of cable cars, horsecar lines, and steam railroads spread the city outward to accommodate them, luring the middle classes to the healthier periphery while newcomers piled into the ramshackle housing near more centralized jobs and factories.

The great Chicago fire of 1871 speeded the outward movement, leaving a more segregated city in its wake. Before the disaster, different social classes had mingled in the same neighborhoods. Residents clustered along denominational rather than economic lines. Afterward, those who could afford to rebuilt in the socioeconomically sequestered enclaves surrounding Prairie Avenue and, later, in the Gold Coast. The poor, too, huddled in their own areas, grouped along religious and ethnic lines. By the 1890s, Chicago had become a crazy quilt of competing cultural worlds, each with its own customs, language, and behavioral norms.

Social problems simultaneously flourished, as slums exploded into an urban wilderness of tenements which were poorly ventilated, overcrowded, and infested with vermin and disease. Epidemics traveled like wildfire through these human warehouses, piling up staggeringly high infant mortality rates, and making tuberculosis an accepted corollary of urban life. Those who were poor, stayed poor, crushed by casualized labor, periodic unemployment, and the cyclical depressions of an industrializing economy.

Gilded Age stewards were reluctant to venture into the slums as casually as their predecessors had. Such work was deemed unpleasant, dangerous, and time consuming. Moreover, those dauntless souls who continued to personally minister to the needy often found that they had little practical advice to render. Unlike the hearty pioneers who used their household talents to run asylums, the pampered ladies of the 1880s had little experience with household drudgery, and when they tried to inculcate skills they themselves had failed to master, the results were often ludicrous. "While I was a Sunday School teacher I was also a teacher in the sewing school," Louise de Koven Bowen ruefully recalled. "I knew very little about sewing and when I was given my first class I found that they were making flannel petticoats, and in my ignorance I had them sew up each side of the petticoat, so that there was no way of getting into it."[1]

Even when personal attention was backed by sound reasoning, the results were not always predictable. Increasing heterogeneity minimized the common ground for understanding between visitors and recipients. Well-intentioned gestures could be misconstrued by immigrants reared in dissimilar cultures, and interpreted as acts of intrusion or hostility. As sociologist Erving Goffman notes, there are "different ways of conveying deference and demeanor, different ceremonial meanings for the same act, and different amounts of concern over such things as . . . privacy."[2]

Sometimes the significance of the gift itself was misinterpreted. In one instance, Bowen gave a hungry family a turkey, and was later "horrified to see the bird dressed up in one of the children's dresses and put in the only bed in the place to keep it warm." As she explained, "Being foreigners [they] did not understand the eatableness of the bird, and therefore, used it as a plaything."[3] Little wonder, with such potentially ungratifying results, that women sought alternative outlets for their energies.

Asylum work had also lost much of its earlier excitement. As the city's Homes grew richer in the aftermath of the war and the Chicago fire, policies ossified, staffs and facilities were enlarged, and much of the responsibility passed to paid workers. Rather than drawing directresses into the slums in search of candidates, asylum work now insulated them from the poor. Ironically, over the decades the city had surrounded the once isolated institutions, and many now stood near the residential enclaves of their wealthy managers. Once a week applicants journeyed there to file past the admission committees, telling their tales of deprivation and woe. But employees did the actual work of investigation, sparing the board the unpleasant task of venturing themselves into unsavory neighborhoods. According to Chicago Home for the Friendless spokesman Lucy Flower, "Until settlements such as Hull-House were opened, the average men and women knew nothing about the dwellers on Halsted Street; they had nothing to take them over that way."[4] Asylum directresses now fulfilled their charitable obligations at a safe remove from the sordid habitats of the unfortunates under their care.

Distaste for direct association with the needy was intensified by the dictates of Society, which frowned upon camaraderie between rich and poor. The Civil War marked a watershed in Chicago's economic maturation, ushering in a period of unprecedented prosperity. Fed by wartime imperatives and underwritten by eastern investors, the city expanded and grew rich. By the end of the Gilded Age, Chicago had become one of the nation's leading producers of foodstuffs, lumber, steel, and clothing, spawning a growing crop of millionaires and nouveaux riches.

While the antebellum urbanite's status depended upon his standing in the church, postwar society used more materialistic yardsticks, measuring the man—and woman—in quantitative terms. Feminine advice books reflected the change, shifting their attention from the ground rules of personalized beneficence to the intricacies of social conduct. Authors now labored to inculcate the necessary skills for maintaining personal status, gauging the backgrounds of new acquaintances, and keeping undesirable strangers at arm's length from marriageable daughters and sons. In the process, the self-sacrificing benevolent lady ceded stage center to the sharp-witted social arbiter as the prevailing feminine ideal.[5]

Moreover, as Society became richer and more well-defined, charitable work lost many of its onerous aspects. In fund raising, large-scale benefits began to replace door-to-door solicitation as the primary means of raising revenues. By sponsoring an opera, musicale, or play in the name of charity, aspiring Society queens could enhance their reputations, sharpen their skills at social one-upsmanship, and fulfill their charitable obligations at a comfortable remove from misery and want at one and the same time.[6]

Other novel alternatives included personal endorsement (the name of a Society leader at the head of a subscription list or a membership roster lent an undeniable cachet to struggling charities), or dispensing alms and money directly to the poor. Mrs. Marshall Field employed an almoner to handle the disagreeable task of dealing directly with supplicants, while her friend, Mrs. N. K. Fairbank, reportedly doled out $10,000 worth of alms each year. Granted full control over their dowries and dividends with the passage of the Illinois Married Woman's Property Act in 1861, matrons were now free to dispose of their funds as they chose.[7]

Women began to donate sums on an ever-increasing scale, inspired by the example of outstanding feminine philanthropists like Britain's Baroness Angela Burdett-Coutts. Aided by skilled advisors like Charles Dickens, the baroness financed a spate of well-publicized undertakings, ranging from ragged schools and housing projects for the poor to urban planning and garden suburbs. Her example was held up to an entire generation of newly rich women as an alternative to the vapid rigors of the social whirl. "The spectacle of a life employed in vast yet unostentatious charities is one which cannot be too strongly commended to women who find emptiness and triviality in their present pursuits," noted the redoubtable Sarah Josepha Hale.[8]

Increasing wealth and newly minted social strictures combined with misgivings about cultural diversity and fears for personal safety aroused by strikes and other civic disorders, reinforcing the insularity of the rich. During the Pullman strike, Nettie Fowler McCormick frantically penned letters to her children in Chicago, begging them to guard against arsonists who might try to torch the family's mansions. "We are filled with dismay and anxiety at the reports from our imperiled city—anxiety for your persons," she agonized. "All trade interests, ours with the rest, must lie prostrate—but the money loss, great as it is, is the *least*. What dangers may come to citizens, I cannot estimate . . . . I fear the worst in every way."[9] Frightened and repulsed by the continual threat of the poor, wealthy Chicagoans began to insulate themselves from the rest of the urbanscape through barriers of privacy and certification. Clubs, private schools, and social registers heralded their retreat, while technological novelties like the telephone enabled them to devise alternative means of communication among themselves, their businesses, and the organizations under their patronage.[10]

In the process, the city outgrew the network of primary contacts and the range of individual perceptions, leaving potential stewards unaware of the magnitude of changing needs. For many, the pungent sights and sounds of the west side tenements were more foreign than the Egyptian bazaars and Parisian cafes which they visited with increasing regularity. This generation faced a dual challenge: the need for more efficient means of gathering the information necessary for intelligent decision making, and the need for newer benevolent ideals attuned to the changing realities of the Gilded Age city.

As the wealthy insulated themselves from the rest of society, clubs and travel began to replace churches as the wellsprings of institutional growth. Clubwork helped to sensitize members to a whole range of problems and solutions, giving rise to a variety of concrete programs, and facilitating the transition from collective doers to collective donors for both men and women alike. These organizations occupied the midpoint between personal benevolence and professionalism. While antebellum elites visited the poor themselves, their Gilded Age counterparts regularly met with peers to discuss the latest trends. During the Progressive era, their sons and daughters would continue to turn to clubs for enlightenment, but they perceived problems differently, viewing them through the eyes of the settlement workers, sociologists, and physicians who lectured there.

Women's clubs had an additional appeal which is often overlooked. The image of the pious Samaritan, so compelling in the prewar years, had been irrevocably tarnished by the Sanitary Commission's highly successful wartime campaign against impulsive humanitarianism.[11] As America swung away from the benevolent ideals of the antebellum years, a "militant crusade for masculinity" gathered momentum.[12] Social Darwinism, the emphasis on violent sports, even the glorification of "the strenuous life," all exuded a virile masculinity foreign to the sentimental ethos of the prewar years. Suddenly, the "separate but superior" rhetoric of Beecher and Hale lost its immediacy, drowned in the clamor of a society devoted to science and expertise. As the home was relegated to the periphery of the social experience, women began to adapt themselves to the imperatives of a masculine world, learning to play by society's rules instead of their own. Clubs, charities, and colleges all served as "school[s] for women in which they might learn how to take their place alongside men in the great work assigned to useful human beings."[13]

European travel gave added impetus to the drift toward stewardship at a distance. Although the European tour was an accepted fact of life for the rich in seaboard cities almost from the outset, Chicagoans entered the tourist circuit more slowly, hampered by their infant economy and the difficulty of the journey itself. In the decades after the Civil War, both situations improved, making European travel an accepted fact of life for the city's wealthy. Eager to enjoy the benefits which their wealth conferred, citizens embarked upon the pilgrimage to European capitals in ever-increasing numbers. What had begun as a trickle in the fifties now became a flood, as the grand tour became a necessary badge of social acceptability.

Although disinclined to pass their time examining the minutiae of municipal management, Chicago's Gilded Age stewards did take time to investigate the workings of the continent's great museums, operas, civic monuments, and symphonies. And upon their return they did their best to reproduce the cultural bastions of the Old World on American soil. Armed with seemingly bottomless purses, Chicagoans pillaged the artistic storehouses of the Old World, proudly transporting their canvases, statuary, and incunabula to the city's newly created museums and libraries, a process repeated in dozens of towns and cities throughout the nation. In effect, clubs and travel shielded elites from direct contact with the welter of problems festering behind the comfortable horizons of the privatized universe, while providing fresh models for their civic undertakings.

As they moved away from personalized beneficence and direct contact with the poor, women began to invade a variety of new areas from which they had previously been excluded, founding hospitals, nursing schools, and art associations. Chicago's first feminine cultural organization, the Chicago Society of Decorative Art (CSDA), and first nursing school, the Illinois Training School for Nurses (ITN), serve to illustrate the course of feminine largesse in the decades after the Civil War.

## II

Despite the popular notion that culture is essentially a feminine preserve, and always has been, Chicago's women assumed responsibility for public arbitership slowly, and through an extremely circuitous route. Few women graced the rosters of the city's antebellum associations. The Chicago Historical Society (1856), the Academy of Sciences (1857), the Mechanic's Institute (1837), and the Young Men's (library) Association (1841) were all organized by men, for men. Kate Newell Doggett, a talented amateur botanist, was the first woman admitted to membership in the Academy of Sciences, shortly after the war. But she was not invited to join the board. The first female member of the Chicago Historical Society, the cultured, gracious Mrs. J. Y. Scammon, wife of one of the organization's wealthiest backers, was not permitted to join until 1867. The Young Men's Association, as the name suggests, was designed for the city's young men, a haven where they could profitably spend their leisure hours, safely removed from the less savory allurements of urban life. Although women were welcomed to the Mechanic's Institute lectures, this organization, too, remained a masculine stronghold. Even in the more liberal postwar era, women were excluded from the board of the Academy of Fine Arts (the Art Institute), and from the ranks of the public library movement.

They played a similarly negligible role in exhibitions. The Mechanic's Institute fairs somewhat condescendingly featured a separate women's division, where feminine handiwork and culinary skills could be displayed. Offerings ranged from wax flowers and bead purses to bread and home-grown beets. A few ladies chose to show their own drawings, paintings, and photographs, but in each instance these entries were more of a reflection of domestic busywork than of fine art. Of the 266 paintings exhibited at the city's first formal art show in 1859, only seven were submitted by feminine donors, including a "Cattle Scene," by Melchior, and "Group of Goats" by Rosa di Tivoli. No women sat on the organizing committees, and none participated in the creation of the Chicago Art-Union in 1860.[14]

Nor did women in other cities fare much better. While men monopolized the realm of high culture, American women shaped the tastes of the masses, flooding the market with sentimental best-sellers and saccharine steel engravings centering on the trials and triumphs of feminine protagonists. Domestic periodicals like *Godey's Lady's Book* led the way. Editor Sarah Josepha Hale used *Godey's* embellishments just as she used its copy, tirelessly reiterating the theme of woman's influence within her appointed sphere. Women were invariably depicted as the focus of attention, the moral sage. Men listened attentively, worshipped from afar, or reverently paid court to feminine beauty and accomplishments. One extremely popular theme was the power of motherhood and the mother's role in inculcating moral precepts in the young. In "Charity," for example, the woman tenderly lifts her babe so that he may drop a coin in a beggar's extended hat, while the child adoringly looks back to her for guidance and encouragement.[15] Other scenes depicted women leading the wayward, aged, and disabled down the path of virtue to physical and spiritual safe harbor. In one of the journal's rare references to the Civil War, the frontispiece illustrated the range and efficacy of feminine benevolence, detailing midnight vigils on the battlefields and in hospital wards as well as more traditional tasks—comforting the poor, consoling the prisoner, and tutoring the young amid the warmth of the domestic circle. One vignette even portrayed an intrepid lady rowing out to succor the victims of a sinking steamboat.[16]

*Godey's* domesticated embellishments, and the countless gift books which reiterated their themes, helped to deflect feminine tastes from the mainstream of American art. These were prints for the parlor, not masterpieces for the gallery. As Hale explained, women had their own, distinctly feminine cultural sphere: " . . . from Painting, we have Drawing, Penmanship, Letter-writing; from Poetry, the art of reading and the taste of selection in literature; from Music, besides household song, which is its natural expression, we have dancing, gracefulness, and propriety of manner and attire, and many of those innocent home amusements which are beneficial to the heart and soul, to mind and body."[17] Reduced from an act of creation to a harmless pastime to while away the hours, artistry was privatized, domesticated, and miniaturized to a distinctly feminine scale.

The Civil War briefly legitimized a more significant role for women through the work of the Sanitary Commission. In order to raise funds for the troops, the commission sponsored a series of mammoth Sanitary Fairs, many of which featured art exhibits. In Chicago, as elsewhere, ladies doggedly combed their city for artworks, borrowing what they could, and occasionally even adding holdings of their own. Although none came from feminine contributors in 1865, six of the 323 works loaned to the Northwestern Sanitary Fair in 1863 belonged to women. Yet, for most the fairs represented little more than an extension of their erstwhile charitable endeavors. Once amassed, the works were sifted and arranged by male connoisseurs like Chicago sculptor Leonard Volk. Women simply collected them. Instead of begging for clothes and coal for orphans, Sanitarians canvassed for Bierstadts and Bonheurs to raise funds for the care of the troops.[18]

More important was the influence of the Philadelphia Centennial

Exposition of 1876. The fair triggered a national stocktaking, in which America's artistic position was surveyed and found to be sadly deficient. While few assailed the superiority of the nation's technological achievements, America's fine arts paled in comparison to the riches of the Old World. The displays from Britain's South Kensington Museum were particularly well received. Viewers marveled at the quality of the magnificent needlework and embroideries of the "poor and painstaking gentlewomen" under the museum's tutelage. As one commentator admiringly noted, this was "real work, to be faithfully performed and duly paid for."[19] The decorative arts movement which developed in the wake of the fair "changed the artistic ideals of the entire country," elevating domestic handiwork to a new level of dignity and respect and moving feminine artistry to the center of the creative process.[20]

Popularized by the exhibition, the movement received additional stature from the endorsement of the revered British art critic and philosopher, John Ruskin, and his disciple, William Morris. Ruskinites regarded handicrafts as the antidote to the sterility of life in an increasingly mechanized world. Beautiful household objects, pleasurably made, would bring joy to both consumer and artisan. The revival of craftsmanship would also help to mitigate the brutalizing effect of factory labor, restoring the worker's self-esteem, and quelling his rebelliousness. In an era of increasing industrial unrest, this prophecy was particularly compelling. Ruskinites fashioned the cause of art into a social and moral crusade, and placed the responsibility for its success squarely in the hands of domestic consumers. Not surprisingly, women eagerly embraced the cause and made it their own.

Founded in June 1877, the Chicago Society for Decorative Art was a branch of a national organization established in New York City shortly after the closing of the fair. As spokesmen explained, the society was both a charitable and a cultural undertaking, designed to aid impoverished gentlewomen by training them in formal courses and creating new markets for their handiwork. Thousands of widows and spinsters flocked to northern cities like Chicago after the Civil War, destitute, alone, and desperately seeking work. By training them to make high quality ecclesiastical robes, carvings, and household items, the society's sponsors hoped to provide them with a permanent means of support which could be executed in the comfort and safety of their own homes.[21]

In addition to aiding the poor, the board aimed to raise the level of popular taste and household decoration. To further this end, they amassed an art library, formed study groups to ponder topics ranging from household decoration to pre-Raphaelite techniques, and staged exhibitions. The directresses were adamant in their determination to upgrade the caliber of feminine art, continually emphasizing that their goal was to emulate "all those features which distinguish the South Kensington School."[22] Wax flowers, "skeletonized leaves," paintings on black panels, and the domestic busywork of "untrained fingers" were rejected out of hand.[23] Articles which passed muster were then exhibited and sold.

Student offerings at these exhibits were regularly augmented by board members' household treasures. Like antebellum asylum directresses, the ladies stocked their programs with whatever was available from their own homes, displaying laces, ceramics, paintings, and tapestries acquired abroad. In the process, they gained invaluable experience in selecting and exhibiting objets d'art, assuming a growing share of responsibility for public cultural arbitership.

Kindled at home, their interest in artistic patronage was sharpened by sojourns abroad. For members like Bertha Palmer and Lydia Hibbard, the journey to Europe marked the beginning of a lifelong devotion to art. Prior to 1875, Hibbard's sole venture into the art world consisted of the purchase of two photographs, of the Colosseum and the Forum, for the parlor of her new home. A frugal woman despite her husband's wealth, this constituted quite a departure for her. As her daughter recalled, these were "the first 'artistic,' not necessary purchases she had ever made."[24] The family's European excursion afforded her her first encounter with fine art. Inspired by what she beheld, her husband began to invest his hard-earned cash in Bonheurs and Bougereaus, while Lydia eagerly accumulated Dresden china and objets d'art.

Although it is impossible to determine the exact number, it is probable that most of the Society's members made the grand tour at least once. Mrs. N. B. Judd had an extended sojourn between 1861 and 1865, when her husband served as Lincoln's minister to the polished court of Berlin. Maria Scammon, Lydia Hibbard, Mrs. Potter Palmer, and Sarah McCormick all went at least once between 1870 and 1875. Some doubled as representatives of the society while on vacation. Emily McVeagh, for example, was appointed "foreign correspondent" to the South Kensington Museum during her stay in Britain. This served the dual function of educating the members and broadening the contacts of the Society. Emily kept the board apprised of every relevant experience. "Since we landed in England," she wrote, "I have tried to . . . look into the history of the old European tapestries, and see for myself as many specimens as possible, in order to have a clear understanding of what they really were, and wherein their greatness consisted. To that purpose, I have examined some hundreds of museum pieces, embracing the best efforts of all the different countries of Europe."[25] In England, she observed the museum's work at close range. Traveling on to Munich, she visited the local art needlework school and enrolled the Chicago Society as a member of the Bavarian Decorative Art Verein. In this fashion, the ladies managed to keep in touch with the latest trends as they developed.

For several years they treaded a fine line between charity and art. Then, in 1888, the organization abruptly shifted course, divesting itself of the class materials and turning exclusively to cultural patronage. Their decision hinged on the question of whether the Society should "dwindle into a bazaar for . . . ordinary fancy work," or "whether it could raise the standard of excellence beyond the range of ordinary competence."[26] In the end, "it was decided to follow the narrow road to art," to "make artistic development, and progress the great object of the Society."[27] Setting aside funds for the purchase of collections to be presented to the Art Institute, they began to acquire oriental and European textiles, later adding other artifacts as well. By the nineties, the Society had become an invaluable adjunct of the Art Institute, and its members significant patronesses in their own right.

Public health also began to feel the gentling hand of feminine influence during the postwar years. Antebellum ladies played an extremely limited role in the city's health organizations, most of which were founded and controlled by businessmen and physicians. William B. Ogden, Walter Newberry, and many of their wealthy, landed peers donated time and money to the creation and maintenance of medical schools and hospitals. Whatever charitable motives may have moved them, they had a vested interest as well. The presence of these institutions proclaimed the town's permanency and maturity, and helped to mitigate its lingering reputation for unhealthiness, giving the illusion that disease, and the poverty it engendered, would be controlled.

Physicians were motivated by more professional aims. Faculty owned and profit oriented, the medical colleges which proliferated throughout the country on the eve of the Civil War competed fiercely for students, and as a result were constantly in need of human "material" to augment their courses. Practicing on the poor in dispensaries and hospitals often provided students with their only practical experience. Not surprisingly, professors from Rush Medical College were among the most vocal proponents of hospitals, like the Illinois General Hospital of the Lake, which they helped to found in 1850. Medical charities satisfied the physicians' civic, social, and professional duties at one and the same time.[28]

Ladies, and their clerical allies, viewed hospitals as arenas for moral regeneration as well as physical cure. Patients were a captive audience, a fact which advice books cannily urged them to exploit. Bored, frightened, and lonely, the sick were generally grateful for attention, even if it came heavily interlarded with Scripture and prayer. The lady who could redeem a sinner before he breathed his last could count her work well done, and many approached the task—both in and out of hospital wards—with a dogged perseverance.[29]

Medical charity had an added appeal in that it seemed to be a logical extension of woman's "natural" sphere, a public version of the informal nursing practices of the home. As Sarah Josepha Hale explained, hospitals deserved to "be placed under the control, or at least under the supervision, of women," for "a woman at the head of one of these public households is as much in her place as a man when in command of a ship or a regiment."[30] Nevertheless, Chicago's ladies made little progress in public hospitals, confining their labors to a single, church-sponsored institution.

Like their counterparts on asylum boards, the directresses of St. James Hospital (1854) visited the patients, prayed with them, saw to their comfort, and did their best to raise revenues through festivals and fairs. In return for a nominal fee, strangers with no one to "watch a sick bed" were promised "that care and attention they will so much need, and will be so little likely to find in crowded hotels, or in their lonely sleeping rooms."[31] Unfortunately, the venture was short-lived. Despite the fact that it did good work, and able physicians and attendants had been secured, the institution was forced to close for lack of funds in 1857.

The Civil War afforded women a chance to participate in medical ventures on a new scale. Hoards of Chicago women volunteered to nurse the boys at the front under the auspices of the Northwestern Sanitary Commission. As they flooded into the hospitals and camps, many were shocked and repulsed by the conditions they found. Tents leaked, bedding was infested with vermin, and patients lay writhing on bare floors, their wounds hideously infected. "Each time some new horror smote my vision, some more sickening odor nauseated me, and I was led out fainting," shuddered CHFF board member Mary Livermore: "The horrors of that long ward, containing over eighty of the most fearfully wounded men, were worse than anything I had imagined, but not worse than scenes in which I afterwards spent weeks and weeks without a tremor of the nerves or a flutter of the pulse."[32]

Livermore and her peers responded to the carnage with a barrage of criticism, attacking doctors who were "not only incompetent, but utterly careless of the comforts of their men," as well as the military bureaucracy which supported them.[33] Undaunted by their own lack of formal training, Sanitarians developed impromptu nutritional programs, cleaned the hospitals, secured necessities and "delicacies" for the boys, investigated the camps, and reported on the conditions which they found. Impressions garnered on the battlefront convinced them of the need for better health care facilities and gave them a personal stake in creating those facilities themselves. Chicago's St. Luke's Hospital and the Hospital for Women and Children were both spin-offs of women's wartime activities.

The highly publicized medical advances of the 1870s and 1880s kept their interest alive and whetted the appetites of their younger sisters and daughters who had not served in the war. It was an exciting time, as one discovery followed another in rapid succession. The use of antisceptic measures and anesthetics was becoming widespread in the 1880s, making surgery and medical care safer and more effective. In 1876, Robert Koch successfully demonstrated that specific bacteria could be linked to specific diseases; six years later he isolated the tuberculosis bacillus. After 1880, the incidence of many of the worst infectious diseases began to plummet, offering mute testimony to the efficacy of scientific advances, and kindling hope for the eventual eradication of disease.[34]

Hospitals, medical schools, and clinics all benefited from the public's growing interest in science. One of the most important feminine innovations was the development of the professional nursing school. As one pioneer candidly explained, when the Illinois Training School for Nurses (ITN) was founded in 1880, "the very idea of training nurses seemed preposterous to some, superfluous to many. Nursing was generally considered one of those occupations which women could assume by nature, like bringing up children or managing households."[35] The movement for nursing education received much of its impetus from the work of Florence Nightingale. During the Crimean War, Nightingale had successfully divested feminine hospital work of its sentimental, charitable connotations and demonstrated that it could be a viable profession for respectable women. In lieu of maternal intuition and self-sacrifice, she insisted that it was to be a skilled employment based on scientific knowledge.[36]

The Bellevue Training School for Nurses in New York (1873) was the first to adopt her principles. Founded by ex-Sanitarians, its curriculum included courses on practical aspects of patient care as well as technical courses on anatomy, physiology, and pathology. Other schools in Boston and New Haven quickly followed Bellevue's lead.[37]

After making the rounds of these eastern institutions, Mrs. Edward Wright returned to Chicago to interest her fellow Fortnightly Club members in creating a similar institution in Chicago. Her clubmates responded enthusiastically, quickly launching the new organization under a prestigious board which included Dr. Sarah Hackett Stevenson, the first female member of the AMA; reformer Lucy Flower; Mrs. N. K. Fairbank, wife of Chicago's millionaire "lard king"; and Mrs. C. B. Lawrence, the spouse of a prominent judge.

The new organization's purpose was twofold: "to train young women to care scientifically for the sick, so establishing a new and dignified profession for women," and to give patients at Cook County Hospital better care than they had been receiving from politically appointed nurses.[38] The founders were adamant in their insistence that nursing must be upgraded to the status of a career for "educated and Christian women," supplanting once and for all "the Sairy Gamps of a former day."[39] "Skilled nursing is an art, and to obtain it, it must be learned," spokesmen explained, adding icily, "it is not obtained by intuition."[40] Until the advent of professional schools like the ITN, nonsectarian and public hospital nursing was generally entrusted to medical students, convalescents, superannuated prostitutes, and charwomen unable to secure employment elsewhere. Naturally, the profession was held in low esteem, deemed unsuitable for respectable women.

Even those who had gained national reputations for their ministrations during the Civil War were unable to parley battlefield expertise into viable careers after the war's end. One of the most pathetic examples was that of Lizzie Aiken. Before the war, Aiken's life had been punctuated by a string of personal disasters. All four of her sons perished, her house was leveled by fire, her husband went insane and squandered their remaining funds, and when her favorite sister came west to console her, she, too, died. Destitute and alone, Aiken enlisted as an army nurse, an occupation at which she excelled. After the war, she secured a job as a city missionary for the Chicago Erring Woman's Refuge through the offices of a friend. Two years later, she was abruptly dismissed in an economy move by the board. "I received the news calmly," she remembered. "I went into my room and held my Bible close to my heart, for it was all that I had weeping all alone."[41]

The plight of women like Lizzie Aiken revealed with jarring clarity the precariousness of gains based on intuitive claims alone. Although many Civil War nurses had excelled in their work, they were unable to translate these successes into permanent gains because they were not grounded in technically certified skills. After the war, in clubs, colleges, and charitable endeavors, women began to vociferously espouse the need for technical training. "The superiority of the trained nurse over the untrained nurse" was viewed as but "another proof of the value of systematic education in all vocations."[42]

In order to ensure that only the best-qualified applicants would be admitted, the board instituted strict requirements and ensured that they were rigidly enforced. Under the sharp-eyed vigilance of superintendent Mary Brown, a former assistant at Bellevue, high school graduates between twenty-five and thirty-five, of good health and moral character (both of which were to be certified in writing by their pastors and physicians), were screened, selected, and trained. "Giddy girls" were rejected immediately. "Imagine a gum-chewing devourer of ice cream and oysters going through a regulation course of medicine, surgery, obstetrics and gynecology, or poring over standard textbooks of anatomy, physiology, and materia medica," one of the directresses conjectured with obvious disdain.[43]

The board members kept a tight rein on the candidates, particularly after the new nurses' home was opened in 1883. "Our responsibility in regard to them as young and homeless in a strange city [creates] the manifest duty of surrounding them with family influences and the wholesome restraints of a real home," announced President Lawrence.[44] Students rose at 6:00 A.M., and had to return before the doors were locked at 10:00 P.M. Visitors were neither allowed at meals, nor in the wards. If called to duty in a private home, they were required to bring back detailed evaluations of their conduct from the families they served. Gossiping about the patient's circumstances was strictly forbidden. "They are also most earnestly charged to hold sacred the knowledge which, to a certain extent, they must obtain of the private affairs of such households or individuals as they may attend," the directresses commanded.[45]

By aiding their middle-class sisters, they helped themselves. Many board members first became aware of the need for better nursing services through their own sufferings, or the deaths of ones they loved. Even the richest knew that she might one day be compelled to stand by watching helplessly as her servants and children succumbed to illness. During the winter of 1868, the wealthy Hibbard clan contracted measles, scarlet fever, and pneumonia. Because no trained nurses were available, and because she, too, was sick, Mrs. Hibbard was unable to care for the family. One son died. Lydia Hibbard later became one of the staunchest supporters of the ITN. Playing on popular fears, the founders underscored the school's dual charitable and social goal, emphasizing that experience gained in nursing the sick poor in Cook County Hospital could later be enlisted in the service of the well-to-do, ready to provide a much-needed extra pair of hands during a family crisis. The association's funding appeals constantly stressed this complex interplay between benevolence and self-interest. "Sooner or later sickness comes to us all," warned President Margaret Lawrence.[46]

Winning new donors was only half the battle. One of the most formidable tasks of the sponsors of the nation's first nursing schools was to convince the medical profession that they had embraced a noncompetitive role and that the confrontations of the Civil War would not recur in hospital wards. Duty and obedience were constantly underscored as the correct demeanor for the professional nurse. "It is the untrained, not the trained nurse, that assumes to be a doctor," insisted ITN spokesmen.[47] The ideal nurse was to be completely disciplined and ready to move into action at the physician's command. Describing a visit to Bellevue, one journalist noted admiringly that "a soldier, pausing in his rounds, presenting arms to his superior officer and listening respectfully for orders, would not have exhibited a more perfect discipline."[48]

The ITN experienced more than just a little difficulty in convincing the city's physicians of their sincerity, literally winning the right to practice in Cook County Hospital ward by ward. The struggle was complicated by the fact that the institution was under political control in a time when women could claim little clout at the polls. The hospital's administration was appallingly corrupt, and the men in authority had no intention of dissipating their power or succumbing to the winds of reform. According to Dr. Sarah Hackett Stevenson, "The dirt was indescribable. It was everywhere and thick. One did not dare sit down nor stand for fear that the vermin which abounded would find a lodging on the clothing."[49] Patients were clad in winding sheets and doctors' aprons. Women about to give birth were not admitted until their labor pains had become almost unbearable. The nurses were "untrained, incompetent, and neglected the patients shamefully." Many were "the mistresses of County Commissioners, kept there drawing salaries and living at the expense of the county . . . in defiance of public decency."[50]

Despite the determined opposition of the warden, the ladies gradually won the right to practice, aided by an "advisory committee" of prominent men. Almost immediately, the ITN claimed to have produced a noticeable improvement in the wards entrusted to their care, "a moral atmosphere . . . that must purify and elevate the inmates, especially the women."[51] Resisting their presence to the end, one politico snarled in frustration:

> In '82 they asked the board to be allowed to put in nurses in the hospital. That was granted. Then they asked for bed and board for their nurses. That was granted. Then they asked for one medical and one surgical ward. That was granted. Then they asked for additional wards. That was granted . . . . They haven't asked yet to be allowed to run the hospital. Why, there are men in the County Board who'd even grant that.[52]

Other organizations quickly followed their lead. Between 1885 and 1889, five new nursing schools were created in Chicago, founded and largely backed by feminine donors.[53]

Ladies began to create and endow medical institutions with ever-increasing regularity during the 1870s and 1880s. Julia Newberry bequeathed $26,000 to the Hospital for Women and Children,[54] Mrs. Mancel Talcott donated a $13,000 addition in 1884, and Mrs. Philip D. Armour was one of several women who volunteered to furnish wards at a cost of several thousand dollars. Julia F. Porter built a children's hospital in memory of her twelve-year-old son in 1882, purchasing a $20,000 building and maintaining it out of her own pocket until its reorganization under a board of directresses twelve years later. Mary Shumway revitalized the Ethical Culture Society's defunct district nursing program, funding it for two years before turning it over to friends as the Visiting Nurse Association in 1889. Jessie Lawson, wife of the publisher of the *Chicago Daily News*, created a lakeside open-air refuge for the summer care of ailing infants, and other hospitals continued to receive sizable grants from feminine donors throughout the period.

The most generous gift was Clarissa Peck's 1884 bequest of $625,000 for a Home for Incurables, providing land, buildings, and endowment in a single stroke. The wife of a Chicago pioneer, Mrs. Peck outlived her husband and her five children as well. Afterward, she lived unpretentiously in the house of a friend, quietly plotting the disposal of her million-dollar estate. Erected on Ellis Avenue between 55th and 56th Streets, Mrs. Peck's memorial provided shelter and medical care for impoverished victims of a variety of lingering ailments, ranging from arthritis to cancer.

Health organizations received the lion's share of feminine gifts in the 1880s, netting over $700,000 in grants of $5,000 or more. By contrast, asylums received only $32,000, and cultural endeavors $18,000. Only one woman, Mrs. Mancel Talcott, consistently donated large sums to the city's Homes. Significantly, her grants replicated antebellum gifts-in-kind, endowing fruit days and shoe days for the inmates. "Goll!" one orphan reportedly exclaimed when he saw his new pair of shoes on Talcott Shoe Day. "This beats the Fourth of July."[55] Noting Mrs. Talcott's benefactions, one group of directresses commented (with unintentional irony), "The example of this noble lady will assist them in walking in the right path thro' the great world which lies before them."[56]

Almost all of the women who donated substantial sums to the Art Institute during the final decades of the nineteenth century were members, or close relatives of members, of the Chicago Society of Decorative Art. The first sizable feminine gift was Mrs. Ellis's $7,400 grant for the purchase of plaster casts in 1887, eight years after the institute was founded. Bertha Palmer labored assiduously under the Society's auspices to strengthen the museum's holdings of medieval textiles. As she explained: "The South Kensington Museum has of course been of inestimable advantage to the artistic development of England and I trust our own Museum may one day be well enough equipped to play a similar role in our part of the world."[57] Later, she would bequeath it $100,000 worth of her choicest canvases. Elizabeth Stickney presented a large collection of engravings in 1888, the first of a series of generous gifts. Later, her niece, Harriet Hammond McCormick, would continue her benefactions. The Society's president, Maria Scammon, also left a $35,000 bequest in 1902, for lectures on the history, theory, and practice of the graphic and plastic arts. But in 1889 their gifts were still modest and few.

Most Gilded Age patronesses were older, nearing fifty at the time of their gifts. Board members, on the other hand, were young, rich, and likely to be engaged in a variety of undertakings. A composite picture of the average member, drawn from the rosters of the ITN and the

CSDA, reveals a woman in her thirties, wed to a wealthy businessman or attorney, the mother of two, and mistress of a household staffed by four servants. Over half (25 out of 40) were also members of the prestigious Fortnightly Club (see table 2).[58]

The contrasts between this group and their antebellum predecessors sharply delineates the magnitude of the changes which had occurred in the intervening years. Less than a fourth (9) were related by marriage or birth to families active in the 1850s, and only one, Mrs. Judd, was a veteran of prewar asylum work. Instead, they represented the new families who came to the city in the 1850s, made their fortunes during the Civil War, and were beginning to enjoy the benefits which their wealth accorded. At least eleven were wed to millionaires, while six others listed holdings in the hundreds of thousands of dollars in the 1899 Cook County Real Estate Assessment List, fortunes far larger than those held by the spouses of the antebellum directresses.

Their wealth enabled them to assume a more managerial role both in and out of the household. While prewar women were fortunate to have one servant, the directresses of the 1880s had a full complement of butlers, maids, cooks, and governesses at their command. Just as they hired and supervised the staffs of their asylums, nursing schools, and art courses, Gilded Age ladies presided over growing hierarchies of domestic employees.

Rich, prominent, and leisured, they assumed a variety of roles, from

**Table 2**
**Characteristics of Board Members of ITN and CSDA, 1880–1889**

| Age in 1880 | Number Children | Number Servants | Husband's Occupation | Children's Ages |
|---|---|---|---|---|
| Under 20 (2) | 0 (3) | 0 (0) | Businessman (17) | Under 1 (1) |
| 20–29 (7) | 1 (4) | 1 (0) | Lawyer (7) | 1–3 (2) |
| 30–39 (8) | 2 (11) | 2 (2) | Financier (3) | 4–6 (6) |
| 40–49 (8) | 3 (1) | 3 (3) | Industrialist (3) | 7–10 (7) |
| 50–59 (2) | 4 (1) | 4 (6) | Physician (2) | 11–14 (6) |
| Unknown (13) | 5 (1) | 5 (5) | Clergyman (1) | 15–18 (5) |
| | Unknown (19) | 6 (1) | Gov. agent (1) | 19–21 (5) |
| | | Unknown (23) | Widow (3) | 22+ (5) |
| | | | Single (3) | |
| | | | Unknown (6) | |

NOTE: Numerals in parentheses = number of women in category.
SOURCES: City directories and 1880 Manuscript Census Reports.

society queen, to philanthropist, to patroness of the arts. Mrs. Levi Leiter's forte was social climbing. Wife of the millionaire partner of Marshall Field, she is best remembered as the mother of Lady Curzon, Vicereine of India. Isabella Blackstone selected a more public-spirited route, becoming one of the city's leading philanthropists after her husband's death in the late 1890s. In addition to endowing churches, medical charities, and family welfare organizations, she constructed the city's first branch library in 1904, the $200,000 Timothy Blackstone Memorial Library in Hyde Park.

Perhaps the most famous was the elegant, wasp-waisted Mrs. Potter Palmer, the undisputed queen of fin-de-siècle Chicago society. The wife of one of the city's wealthiest men, she was an avid art collector. Guided by the sage advice of her friend, artist Mary Cassatt, Palmer began to collect in earnest on the eve of Chicago's Columbian Exposition. Between 1891 and 1892, she purchased scores of canvases while touring the courts of Europe as part of her duties as chairman of the fair's Board of Lady Managers. Unlike most Americans, her collection was bereft of old masters, consisting primarily of impressionists and the works of American painters. Her faith in contemporary art was vindicated at the fair, where the collection was extremely well received. Aided by Cassatt, Palmer helped to engineer the acceptance of French impressionism in the United States.

Others, like Ellen Henrotin and Lucy Flower, became leading clubwomen and noted reformers. Both held the presidency of the Chicago Woman's Club, both helped to found the nation's pioneer juvenile court in 1899, and both were later drawn into the orbit of Jane Addams and Hull-House, contacts which lured them into a variety of crusades. Ironically, they hailed from radically different backgrounds. An orphan, Flower supported herself as a teacher before her marriage to a prominent Madison attorney. Henrotin, on the other hand, was the child of wealth and luxury, reared in New Haven, London, Paris, and Dresden. While Flower presided over the ITN and engaged in a variety of child-oriented reform movements, Henrotin immersed herself in women's organizations, eventually chairing the Illinois Woman's Suffrage Association, the General Federation of Women's Clubs, and the Woman's Trade Union League.

Only one was a career woman. The ITN directress, Dr. Sarah Hackett Stevenson, began her career much as many of her antebellum predecessors had, by teaching school. The daughter of a rural Illinois merchant, she graduated from the Illinois State Normal University and taught for several years in a string of small midwestern towns before deciding to pursue a medical career at the recently created Chicago Woman's Medical College. Later, she capped her education with a year at London's prestigious South Kensington Science School, where she reportedly was one of Thomas Huxley's brightest protégés. Huxley's faith was vindicated, for Stevenson went on to list several pathbreaking efforts to her credit, including her appointments as the first woman member of the ultraconservative American Medical Association, the first on the staff at Cook County Hospital, and the first to sit on the Illinois State Board of Health. She was also the clubwoman par excellence: a Fortnightly member, president of the Chicago Woman's Club, and chairman of the national hygiene committee of the Women's Christian Temperance Union.

Better educated than most of her fellow board members, Stevenson was one of only two college graduates. The rest were educated in much the same fashion as the earlier group, trained in public schools, tutored at home, or "finished" in fashionable boarding schools. The curricula of these boarding schools was notoriously arid. "I never learned the significance of things," bewailed one alumna, "and the quality of impressions received and stored, gave me no joy or interest in aiming at any special distinction. It was simply and inevitably the principle of conformity to rules and text-books."[59] Coursework generally consisted of languages, basic skills like reading and penmanship, drawing, music, and a smattering of history, mathematics, and science. Mrs. Potter Palmer mastered the politely useless arts of towel hemming and the making of wax camellias. "By the time I made my entry into society I was ignorant in everything and accomplished in nothing," lamented her contemporary, Louise de Koven Bowen.[60]

For women such as these, the club became "the mature woman's college."[61] Feminine study groups, salons, and early club meetings are frequently passed over by historians as a rather inane prelude to the real business of reform.[62] But this overlooks the fundamental role they played in socializing adult women to new levels of cultural and charitable responsibility. Clubs galvanized women's skills, prejudices, and energies into new forms of social action, giving members the self-assurance they needed to move beyond the narrow limits of the home, and encouraging them to pool their resources to found and fund new institutions. As one member proudly pointed out, "The Chicago Woman's Club is a finely equipped training school, wherein one thousand thinking women absorb the knowledge which is power—power in the civic life of Chicago."[63]

The Woman's Club is a case in point. At first, the club adopted a fairly passive role, discussing issues but eschewing concrete plans. Discarding the intuitive wisdom which shaped the actions of the antebellum generation, members eagerly devoured the writings of Pestalozzi, Froebel, Spencer, Rousseau, Charles Loring Brace, and Enoch Wines. As one member explained, the club was founded upon the "desire to enlarge our vision, to enable us to share in the wider interests of the community,"[64] but "it took time to educate the members up to the required degree of courage and experience."[65]

The early years were a time of learning and self-discovery. By the eighties members were chafing at the bit, ready and anxious to move into larger roles within the community. As Henriette Greenbaum Frank explains, "There was manifest among the members of the Committee on Philanthropy a strong desire to do something which should make them a Committee of Philanthropy in fact as in name."[66] The turning point came in 1883, when members asked, "Shall the Club Do Practical Work?"[67] In the ensuing discussion, "the conversation having continued past the hour of adjournment," they resolved "that in undertaking such practical work it is not the purpose of the club to become a charity organization, but rather a discoverer of the best methods of advancing humanitarian principles, and of helping individuals and organizations to become self-sustaining; that it will receive and become the custodian of any contributions from its friends for specific purposes."[68] This resolution was a milestone for feminine charity in Chicago, for it stressed a new commitment to experimentation and innovation rather than institution building, monetary aid rather than service. During the ensuing decade the club sponsored a kindergarten and a protective agency for women and children, initiated the hiring of women matrons for female prisoners, and financed a dormitory at the new University of Chicago.

By the late 1880s, the growing ranks of formerly autonomous women's groups were coalescing into a coherent national network, linked by overlapping memberships, joint projects, and umbrella organizations like the National Council of Clubs and the General Federation of Women's Clubs. Like the older American Female Guardian Society, these Gilded Age organizations bound members together in sisterly pursuit of shared goals and ideals. As they grew in power and influence, clubs supplanted the influence of the church as the medium through which women were conscripted and informed, funneling feminine volunteers into a plethora of secular charities, cultural undertakings, and reforms.

"We have been limited for so long to orphan asylums and hospitals that we are 'taking to' ... the founding of scholarships, libraries, art galleries and gymnasiums," noted one clubwoman.[69] The focus of feminine beneficence had broadened considerably by 1889, as women began to take the lead in upgrading the city's charitable resources, public health, and popular taste. Freed from household (and charitable) drudgery by servants and the city's growing wealth, and motivated by a changing feminine ideal, they began to move away from the personal service of their mothers' generation.

Several factors contributed to their development as managers and patronesses. National events, like the Civil War and the Centennial Exposition, sensitized them to the need for better health care facilities and cultural amenities, giving women a personal stake in their creation. Travel broadened their range of vision, providing fresh alternatives for civic undertakings. Newly codified married women's property acts gave them the financial power with which to back their projects. Women's organizations played a crucial role, encouraging members to give sums as well as service, to initiate innovative projects, and to replace household wisdom with informed, pragmatic action.

Rejecting the sentimental formulas of an earlier age, Chicago's Gilded Age managers and patronesses replaced the intuitive solutions of their mothers' generation with the drive toward feminine education and expertise. In the process, they brought themselves more in line with the values and practices of the larger society. Donating sums on an increasingly generous scale, ladies assumed a more administrative role within the charities and cultural endeavors under their command. They also demonstrated a growing sensitivity to the needs of the "fit," fashioning ladders of self-improvement for their aspiring sisters much as Andrew Carnegie recommended in his Gospel of Wealth.

And yet, many significant issues remained unresolved. Most of the city's agencies continued to be rigidly segregated by gender well into the twentieth century. Although feminine largesse was on the upswing, feminine donors still gave less, and less consistently, than their masculine counterparts, tending to focus on traditional areas of domestic concern. While men formulated policies affecting the city as a whole, women continued to confine their attention primarily to the needs of other women, the elderly, and the very young.

Men, rather than women, ultimately knit the city's sprawling array of charities and cultural organizations into a cohesive, comprehensive system through their clubs, overlapping directorates, and the prestigious Chicago Relief and Aid Society, from which women were rigorously excluded. Thus, despite significant gains in a variety of new fields, Chicago's Gilded Age managers and patronesses remained at the periphery of the decision-making process, pioneering, claiming new prerogatives, but still isolated within the sheltered idiom of gender and sphere.

William Butler Ogden (1861). Courtesy of the Chicago Historical Society.

# 3
# CHRISTIAN GENTLEMEN & SELF-MADE MAGNATES

First as servants, then as donors and managers, feminine stewards played an integral role in developing Chicago's charitable resources. Yet, had their fellow townsmen been polled prior to 1894, most would have cited the male-dominated Chicago Relief and Aid Society (CRA) as the city's most important charity. Founded in 1850, the CRA quickly attracted the backing of Chicago's leading Christian Gentlemen. Educated, respected and refined, the city's first generation of masculine civic stewards were essentially volunteers. Like their feminine counterparts, CRA trustees personally visited the homes of the poor to minister to the impoverished families entrusted to their care.

There the similarity ended, for antebellum CRA board members held positions of authority in a far more diversified array of business ventures, civic, religious, and cultural undertakings than their feminine counterparts. These men built the city; every aspect of its growth and health was as familiar to them as the lists of their investments and the inventories of their possessions. The rite of succoring the poor, like luring new settlers or bargaining for a new transportation route, was merely another component in their overall drive to ensure the city's continued social and economic viability.

The Chicago fire of 1871 heralded the maturation of a substantially different generation of leaders, men who had arrived in the 1850s and amassed substantial fortunes during the Civil War. Eschewing the direct personal service of their predecessors, postwar CRA members used the fire relief funds to fashion a comprehensive welfare system firmly implanted under their own control. Centralization, self-help, efficient management of the chronic poor: these were the charitable goals of Chicago's self-made magnates. In effect, although the fire ushered in a new era of plutocratic rule for both men and women alike, CRA trustees translated their newly acquired prerogatives into a system which was elitist, aloof, and tightly centralized under masculine control.

Chicago was just beginning to emerge from the chrysalis of village life when the Chicago Relief Society was founded in 1850. As rail links were forged with the east, and the canal route to the Mississippi River was completed, travelers and settlers began to pass through the city at an ever-increasing rate. In the process, its complexion changed. Although the first settlers were mainly Yankees from New England and New York, by 1850 52% of the population was foreign born. The older residents keenly resented these "poor and vicious foreigners" who squatted on private property and pilfered timber to warm themselves.[1] Clannish and poor, they huddled in shantytowns with quaint names like New Dublin, Swedetown, Conley's Patch, and the Sands. The reality was something else. Peppered with saloons, gambling dens, and brothels presided over by fierce prostitutes like the Bengal Tigress, these slum towns were suspiciously regarded as the seedbeds for the city's rising tide of pauperism and crime.

Public resources for the care of the poor were limited and grudgingly rendered. The first county poorhouse, built in 1836, quickly fell into disrepair and was replaced by a newer one in 1841. Dilapidated and unsanitary, it was viewed as a place of last resort. The county government also dispensed outdoor relief funds, but when the treasury was low this service was often among the first to be discontinued.[2]

Between 1848 and 1850, years marked by endemic cholera and increasing immigration, the impoverished government belligerently refused to make any relief grants. Faced with a mounting crisis, Chicago's private citizens banded together to cope with the problem themselves. Founded on December 28, 1850, the Chicago Relief Society was designed to render temporary aid, advice, and care to the "worthy" poor. In order to circumvent the spread of street begging and pauperism, doles were to be solely in the form of food, fuel, and clothing. The founders stressed that money was not to be given under any circumstances.

Like later organizations, they hoped to systematize the city's growing network of charities through careful supervision and observation of the poor. The city was promptly districted, with each section entrusted to a volunteer who would investigate applicants, carefully record their names and nationalities, and "endeavor to discourage vicious habits, procure the education of children, and promote industry, cleanliness, economy and virtue."[3] Contributions "of any sort, or kind, and however trifling" were solicited from the public at large, including clothing made by ladies' benevolent societies. In return, donors received cards to deflect importuning beggars to the society's doors.[4]

Despite a promising beginning, the organization was discontinued when county relief payments were resumed in 1851. Six years later, it was briefly revived as the Chicago Relief and Aid Society during the financial panic of 1857. Once again, relief and moral instruction formed the major thrust of the society's activities. Inveterate paupers, able-bodied workers, and the poor who had migrated from other cities were not deemed suitable candidates for aid. Only the sick and temporarily impoverished received assistance from the society's representatives. When the crisis had passed, the CRA once again lapsed into inactivity.

Chicago's relief agencies have often been compared to the New York Association for the Improvement of the Condition of the Poor (AICP), founded in 1843. Like the CRA, the AICP was designed to curb pauperism through constant vigil and niggardly aid. The AICP director, Robert M. Hartley, spent a year studying relief techniques in American cities and abroad before implementing his program in New York. The result was a carefully delineated system for grading the poor. Those reduced to poverty by infirmity, sickness, old age, or unavoidable misfortune were to receive immediate, albeit limited, aid. Dissolutes brought to the brink of ruin through their own antisocial habits and pastimes would get more advice than material assistance. Hartley sternly advised that "alms should, as far as possible, be withheld from the drunkard."[5] Sturdy beggars and professional vagrants, the lowest rung on the ladder, were unworthy and ineligible for aid. They were to be recorded and watched.

The keynote of the AICP was uplift, the cornerstone visitation. In addition to relieving want, visitors sought out jobs, discouraged vicious habits, fostered notions of cleanliness, thrift, and piety, and enjoined parents to educate their young, all under the patina of friendliness and neighborly concern. Hartley repeatedly cautioned his visitors to "avoid all appearance of harshness, and every manifestation of an obtrusive and a censorious spirit."[6] In addition to reforming the poor, the trustees hoped that personal service and ongoing supervision would restore the city's rapidly waning sense of community, encouraging social interaction by bringing urbanites into contact with people of different social strata. The injunction to seek out the poor in their own homes promised to restore the network of primary relationships, even in an immense city like New York.

Their desire to build a personal bridge between the classes was kindled by the changing urban scene. New York had shed most of the earmarks of village life by 1850 and turned into a sprawling giant. Congested streets, inadequate interurban communications systems, and even the lack of suitable communal meeting places contributed to the growing sense of fragmentation. As the population grew, nearing the million mark by 1860, transit systems spread the city outward, making interpersonal communications increasingly elusive. Omnibuses appeared as early as 1827, and within a decade were augmented by the more efficient horse-drawn street railways. Each transportation innovation reduced commuting time to the central business area, luring homeowners farther into the periphery. A cyclical process, each new spurt of urban expansion fostered greater social and economic segregation. Although falling short of the rigid stratification of the postwar decade, New York was fast becoming a city divided by class and caste.[7]

Chicago was just beginning to experience these problems in the 1850s. One of the nation's fastest growing cities, its 100,000 population figure (1860) still lagged far behind New York. Nor was its pattern of spatial distribution as sharply defined. The first omnibus service was not introduced until 1852, stretching the city from a modest nine square miles to thirty-five by 1871. Shanties still loomed near the stately homes of the rich, and many neighborhoods retained the heterogeneous populations of the village until the fire of 1871.

Chicago's problems were not as great, nor its solutions as permanent. As the society's spokesmen explained, the CRA "has sprung up at the sound of distress, as the winter advances, elected its officers, secured such agents as could be obtained, and worked with eagerness until the opening of spring, when it ceased acting entirely and remained dormant until winter again, when it wakes up as before."[8] Despite their obvious attempt to emulate the ACIP, the CRS and the CRA failed to achieve the longevity of the parent organization. Spurred to action during periods of acute distress, they were quickly disbanded when the immediate crisis had passed.

Nevertheless, they won the backing of some of the city's leading citizens. Of thirty trustees, twelve were prominent businessmen, eight were lawyers, four bankers, and three doctors and government employees. Fourteen were listed as landholders in the 1850 manuscript census and tax lists. Their holdings varied widely, ranging from $250 to over $250,000, with most in the $10,000 to $50,000 bracket. Their religious affiliations were equally varied, including seven Presbyterians, five Episcopalians, three Methodists, two Baptists, and one Universalist and Congregationalist. The majority (nineteen) were Yankees, hailing from New England and New York, born between 1800 and 1817, and arriving in Chicago between 1832 and 1840. Over half (17) served in the city government, including four former mayors.

Many participated in a variety of charitable, humanitarian, and religious programs. Ten sat on asylum boards, and an equal number were directors of the Chicago Bible Society and the City Tract and Missionary Society. Still others enlisted in the temperance and antislavery crusades. Former mayor B. W. Raymond, a Finney convert, was a founder of the Presbyterian college in Lake Forest; Dr. N. S. Davis, a lifelong temperance crusader, taught Sunday school and served as a trustee of the Methodist's Northwestern University; marble merchant A. S. Sherman founded a Methodist mission church in 1843; and Philo Carpenter became involved in a welter of benevolent undertakings.

Carpenter was a model moral steward. The son of a distinguished New England family (his grandfather directed West Point during the Revolutionary War), he was born in Savoy, Massachusetts, in 1805, and settled in Chicago at the age of twenty-eight. Shortly after his arrival, the enterprising druggist opened the city's first Sunday school, organized the First Presbyterian Church, and launched the Chicago Temperance Society. Not a man to shun responsibilities or sidestep risks, he opened his home to the underground railroad, conscientiously visited the poor to distribute Bibles and tracts, and personally ministered to countless victims during the cholera ridden summers of 1849 and 1850. After suffering excommunication from the Presbyterian congregation for his antislavery activities, Carpenter established the city's first Congregational Church, later donating a healthy $50,000 to ensure its continued prosperity. A generous man, he also gave at least $110,000 to the Chicago Theological Seminary, bequeathing more modest sums to Oberlin College, Berea College, the Chicago City Missionary Society, and the Chicago Historical Society.

Although church attendance was synonymous with respectability during this era, and all of the trustees were conscientious churchmen, some opted to express their civic consciousness through more secular pursuits. Mark Skinner, the college-educated son of the governor of New Hampshire, sat on the boards of Rush Medical College, the

Chicago Historical Society, and the Young Men's (literary) Association. Richard K. Swift, a former pawnbroker who had risen to head his own bank, was active in the Academy of Sciences. After briefly dabbling in academia and medicine, Mayor James H. Woodworth established a successful dry-goods business in Chicago, devoting his leisure time to the Academy of Sciences, the Astronomical Society, the University of Chicago, and several asylums.

William B. Ogden had a hand in every worthy undertaking. The son of a prosperous upstate New York manufacturer and lumber dealer, Ogden was Chicago's wealthiest citizen and largest landholder. After briefly flirting with a legal career, and serving a stint in the New York Senate, he came to Chicago in 1835 to manage the extensive real estate holdings of his brother-in-law, Charles Butler. Butler was a prominent New Yorker, the law partner of Martin Van Buren, and a well-known philanthropist who numbered membership in the AICP among his many organizational ties.

Ogden occupied a similar position in Chicago. In addition to serving as the city's first mayor, he sat on the boards of the Chicago Historical Society, the University of Chicago, Rush Medical College, the COA, the Erring Woman's Refuge, and the Astronomical Society. Although Episcopalian, he donated twenty acres of land to the Presbyterian Theological Seminary in 1859, and helped to underwrite several Catholic projects as well. Any undertaking which promised to benefit Chicago elicited his attention and support. He financed the construction of miles of streets out of his own pocket, designed the city's first swing bridge, and sponsored the construction of the Galena and Chicago Union Railroad in 1848. Yet, despite his far-flung business activities, Ogden "never forgot in his busiest days to visit the suffering, and always took with him the choicest products of his fruit and green-houses."[9]

Rather than remaining aloof from society, wealthy citizens like Ogden regularly made the rounds of the homes of the poor. Most of the trustees of the CRS served as volunteer visitors, and they were joined by many of their equally well-to-do peers. Antebellum treatises and sermons constantly enjoined the wealthy merchant and his brother of lesser means to honor their civic and spiritual obligations.[10]

Whether rich or poor, men were expected to perform acts of personal charity. Training for this role was to begin as early as possible. "Benevolence should be taught and inculcated early," admonished one source. "If the seed is not sown, there will be no harvest."[11] No one was too old, or too young, to be charitable. McGuffey readers urged schoolchildren to perform good deeds, reminding them that even the great Washington was not too exalted to enter the hovels of the poor in times of need. "Can evil ever come from being benevolent?" one passage queried. "Are there many who are really so poor as not to be able to do something for others?"[12]

The impulse to do good was fortified by religious injunctions. Theologians continually reiterated the obligations of stewardship. Moved from the center of the governmental process by the Revolution, they looked to individual conversion to combat the moral declension which seemed to threaten the social fabric of the new republic. If government could not control social behavior, the individual must be made to control himself. By the 1820s revivalism had become the raison d'être of much of the American ministry. Reared in an atmosphere of heightened religious emotionalism, many Chicagoans had matured into dedicated churchmen. Fired with missionary zeal, and a keen appreciation of the perils of sin, they determined to become their brothers' keepers.[13]

Great revivalists like Charles Grandison Finney labored tirelessly to inspire charitable voluntarism on a national scale, among all levels of society, by demanding that social action follow conversion. Preaching hellfire and damnation, Finney harvested souls by the hundreds as he made his way across New York State, and his converts carried his teachings to the cities of the frontier. His aggressive evangelism catalyzed wave upon wave of humanitarian activity among his followers, laying the groundwork for the Benevolent Empire.

Men of wealth were continually urged to be Christian Gentlemen. As Paul Goodman explains: "In a republic, business enterprise was appropriately the chief means of acquiring great wealth because virtue and talent were rewarded, giving every citizen an opportunity to prosper. Those who accumulated riches did so, it was argued, because they possessed personal merit, not hereditary advantage. The successful were obligated to serve the community in which they had prospered."[14] The necessity for this type of responsible behavior was quite plain to the men of the post-Revolutionary generations. If excess riches could be siphoned back into the community, then rampant materialism would be checked. If leisure were employed to enhance the quality of city life, rather than being wasted in dissipation, virtue and simplicity would flourish. If the rich were willing to personally devote time and energy to aiding their fellow men, then class lines would not harden into caste lines, and the well-to-do would not be insulated from the rest of society by their wealth.

The model gentleman was cultured, charitable, and a ready patron for any project which would benefit his city. Although wealthy, he was neither ostentatious nor unduly acquisitive, for "the great danger was that one might become too greatly absorbed in the quest for treasure, neglect other pursuits and stain one's character."[15] Speculative ventures, which brought wealth without hard work, were frowned upon. Self-culture, devotion to family and community, charity, and cultural patronage were means of curbing the acquisitive spirit while justifying the process of acquisition itself.

Contemporary writers celebrated the virtues of the Christian Gentleman, extolling the exploits of particularly exemplary individuals. Freeman Hunt's popular books consisted of vignettes of conscientious businessmen like Stephen Girard. The French-born Girard, an active Philadelphia councilman, rendered heroic service during the yellow fever epidemics which swept the city in 1793 and 1797. Aided by Thomas Pym Cope, Girard took charge of the contagious hospital, nursed the inmates himself, sought out others who needed help, and supplied the poor with food and fuel. His work brought him into contact with many orphans. Upon his death, he bequeathed a substantial amount to his adopted city for municipal improvements and founded the celebrated Girard College for poor orphan boys. In appraising Girard's bequests, Hunt commented approvingly, "The savings of the years of toil were . . . dispensed in bulk upon the community in the midst of which he had gathered them."[16] But it was clear that Girard had also been singled out for his extraordinary personal charity during his lifetime. "What is a man worth?" queried Hunt. "He is worth precisely just so much as he has capacity and inclination to be useful."[17]

Men of prominence knew that at life's end their achievements and shortcomings would be candidly dissected and reviewed in pulpit and press. In his excellent study of philanthropy in Tudor-Stuart England, Wilbur K. Jordan suggests the significance of funeral sermons in spurring emulative charities. Like these sermons, obituaries unsparingly analyzed the decedent's activities for all the world to see, and charity and civic responsibility ranked very high on the list of evaluative criteria. Indeed, when Ogden died, leaving what appeared to be only a pittance for charity, the journalistic attacks were so vitriolic that his friends felt compelled to step forward and defend his good name. It is possible that this kind of publicity served to reinforce the demand for civic responsibility embodied in the gentlemanly ideal. As Hunt concluded, "Neither polished marble nor lying epitaph can ever preserve the memory or ennoble the life of him who, dying, leaves behind no monument of mercy, and no remembrances of generous and benevolent worthiness."[18]

The model for the Christian Gentleman was more than merely a self-serving justification for the stature of the very rich. When transferred to the newer, less-stratified cities of the west, it became a means of socializing new leaders to the responsibilities of stewardship. Even in a city as brash and notoriously materialistic as Chicago, men attempted to conform to this role model as soon as wealth and leisure would permit. In assessing each other's achievements, wealthy Chicagoans continually stressed their gentlemanly qualities rather than material accomplishments. Erudition, bibliophilia, charity, cultural patronage, and refined but modest life-styles were the qualities most frequently singled out for commendation.

The Civil War shattered the benign ideals of the antebellum generation, giving rise to a far harsher, tooth and claw interpretation of noblesse oblige. The carnage of the war blunted the nation's sensitivity to human suffering and discredited the intuitive, sentimental, impulsive beneficence of the prewar decades. Calls to refined benevolence no longer seemed germane to the harsh realities of a rapidly industrializing society. In their stead rose Social Darwinism. Constructed on the scientific reasoning of Charles Darwin, shaped by the philosophizing of Herbert Spencer, and popularized by the Yale professor William Graham Sumner, it served to legitimize the actions of a brutal age with the rallying cry of survival of the fittest. "It is out of the question to go back to . . . the sentimental relations which once united baron and retainer, master and servant, teacher and pupil, comrade and comrade," Sumner sharply advised.[19] Discussed and avidly debated by the press, in colleges and clubs, the new philosophy quickly gathered a vast following among the public at large.

The hero in the Social Darwinist scenario was the self-made man.[20] The antithesis of the Christian Gentleman, he was at heart a buccaneer. A ruthless centralizer who cared not a whit about staining his character (or anyone else's, if ample profits were involved), and materialistic to the bone, he was the victor in the race for riches, the epitome of the "fit."

The archetypal self-made man was steel baron Andrew Carnegie. A poor Scottish immigrant when he arrived on American shores as a child, Carnegie had become one of America's wealthiest men through what contemporary authors were fond of labeling "pluck and luck." In his classic treatise on plutocratic benevolence, "The Gospel of

Wealth," published in 1889, Carnegie reasoned that the self-made businessman was ideally suited to redistribute the excess riches he had garnered from the community, investing it where the money would do the most good. This entailed aiding the "fit" who were anxious to help themselves, placing within their reach "the ladder upon which the aspiring can rise." Poverty was not only inevitable but an essential corollary of the system, for poverty bred the ambition and determination which ultimately led to success. "To abolish honest, industrious, self-denying poverty would be to destroy the soil upon which mankind produces the virtues which enable our race to reach a still higher civilization than it now possesses," Carnegie sanctimoniously declared.[21]

Having made the transition from rags to riches himself, the industrialist wasted little sympathy on those who failed to emulate his example. As he explained, "It were better for mankind that the millions of the rich were thrown into the sea than so spent as to encourage the slothful, the drunken, the unworthy."[22] Inveterate paupers were to be strictly "isolated from the well-doing and industrious poor, who are liable to be demoralized by contact with these unfortunates."[23] Much as one would quarantine a house of cholera victims, poverty was to be contained.

Unlike the prewar advocates of individualized beneficence, men of Carnegie's ilk envisioned a society held together by institutions bestowed by the rich and patronized by the "fit." The endowment of universities, art galleries, public parks, and concert halls all fell within the patron's appointed sphere. If great wealth were properly administered, Carnegie claimed, "the ties of brotherhood may still bind together the rich and poor in harmonious relationship."[24] Through these institutional bonds, "the millionaire will be but a trustee for the poor, entrusted for a season with a great part of the increased wealth of the community, but administering it for the community far better than it could or would have done for itself."[25] Rather than personally mingling with the poor, the self-made man would remain aloof from squalor and want. His task was to bestow, not to befriend.

The great Chicago fire completed the work which the Civil War began, burning away the ideals and accomplishments of Chicago's antebellum gentlemen and clearing the way for plutocratic rule. Kindled in a ramshackle barn in an impoverished immigrant section on the city's west side, it blazed relentlessly, consuming the central business district and the wealthy residential areas of the north side.

Descriptions of the inferno read like a vision from hell. Prostitutes and thugs careened drunkenly about, snatching what they could from stores and businesses in the fire's path. Night turned to day as the sky filled with the lurid yellowish red glare of the flames. Some died in the streets, clutching possessions or crucifixes before their eyes as the fire consumed them. Others managed to escape. As one wealthy north sider recalled:

> The flames ran in our direction, coming faster than a man could run. The rapidity was almost incredible, the wind blew a hurricane, the air was full of burning boards and shingles flying in every direction, and falling everywhere around us.... We had just time to dress ourselves, tie up a few valuables... and run for our lives.... I fled with my children clinging to me, fled literally in a shower of fire. You could not conceive anything more fearful. The wind was like a tornado, and I held fast to my little ones, fearing they would be lifted from my sight. It seemed as if the whole world were running like ourselves, fire all around us.... On we ran... till we reached Lincoln Park. There among the empty graves of the old cemetery we sat down [until] the dry leaves and even the very ground took fire beneath our feet, and again... [we] travelled with thousands of our poor fellow mortals on and on.[26]

When the debris was cleared and the losses tallied, most of the central business district and the north side lay in ashes. The losses were staggering. Nearly three hundred were dead, another hundred thousand homeless, and over $200,000,000 worth of property had been destroyed. Most of the survivors from the north side had clustered into Lincoln Park, at the northern edge of the fire. An eerie sight, they milled about, dazed and disoriented, among the open graves of the cemetery, which was in the process of conversion to parkland. A journalist recorded the scene:

> Here is a refined and handsome lady, all alone, with a bundle of dresses.... Here is a strong, able-bodied man, recognizable as a banker, sitting sadly on a grave, with his hat over his aching eyes, gazing thoughtfully into a frying pan which he holds in his hand. Every-where are rushing crowds, exclamations, salutations of woe in every language under heaven.... Here comes a young man who exhibits an ice pitcher and laughingly declares that it is all he possesses in the world. There are no strangers here. There are no ceremonies. The cement of a kindred sorrow has done its work.[27]

The nation's, and the world's, response was genuine and immediate. The disaster proved the beneficial power of technology beyond a doubt. News of Chicago's disaster was speeded over telegraph lines even before the flames had cooled. Trade rivals, like St. Louis, briefly gloated, and then turned to the serious task of marshaling monetary and material aid for their stricken foe. In New York, Chicago's primary economic ally, $500,000 was raised in thirty hours; $2,000,000 in three weeks. Aid poured into the city from around the world. Touching gifts, like paintings from artists and tiny sums from remote villages and towns, attested to the genuine sympathy which the disaster had inspired. In a nation recently sundered by the bitter conflict of the Civil War, Chicago's recovery became a welcome symbol of unity. "We could not afford to do without the Chicago fire," evangelist Henry Ward Beecher perceptively explained.[28]

The relief funds were entrusted to the CRA, which had been reorganized and started anew on a permanent basis in 1867. Most of Chicago's Gilded Age millionaires would serve on the board at some point in their careers. At the time of the fire its roster included, among others, department store magnate Marshall Field; industrialist George Pullman, originator of the Pullman Palace Car; N. K. Fairbank, the "lard king"; and millionaire foundry master Richard Teller Crane. Industrialists, businessmen, professional men, the majority were wartime nouveaux riches who had arrived in Chicago in the 1850s, made their fortunes in the 1860s, and were just beginning to assume a public role at the time of the fire. Their rise to prominence was hastened as the older generation of leaders, no longer young or resilient enough to begin again, resignedly deferred to these "younger men . . . who have not had their enthusiasm burned out of them."[29]

There was surprisingly little continuity between the rejuvenated board and its predecessors, a break which was reflected in other postfire boards as well. Only one man, E. C. Larned, served in both the 1857 CRA and the fire relief committee of 1871–72. Larned's son, Walter, an alumnus of Harvard Law School and son-in-law of New York publisher Charles Scribner, was one of the few children of the original board members to serve in the CRA in the ensuing decades. This discontinuity is particularly intriguing since one would normally expect the sons of the rich to inherit their fathers' positions on charitable boards.

Time, the war, and the fire all took their toll. Many of the early settlers were old men by 1871. Ogden and Carpenter were sixty-six,

Woodworth sixty-seven, Raymond seventy. Some suffered irreversible losses in the fire and the financial panics of 1857 and 1873. Ogden received a dual blow, simultaneously losing his Chicago holdings and his extensive lumber business in Peshtigo, Wisconsin, in blazes sparked on the same day. Too old to begin again, many of this generation drifted west, or returned to the homes of their youth. Ogden retired to Boscobel, his magnificent New York estate. R. K. Swift set out for Colorado after his bank failed in 1857, finally settling in Lawrence County, Missouri, where he died in 1883. Carpenter moved to Aurora, Illinois, in 1865, two years after railroad president Henry Farnum returned to New Haven, where two of his sons served on the faculty of Yale. New Haven's gain was Chicago's loss, for Farnum later became a major contributor to the university.

Five of the original trustees died between 1865 and 1875, and eight more perished during the ensuing decade. Some undoubtedly lost sons in the war. Others, like Mark Skinner and Philo Carpenter, left broods of daughters but no sons to succeed them. Some waited until literally the last moment to marry. Ogden wed for the first time in 1875, a scant two years before his death, and left no children to succeed him. All of these factors combined to ease the transition between Chicago's antebellum Christian Gentlemen and their Gilded Age peers. The clashes between old and new wealth which marked the experiences in eastern cities were far more muted in Chicago.

The fire relief committee of 1871–72 was richer, younger, and more ambitious than its antebellum predecessors. While the prewar generation had built a city from a prairie swamp, this group would fashion Chicago into the second largest city in the nation, the hub of a network of national and international business concerns. The composition of the board graphically reflected the change. While none of the earlier trustees had been engaged in manufacturing, eight of the fire relief board were industrialists, engaged in building enormous fortunes in iron, railroad supplies, and the byproducts of the packing industry. Seven were businessmen: commission merchants, railroad officials, lumbermen, department store owners, and wholesalers tapping an ever-widening economic hinterland. Four were the lawyers who served them; one a banker; and one the popular "society" doctor, Hosmer A. Johnson. Protestant Yankees born in New England and the Middle Atlantic states between 1825 and 1840, almost all arrived in Chicago in the 1850s, just in time to take advantage of the windfalls of the Civil War. At least five were millionaires by the 1880s, and the figure may have been much higher. Unlike their predecessors, they were not public servants. While fifteen would hold overlapping directorates in other charitable and cultural undertakings at some time in their careers, only two served in local government.

> Julius Rosenthal was the only immigrant, and the only Jew. Few could match Rosenthal's academic credentials. Born in Germany in 1828, he held degrees from both the universities of Heidelburg and Fribourg, a rarity in a period when few Americans pursued their studies beyond the academy. His Chicago career began modestly, with a position as a clerk in R. K. Swift's bank in 1854. Studying law in his spare time, Rosenthal was admitted to the bar in 1860, and quickly gained a reputation as one of Chicago's most distinguished attorneys. In addition to acting as vice-president of the newly created public library, he was a leading figure in the city's German and Jewish charities, the boards of the German *Altenheim*, the German Relief Society, the United Hebrew Relief Association, the Jewish Training School, and Michael Reese Hospital.

Several other trustees rose to prominence from relatively modest beginnings. Although most were descended from colonial families, none seems to have been as directly related to prominent eastern clans as Ogden, Skinner, Carpenter, and Kinzie had been. T. W. Harvey began as a carpenter's assistant and went on to head a lumber firm and the Harvey Steel Car Company. N. K. Fairbank, the millionaire manufacturer of oil and lard, was apprenticed to a bricklayer at the age of fifteen, later working as a bookkeeper in Rochester before coming to Chicago in 1855 as the western representative of a New York grain commission house. Like Rosenthal, he gradually became involved in a wide variety of charitable and cultural enterprises, including the Newsboy's and Bootblack's Home, St. Luke's Hospital, the Academy of Design, the Orchestral Association, the old University of Chicago, and the Chicago Manual Training School.

Marshall Field's experience is a case in point. A farmboy with no taste for the anonymity of farmlife, he found his first job in a general store near his family's home in Conway, Massachusetts. In 1856, he followed his brother Joseph to Chicago, where he was soon employed in John V. Farwell's store as a combination clerk and traveling salesman. As Farwell admiringly noted, Field had the merchant instinct. The ladies admired his icy courtesy and handsome appearance, while his unshakable rectitude won the trust of the men. Field is said to have arrived with a tiny stake of $500, saved from his Pittsfield job, to which he quickly added another $200, saving half of his first year's salary by sleeping in the shop and practicing rigid self-denial. Frugal to the bone, he detested extravagance in others. As he explained, "The five, ten or fifteen cents a day that is squandered, while a mere trifle apparently, if saved, would in a few years amount to thousands of dollars and go far toward establishing the foundation of a future career."[30]

Heeding his own advice, Field soon amassed enough to strike out on his own. By 1860, he had moved up from clerk to partner. Five years later, he started his own store with Levi Leiter and Potter Palmer, and by 1866 they were doing $9,000,000 worth of business per annum. The firm continued to prosper, and by the time of his death in 1906 Field was one of the wealthiest men in America, worth an estimated $120,000,000. Having succeeded himself, he took a hard line against the dissolute and poor. "The man who is characterized by want of forethought, idleness, carelessness or general shiftlessness cannot expect to succeed," he sternly declared.[31] Like a latter-day Ben Franklin, he ticked off the elements of success: energy, common sense, conscientious labor, careful choice of companions, honesty, self-control, economy, self-reliance, frugality.

Few of his peers would have quibbled with this formula. Field's former employer, millionaire retailer John V. Farwell, devoted lifelong support to the YMCA in the hope of instilling precisely those qualities in the city's young men. George Pullman's celebrated planning experiment in the 1880s had much the same aim, albeit with a greater profit margin. With decent housing, aesthetically pleasing surroundings, and a noticeable absence of drinking establishments, Pullman was designed to be the crucible of an improved citizenry and a better class of workers.[32]

This blind faith in the openness of the system and the power of the ambitious individual to make his own way made the board members intractable foes of unionization and labor unrest. When Pullman became the focus of one of the nation's most notorious strikes in 1894, he opted to starve the workers out rather than cutting profits or acceding to their demands. Similarly, when the question of pardoning the condemned Haymarket anarchists was raised in 1887, it was Field's dissenting voice which quelled the amnesty movement. Employing workers on a scale undreamed of by the previous generation, Chicago's Gilded Age trustees hoped to create an ideal work force: available and cheap when needed, docile and stoic when unemployed.[33]

The new CRA reflected the shift in emphasis from personal regeneration to a disciplined labor force. Organized on a permanent basis in 1867, it also had a permanent director, O. C. Gibbs. Shortly after Gibbs was secured, the trustees sent him to Philadelphia, New York, St. Louis, and Boston to observe relief operations at close range with an eye to their applicability in Chicago. Upon his return, he promptly established a wood yard where paupers could work for their meals, and urged the county poorhouse to do the same. Visiting was consigned to a salaried visitor, while the trustees raised the necessary funds.

As Gibbs explained, citizens had a duty to aid unemployed workmen and their families, for "their labor is needed here in the summer, and they cannot go elsewhere in winter."[34] Aid was to be strictly temporary, consisting of small quantities of necessary articles, and never rendered without preliminary investigation. When Methodist minister and former Iowa businessman Charles G. Trusdell assumed the directorship in 1872, the association's policies were already well formed. Like the trustees, Trusdell evinced a keen appreciation of the threat of the unemployed. As he admitted with arresting candor, "Charity has a twofold character. It is the practical expression of sympathy with the afflicted, and the price that society pays for its own safety."[35]

The fire relief funds arrived in the CRA's coffers through a rather circuitous route. Before the ashes had even begun to cool, the mayor appointed an impromptu relief committee consisting of Gibbs, Fairbank, and attorney Wirt Dexter, another CRA board member. Three days later, on October 12, the committee proposed that the funds be turned over to the CRA. On October 13, the work was formally transferred to the agency, and the arduous task of succoring the victims was begun.

The board quickly coalesced into committees and set about the enormous task of distributing over $5,000,000 in relief funds. "The board gave their entire time," recalled superintendent Trusdell. In the process, they "came in personal contact with thousands upon thousands of applicants of every grade and for all imaginable things. They had opportunities to study this whole question, such as no body of men ever had before."[36] Within six months winter shelter had been built, small loans granted to businessmen, and jobs, food, and tools distributed among the remainder of the populace.

The largest sums were given to existing institutions. Some of the asylums on the city's periphery managed to escape the holocaust, and these were conscripted as temporary shelters and distributing centers for relief. Hospitals, too, were quickly reestablished to care for the injured and the sick. Yet long after the initial emergency had passed, relief money continued to flow into institutional coffers.[37]

It was accepted with a sense of bitter irony. During the brief flurry of affluence between Appomatox and the fire, an expansionist mentality had dominated all of the city's voluntary organizations as newly rich Chicagoans began to donate unprecedented sums. Even visitors remarked that "the growth of [Chicago's] churches, charities, and Sunday-Schools is almost as astonishing as the increase of her trade."[38] Staffs were augmented, buildings purchased, and money borrowed in anticipation of future largesse. The ensuing fire left them financially crippled, faced with worthless pledges and mountainous debts.

The CRA paid the debts, built longed-for additions, provided income-producing properties as a hedge against future catastrophes, and helped the city's asylums, hospitals, and dispensaries through the economic crisis of 1873. St. Luke's Hospital was a case in point. Two years before the fire it was overcrowded and desperately trying to secure new facilities. "We MUST make an effort to better ourselves, either by renting a more suitable house, or by building," the trustees declared. The inadequacy of our present building, its inconveniences, and its want of sanitary surroundings, etc., demand that some immediate steps be taken to secure a building better suited to our purpose."[39] Upon receipt of a $28,000 grant, they burst into a litany of gratitude, earnestly reiterating how "the Chicago Relief and Aid Society . . . generously offered to assume the larger part of our expenses. They furnished the remainder of our house. They supplied us with every possible want, and we were enabled to do far more good than before. Every debt we owe is paid, and our property is entirely free from encumbrance."[40]

In return, applicants agreed to submit detailed information on their income, property holdings, means of support, expenses, population, and "whether your work could be enlarged if you had the means."[41] Other requirements were tailored to suit the recipient. The Society insisted that no barriers of race, creed, or nationality be allowed to stand in agencies under their patronage. They also demanded control over a varying number of bed rights. Representatives of the Old Ladies Home were required to "enlarge its objects, and place it under the control of business men such as the Relief and Aid Society shall approve."[42] This entailed ousting clerical trustees and filling the vacancies with CRA board members, giving the CRA final approval over all plans and managerial procedures, and opening its doors to men as well as women inmates.

Few could afford to refuse their generosity. Chicago Nursery and Half-Orphan Asylum directresses independently canvassing eastern cities were repeatedly told "that [the money] had already been telegraphed to the Relief and Aid Society."[43] The few intransigents who balked at the restrictions paid dearly for their resistance. When representatives of the Jewish Hospital temporized about ceding bed rights in exchange for $15,000, the CRA withdrew its offer, and the hospital was unable to reopen.[44]

Postwar demobilization, the fire, and the economic depression which ensued left many jobless men and children loitering in the streets, providing ready tinder for street-corner agitators. The era was punctuated by violence: the railroad strikes of 1877, Haymarket, the Pullman strike. During the riot of 1877, middle-aged businessmen, lawyers, and bankers clumsily shouldered muskets to defend their homes from pillage and the torch. One ingenious merchant equipped his home with a novel device which enabled him to "punch a button marked 'Fire' and summon the fire department. He could punch another button marked 'Mob' and summon the police."[45] Unwilling and unable to inspect the problems of the hostile poor at close range, the members of the CRA faced the challenge of devising efficient methods for dealing with poverty at arm's length.

As the economic situation worsened after the panic of 1873, a group of workmen stormed CRA headquarters, demanding that the remaining funds be surrendered to city aldermen for distribution to the poor. Trusdell slyly defused the situation by offering agency jobs to some of the insurgents, but little else was done for the poor after the initial emergency had passed. With the closing of neighborhood stations early in 1872, only widows with small children, the sick, and aged and infirm were deemed worthy of aid. Impoverished families with able-bodied schoolchildren were sternly turned away with instructions to set the children to work, while sturdy beggars and chronic paupers were promptly consigned to the county poorhouse, where they faced the grim prospect of being farmed out to the lowest bidder. In phrases that smacked of the rhetoric of Carnegie and Sumner, one trustee explained that "to aid the willingly idle man or woman, or anyone who can help himself, is in the highest degree hurtful to the person aided and to society at large."[46] Relief, asylums, hospitals, and almshouse care were the primary components in the system of private social control in Gilded Age Chicago.

Armed with the fire relief funds, the men of the CRA knit the city's charities into a centralized system providing minimal monetary assistance and institutional shelter for the poor. Well on the way to becoming some of the nation's leading industrialists and merchant princes, they transposed the techniques of the business endeavors in which they excelled onto the sentimental ventures of a preindustrial age. The information garnered in the course of distributing the relief money gave them a superb overview of the city's needs and resources, a perspective which shaped their activities in the ensuing decades. The conditions which they demanded in return for grants gave them nominal control over institutional admissions, updated asylum administration, refashioned the institutions along business lines, and put them in the black. Field, Crane, Pullman, and several of their peers later made substantial gifts to local asylums. Bound by financial and personal ties, these formerly autonomous charities were welded into a loose system through which the poor could be quickly and efficiently treated. Whether doles or institutional care was deemed proper, the CRA had the necessary resources instantly at its command.

Those foolish enough to criticize their techniques or challenge their hegemony were dealt with quickly, effectively, and as mercilessly as the most irksome business competitor. When a rival Charity Organization Society (COS) was founded in 1883, CRA spokesmen instantly howled in protest, pointing out that they had already coordinated the city's charities in accordance with the best business principles, and were thus "enabled to know what work is being done by each, AND PREVENT, TO A LARGE EXTENT, THE DUPLICATION OF AID."[47] Next, a merger was proposed. Completed in 1887, it sounded the death knell for the COS. The board quickly divested the new organization of its "scientific" innovations and returned to its former almsgiving practices. Chicago was one of the few major cities which did not have a strong COS movement in the 1870s and 1880s.

The Christian Gentlemen of the antebellum years had ministered to the poor themselves, visiting them in their homes, and garnering invaluable first-hand knowledge of developing urban conditions in the process. Since many were simultaneously active in city government, charitable work enhanced their ability as decision makers. Moreover, overlapping directorates provided a necessary degree of centralization in an era when more formal lines of communication were few and weak.

Although marshaled by similar religious injunctions and biographical models purposefully limned by socially conscious crusaders like Hunt and Hale, men assumed a far more worldly stance than their benevolent wives. Masculine largesse preserved the republic, the religious establishment, personal character, business integrity, and private investments in a single stroke. Self-sacrifice, the raison d'être of feminine charity, was a negligible theme in the clarion call to masculine stewardship. Personal service, mutually reinforced by economic duress, was the common thread uniting men's and women's charitable endeavors on the eve of the Civil War.

As America swung from the benign social philosophy of the Christian Gentleman and his benevolent spouse to the plutocratic vision of men like Sumner and Carnegie, intuitive, sentimental, impulsive individual action was supplanted by the administrative orientation of the Gospel of Wealth. Although certain sectors of society were still urged to participate, the emphasis on broadly based mutual aid disappeared. Predicated on monetary largesse and managerial skills honed in the process of day-to-day business transactions, Carnegie's dictum was essentially a masculine doctrine tailored to the needs of the rich. For Chicago's feminine stewards, the Gilded Age was an era of expanding managerial and monetary opportunities, while the masculine leitmotivs were centralization and control. Businessmen, rather than women, were accorded the central role in the Social Darwinist scenario.

Using the world's generosity, and later their own, Chicago's Gilded Age plutocrats knit the formerly autonomous institutions of an earlier generation into a comprehensive network providing opportunities for the worthy, and an informal check on the menace of the "unfit." Ironically, for many, the hectic months of fire relief distribution in the wake of the disaster afforded their final opportunity for direct contact with the poor. In the ensuing decades, CRA veterans would continue to draw upon these insights, using them as guidelines for the creation of a welter of new civic endeavors. Rather than emanating from the populace as a whole, Gilded Age charity and culture were to be bestowed.

Philip Danforth Armour (ca. 1880s). Courtesy of the Chicago Historical Society.

# 4 CULTURE & COMMUNITY

In cultural matters, as in charity, the fire of 1871 marked a watershed between the efforts of antebellum volunteers and their wealthy, administrative successors. Like Puritans in the wilderness, Chicago's Christian Gentlemen had set about replicating the institutions they had left behind almost at once. Moved by an earnest desire to create an intellectual island amid the harsh prairie of the western frontier, they built the city's first libraries, learned societies, and galleries with their own hands. Their motives were varied and complex, embracing democratic aims, boosterism, and a desire to curb growing materialism and unrest. As one proponent explained, without "culture, taste, beauty, art [and] literature . . . there is a danger that our city will become a town of mere traders and moneygetters; rude, unlettered, hard, sharp, and grasping."[1]

While Christian Gentlemen labored to keep the spirit of learning and refinement alive among their own cliques, their Gilded Age successors took a more inclusive stance, creating elaborate institutions to serve as neutral meeting grounds for the "fit" of all classes. Laboring against a backdrop of endemic social and economic conflict, Chicago's self-made magnates sought to reunite class and caste in the collective pursuit of knowledge and self-culture.

As has already been noted, Chicago's women entered the cultural arena more hesitantly, hampered by popular disapproval of bluestockings, legal restrictions which limited their role as patronesses, and the appeal of a genre art carefully calibrated to their tastes and domestic interests. When they finally began to demand an enhanced role in the 1870s, they did so by initiating quasi-charitable arts organizations designed to foster the cause of domestic art and aid their own sex. Differences between masculine and feminine styles of patronage remained sharply delineated well into the 1890s.[2]

While women were relegated to the periphery of the cultural arena, cultural philanthropy became an increasingly popular outlet for masculine stewards. The cultural aims espoused by Chicago's antebellum Christian Gentlemen sharply counterpointed the mores of the frontier. Before the influx of eastern merchants and speculators in the 1830s, Chicago had a mongrel population of French and English fur traders, half-breeds, and soldiers garrisoned at Fort Dearborn. Taverns served as the focus of community life, comfortable places where residents could spend their spare hours playing cards, drinking, and swapping yarns. Cultures mingled promiscuously in this setting, as women swilled whiskey shoulder to shoulder with Indians and traders, and Potawatomi dances alternated with French cotillions. As one historian has noted, "There was hardly a man in Chicago in 1832 who did not know how to paint his body, decorate his hair with eagle feathers, and leap in frenzied exultation, terrorizing effete easterners."[3]

Incoming settlers viewed the traders and their Indian friends as little better than savages. The Treaty of 1833, signed in the aftermath of the Blackhawk war, ceded the title to the lands west of Chicago to the Mississippi River to the United States government, ending years of bloody disputes between Indians and whites. As easterners flooded into the city after its passage, they quickly established the familiar institutions of their youth. Churches, libraries, and reading rooms began to challenge the centrality of the tavern, and churchgoing became an indispensable sign of respectability. If the frontier symbolized disorder and fraternization, the transposed culture of the east signalized permanency, self-restraint, and the imported values of a more settled society. It was a bulwark against the threat of the frontier: the descent into savagery.

Democratic imperatives shared the stage with local aims. The rise of Jacksonian democracy and the broadening franchise unleashed attendant fears about the rise of demagoguery and mob rule. Only by educating the citizenry, it was argued, could democratic institutions be preserved. Only by fostering knowledge, temperance, refinement, and virtue through mass literacy and intellectual activity could the future of the republic be assured.

The threat loomed from above as well as below. America was becoming richer, and much of this new wealth was concentrating in the hands of urban merchants and professional men, raising the specter of rampant materialism and ostentatious display. Nineteenth-century critics continually searched for socially responsible uses to which these excess profits might be applied. As one historian points out: "In the eyes of the church it was a sin for the wealthy to waste their substance on luxurious clothing, lavish entertainment, great mansions, and other forms of ostentatious display . . . [the rich man's] money was simply held in trust to be used in doing God's work . . . this meant support of schools, libraries, museums, orphanages, hospitals, churches, and similar beneficent institutions."[4] If the rich invested their surplus wealth in the instruments of personal and civic refinement, virtue would flourish, and both individual and community would gain.

Libraries, schools, and lyceums were deemed absolutely essential accoutrements in a democracy, for these were the crucible in which society's "natural aristocrats" were sifted, shaped, and trained. If such institutions continued to be maintained on a democratic basis, open to men of talent whatever their station in life, then the Jeffersonian ideal of careers open to talent would become a reality. Educated and nurtured by society, the best qualified would rule.

And the rest of the population would lead enriched lives. As Carl Bode explains, "If there was ever an American dogma during these decades, it was the desirability of personal improvement."[5] Familiarity with art, with literature, and with the ideas and aspirations of the nation's leading scholars and philosophers was claimed as a national prerogative. American technology was still in its infancy, and even the most arcane operations were still comprehensible to the average layman. As a result, citizens claimed the right to be informed on every subject, no matter how unusual. It was an age of intense curiosity, an age rallying to the collective cry of "show me!" Lyceums, lectures, libraries, and art-unions brought the world of scientific and scholarly endeavor within the reach of the average citizen.

The presence of cultural institutions could also shore up a city's sagging image, revivifying its competitive edge even as its economic supremacy waned. Hundreds of towns and hamlets were founded throughout the midwest during the first decades of the nineteenth century, each vying for settlers, businesses, and, ultimately, survival. Competition between leading cities like St. Louis, Chicago, and Cincinnati was intense. Although economic considerations were paramount, cultural clout was also extremely important, as each in turn cast its bid for the title of "Athens of the West." Beyond the spiritual considerations, the aggressive development of cultural amenities made good business sense. It was a sound investment, luring students, visitors, and settlers who might otherwise have located elsewhere.[6]

Each of these broader concerns—democratic aims, the desire to provide a check on materialism and unrest, to educate the masses, and boost the city's image—merged with more personal considerations to foster the rapid development of cultural patronage in Chicago. Many of the city's most dedicated patrons were property holders, men who stood to benefit from anything which promoted the city's welfare, be it curbing crime and unrest or attracting new citizens to spark the growth of the economy. Moreover, the presence of such institutions helped to mitigate Chicago's unsavory reputation for ruthless materialism. By personally dedicating themselves to the well-being of their libraries and learned societies, citizens demonstrated to the rest of the world that they did not have account books for hearts. In the relaxed atmosphere of their reading rooms and institutes, weary businessmen and professionals could set aside fiscal worries and briefly don the mantle of the gentlemanly scholar, pursuing cherished avocations in the company of like-minded peers. Friendships cemented under such favorable conditions could later be tapped for business and professional purposes, adding personal gain to personal satisfaction.

Some of Chicago's early cultural boards were fairly inclusive, others were not.[7] Men were conscripted according to interest, background, and ability rather than wealth alone. The Young Men's Association (YMA, 1841) was the most democratic, actively seeking out newcomers and granting library privileges to nonresidents in order to shield them from theater, brothel, and saloon. Many of the organization's officers were but recently arrived themselves. Of those who served in the 1850s, over half (27 of 45) moved to Chicago after the beginning of the decade, and eight of those left before the decade's end. They were a fairly heterogeneous lot, comprised mainly of businessmen, professionals, and upwardly mobile clerks. The only manual laborer, a cooper, would soon own his own lumberyard. Socially and geographically mobile, their roots within the community were still relatively tenuous. Seventeen played leading roles in other organizations, and about a fourth (11) were listed as landowners of tracts valued at $100 or more (see table 3).

Like the leather-apron men of Benjamin Franklin's Junto, each of the two hundred charter subscribers was asked to contribute a volume from his own holdings to form the nucleus of the association's library. Some responded more generously than others. Young Walter New-

**Table 3**
**Characteristics of Participants in Selected Cultural Undertakings, 1850–1859**

| | YMA | ART | CHS |
|---|---|---|---|
| Occupation: | | | |
| Lawyer | 14 | 8 | 5 |
| Businessman | 13 | 6 | 3 |
| Physician | 0 | 3 | 1 |
| Banker | 2 | 2 | 1 |
| Clergyman | 0 | 1 | 1 |
| Artist | 0 | 2 | 0 |
| Engineer | 0 | 1 | 0 |
| Industrialist | 0 | 1 | 0 |
| Government employee | 0 | 0 | 1 |
| Bank teller | 3 | 0 | 0 |
| Clerk | 2 | 0 | 0 |
| Librarian | 1 | 0 | 0 |
| Dentist | 1 | 0 | 0 |
| Builder | 1 | 0 | 0 |
| Cooper | 1 | 0 | 0 |
| Educator | 1 | 0 | 0 |
| British counsel | 0 | 1 | 0 |
| Unknown | 6 | 4 | 0 |
| Year of Arrival in Chicago: | | | |
| 1830s | 2 | 9 | 8 |
| 1840s | 14 | 11 | 2 |
| 1850s | 27 | 5 | 2 |
| Unknown | 6 | 4 | 0 |

| | YMA | ART | CHS |
|---|---|---|---|
| Property Listed in 1850 ($100 or More): | | | |
| $100–$2,499 | 8 | 5 | 2 |
| $2,500–$4,999 | 2 | 1 | 1 |
| $5,000–$9,999 | 1 | 1 | 1 |
| $10,000–$24,999 | 0 | 3 | 1 |
| $25,000–$49,999 | 0 | 2 | 1 |
| $50,000–$99,999 | 0 | 2 | 2 |
| $100,000 to $500,000 | 0 | 1 | 1 |
| Not listed | 34 | 14 | 3 |
| Founders or Officers of Other Organizations: | | | |
| 1 organization | 11 | 7 | 1 |
| 2 organizations | 4 | 1 | 3 |
| 3 organizations | 2 | 2 | 6 |
| 4 or more organizations | 0 | 3 | 1 |
| Nonparticipants | 28 | 16 | 1 |

SOURCES: City directories, annual reports, random biographical data, 1849–50 property tax lists for the City of Chicago, Chicago Historical Society.

KEY: YMA = officers of Young Men's Association, 1850–59; total number, 45. ART = board members of 1859 exhibit and Chicago art-union; total number, 29. CHS = founders and officers of the Chicago Historical Society, 1856–59; total number, 12.

berry, an avid bibliophile who had served on the executive board of the Detroit Lyceum before coming to Chicago, donated scores of tomes from his own shelves. Others lectured or led debates. Open to the public, these programs were extremely popular. Initially, local physicians and attorneys served as the speakers, but by the 1850s the podium had been surrendered to itinerant lecturers of national renown, including Wendell Phillips, Ralph Waldo Emerson, Horace Mann, Charles Sumner, Clara Barton, Elizabeth Cady Stanton, and Susan B. Anthony, secured through the efforts of dedicated members like Samuel Dexter Ward and Edwin S. Wells, who served (without remuneration) as booking agents for the Metropolitan Literary Union.

The visual arts fared less well. Few permanent galleries were established in Chicago before the Civil War, and local exhibitions subsisted primarily on loans from private collections. The earliest exhibits were barely exhibits at all, held at the Mechanic's Institute Fairs, where canvases dangled promiscuously amid homemade foodstuffs, knitted novelties, and amateur inventions. In 1859 the first general exhibition, comprised of over two hundred paintings garnered from the walls of Chicago collectors, was staged jointly with the Chicago Historical Society, "to afford the public . . . an opportunity to gratify and improve their taste in Art matters."[8] A resounding success, drawing over twelve thousand patrons during its brief run, the exhibition graphically demonstrated the public's appetite for high culture. Encouraged by the hearty response, the city's neophyte patrons launched the Chicago Art-Union (1860), for the encouragement and advancement of fine art in the west.

The typical art patron of the 1850s arrived in the 1830s or 1840s and was well established in business or the professions by 1859. Collectors themselves, many were also members of the American Art-Union, a national organization dedicated to the popularization of the visual arts. Civic leaders like William B. Ogden gravitated toward the role of the connoisseur with ease, regularly corresponding with artists to commission works for their private galleries, and occasionally even luring internationally renowned artists like G. P. A. Healy to their prairie town. In the process, art patronage served both civic and personal aims, reflecting a pronounced admixture of boosterism and self-conscious cultural expertise.

Artists played a more limited but nevertheless important role. Sculptor Leonard Volk served as the official arbiter of the 1859 exhibit, sorting and assembling contributions for display. Born in Wellstown, New York, Volk was the son of a marble cutter, and the cousin of Illinois famed senator, Stephen A. Douglas, the "Little Giant." Douglas became Volk's guardian angel, footing the bill for two years' study in Italy, helping him to set up a small studio in Chicago upon his return, and netting him several commissions for public statuary to grace the state's capital. Volk displayed his wares at the 1859 exhibit, served as the moving spirit behind the creation of the art-union, volunteered to direct the Sanitary Commission's art fairs during the Civil War, and was instrumental in the creation of the artist-sponsored and owned Academy of Design. Although few in number, professionals like Volk often played an important role in marshaling public support for particular forms of cultural enterprise.

Occasionally, interested laymen filled the same role. The Chicago Historical Society (CHS, 1856) was the brainchild of retired Congregational minister William Barry. Barry personified the gentlemanly scholar. Born of an old Boston family, he graduated from Harvard's Divinity School in 1826, capping his education with two years at the Universities of Gottingen and Paris. His professional duties carried him through a string of New England pastorates, during which time he penned several voluminous town histories. Like so many of his ministerial colleagues, Barry's health was frail, eventually causing him to abandon the cloth and seek renewed health in the west. Settling in Chicago, he promptly set about marshaling support for a local historical society. Serving as both secretary and librarian until his retirement in 1868, the former clergyman labored tirelessly to promote the society's interests.

Well born, well bred, well traveled, and a prolific author in his own right, Barry was a welcome addition to the ranks of Chicago's cultured leaders. The men he gathered about him were among the city's most distinguished. Pioneer settlers who had shaped Chicago's history themselves, they had a personal stake in preserving the relics of its past. As a group, they were richer, more settled, and more active in civic undertakings than members of any of the other boards. Only two of the officers and founders arrived in Chicago in the fifties. Nine were property holders in 1850, and seven were veterans of municipal governmental service. Ogden was a member, as was Jonathan Young Scammon. The college-educated son of a Maine clergyman, Scammon was a man of many talents, editing a newspaper, heading a law firm, an insurance company, and a bank, all within two decades of his arrival in 1835. "Always the refined, instructive and courteous gentleman," he divided his leisure hours between scholarly pursuits and public service.[9] His governmental record included the presidency of the school board and several aldermanic terms, while the list of his charitable and cultural commitments encompassed seats on asylum and hospital boards, the Academy of Sciences, and, later, the Chicago Astronomical Society, to which he donated $30,000 for the erection of Dearborn Observatory in 1864. Men like Scammon had a wealth of documents, reminiscences, and memorabilia to bestow, filling the society's archives with their own, very personal gifts-in-kind. By celebrating Chicago, they celebrated themselves.

Inspired by eastern examples and the proselytizing of cultural missionaries like Barry, Chicago's Christian Gentlemen self-consciously set about shaping the city's intellectual resources, pooling their books, paintings, and memoirs to lend a patina of refinement to their adolescent prairie town. In many respects, their organizations were little more than clublike affinity groups, catering to the interests and needs of specific segments of the city's population.

Just as it had for the city's charities, the fire marked a turning point in Chicago's cultural development. With their charitable counterparts, cultural associations had embarked on a headlong program of expansion in the late 1860s, only to have their collections and newly acquired "fireproof" buildings reduced to ashes in the blaze of 1871. Afterward, the men of Ogden's generation stepped aside, opening the way to younger, more resilient men. In the process, many of the businessmen who marshaled the CRA assumed responsibility for cultural patronage as well.

The Chicago Atheneum was one of the first cultural institutions to attract the collective support of men like Pullman, Field, and Richard Teller Crane. Organized in the wake of the fire, in October 1871, it was initiated by representatives of the Boston Young Men's Christian Union to distribute emergency relief funds and provide a social center for unemployed fire victims. Although conceived as a religious undertaking, the Atheneum quickly adopted a more secular stance, modeled on New York's Cooper Union and English Workingmen's Colleges. A self-proclaimed "People's College," it offered courses on everything from mathematics and bookkeeping to Latin and music appreciation. Its "Dime Course on Art Topics" featured distinguished lecturers like architect William Le Baron Jenney, father of the modern skyscraper, and periodic talks were scheduled with local luminaries like Jenney, Volk, and Dr. Mary Thompson. Manual training courses, sociables, and the gymnasium rounded out the Atheneum's early offerings.

Although they did not dominate the board, Gilded Age millionaires John Crerar, R. T. Crane, Marshall Field, Levi Leiter, O. S. A. Sprague, George Pullman, Murry Nelson, and Charles Hutchinson were among the Atheneum's early backers. Its programs appealed to them for a variety of reasons. Classes afforded the ladders of self-help to the aspiring poor at a minimal cost, a powerfully appealing idea to men of this generation. The more educated the worker, it was reasoned, the less likely he would be to riot and rebel. And, as department store executive Harlow Higinbotham explained, courses "which the ambitious boy or young man may follow in his leisure hours . . . add directly to his business efficiency."[10] The spectacle of over one thousand workers devoting their spare hours to self-culture and moral uplift under the Atheneum's auspices must have been immensely gratifying to men like Pullman and Field, for it gave flesh and substance to some of their most cherished values.

Outlining his version of the *Elements of Success*, Field emphasized,

> Next to the selection of occupation is that of companions. Particularly is this important in the case of young men beginning their career in strange cities away from home influences, as too often it is the case that young men of excellent abilities are ruined by evil associates; a young man therefore cannot too early guard against forming friendship with those whose tendency is to lead him on the downward path. To every young man I would say, seek at the start to cultivate the acquaintance of those only whose contact and influence will kindle high purposes, as . . . a sterling character [is] one of the fundamental principles of true success.[11]

Like the YMA, the Atheneum protected the young from less edifying pastimes and shielded them from unwholesome companions. Good moral character was the only requirement for continued membership. "Any person guilty of improper conduct, or whose personal character may be found objectionable" faced immediate expulsion.[12] While the literary society provided uplift and a home away from home for the lonely, the gymnasium served as "one of Nature's temperance societies," upgrading health and luring "young men away from the haunts of vice and dissipation."[13] Thus, the Atheneum served a dual function, both a shelter and a school.

It was also a community meeting ground. To those meeting its minimal requirements, the Atheneum's doors were opened hospitably wide. Centrally located within a block of many of the major streetcar lines, it was directly (and intentionally) accessible to all parts of the city. Unlike earlier organizations, it welcomed women as well as men, young and old, rich and poor, Christian and Jew. While an estimated 90% of the students were drawn from the working class, the Atheneum actively sought participants from other social strata as well, offering "to ladies and gentlemen of leisure . . . the very best instruction in languages, in music, and in art . . . at prices which they must almost blush to pay."[14] Drawing both rich and poor together in the common pursuit of culture and self-improvement, the Chicago Atheneum offered something for everyone.

While Chicago's Gilded Age millionaires quietly supported the Atheneum, they eagerly wrested the task of cultural arbitership from the ailing Academy of Design in a blatant power coup. Founded in 1866 by a group of local artists, including Volk, the academy was the third of its kind in the United States. Before the fire, it maintained an art school and studios and staged several exhibitions designed to popularize the fine arts. All were lost in the blaze. Afterward, it limped along in rented quarters until 1878, when the burden of its debts compelled the trustees to enlist the aid of some of the city's art-minded businessmen. The alliance was strained and short-lived, for it quickly became apparent that the artists had rebuilt their organization upon a foundation of highly questionable business practices. In the words of one disenchanted backer, the institution was "rotten to the core . . . [the former officers] had mortgaged the property of the Academy to themselves, and had spent the money of the school in a reckless and hasty manner."[15]

Thoroughly disgusted, the businessmen abandoned the artists to their fate and formed a rival institution of their own in 1879. Among the incorporators and officers were Marshall Field, art collectors Samuel N. Nickerson and James Dole, Nathaniel K. Fairbank, and wealthy banker Charles Hutchinson. The trustees pointedly underscored the distinction between their own well-managed undertaking and its ill-fated predecessor. "The Academy of Fine Arts is on a good, solid, substantial basis, while the Academy of Design is entirely bankrupt," snapped Hutchinson.[16]

As some of the city's leading businessmen, they were profoundly interested in fiscal affairs and economic viability. Of the nineteen founders and officers who served between the organization's inception and 1889, at least five were millionaires. Unlike the trustees of the Boston Museum of Fine Arts, they were not descendants of wealthy families. Only two were the sons of rich Chicagoans, and neither of them had had the benefit of more than a high school education. Nor were they the sons of pioneers. All arrived after 1850, coming to prominence in the aftermath of the Civil War.[17]

Many were avid collectors themselves. Notions about the relationship between the collector and the public were in a state of transition during the 1880s. Art patrons like Charles Hutchinson, Samuel Nickerson, and James W. Ellsworth clung to the practices of an earlier era, opening the doors to their domestic galleries to public inspection, and generously loaning their treasures to the endowment-starved Art Institute much as Ogden and Skinner had exhibited their holdings in 1859. The museum could not have survived without their aid, for until the 1890s it had no endowment, paying operating costs from the annual dues collected from its broadly based membership.

For Gilded Age connoisseurs like Hutchinson, the museum became an extension of their own homes, and they exhibited their prizes with an unmistakable air of possessive pride. Field, it is said, donated several important items because he liked the way they were displayed. Hutchinson was famous for his discourses on Rosetti's *Beata Beatrice*, which he periodically loaned to the Art Institute. According to one source, he habitually buttonholed visitors to tell them of the painting's history and outline the significance of its style.

Hutchinson did more than lecture unwary visitors. He dedicated himself heart and soul to the task of keeping the museum alive during the first years before it began to amass an endowment. Born of an old American family (he numbered Anne Hutchinson and at least one colonial governor of Massachusetts among his ancestors), he was the son of Chicago's notorious speculator, Benjamin P. Hutchinson, better known as "Old Hutch." In the best tradition of the Chicago elite, Old Hutch was born in 1829, came to Chicago in the 1850s, and was rich by the 1870s. He founded a packing house, controlled several banks, and was a brilliant grain speculator, achieving a corner on wheat in 1888. According to legend, brokers at the Board of Trade used to hum a jingle when they saw him coming:

> I see Old Hutch start for this club,
> Good-bye, my money, good-bye.
> He's given us all a terrible rub,
> Good-bye, my money, good-bye.[18]

Old Hutch may have been accused of many things in his lifetime, but no one ever called him a Christian Gentleman.

His life ended tragically. Always eccentric, in his later years he was adjudged insane and died in an institution. But his son inherited much of the father's financial genius. The elder Hutchinson gave each of his children $1,000,000 to start them off in life, and within a short period Charles had parlayed this into a multimillion-dollar estate. Charles was not the usual rich man's son. Although he yearned for a college education, his father firmly resisted the boy's entreaties, believing that a diploma from the Chicago public high school was as much as Charles would need for a successful business career. Immediately after graduation, the boy was given a job as a cashier in his father's Corn Exchange National Bank for the modest sum of $3 per day. By the 1880s, Charles was president of the bank and richer than his sire.

In his spare time, he worked at the Burr Mission, helping children in a squalid section of town, and by the 1880s he was president of the Art Institute as well. Hard-bitten businessman that he was, Old Hutch never fully understood Charles's fascination with art and used to needle the boy about his acquisitions. When Charles purchased a $2,500 painting of five sheep in a meadow, Old Hutch jokingly exclaimed to a friend, "A son of mine! He paid $500 apiece for five painted sheep and he could get the real article for $2 a head!"[19]

In spite of his father's opposition (or perhaps because of it), Hutchinson became a dedicated art collector, traveling the world with his friend, Martin Ryerson, in search of new treasures for the Art Institute's walls. His diary reads like a Baedecker guide to international museums. In 1881, he journeyed to the Metropolitan Museum of Art, the Boston Museum of Fine Arts, and the Lenox Library. Later, he toured the great repositories of Europe, including the South Kensington Museum in London, which he enthusiastically labeled "the greatest of all modern institutions for the advancement of art."[20] Ever the connoisseur, he ranked cities by the quality of their museums. Toledo was "superb," Madrid less so, Paris's Louvre "magnificent." "How I wish we had some of the fine monuments and museums in Chicago," he enviously sighed. "Sometime I hope we may."[21]

Accompanied by the Art Institute director, William M. R. French, or other trustees, Hutchinson regularly visited the art dealers of Paris, Italy, and London, making purchases and garnering useful information on museum management. One of his greatest coups was the purchase of the Demidoff collection of old masters, including rare

Rembrandts and Holbeins. Although upstaged at the opening by an enormous painting of the Brooklyn Bridge, the acquisition signaled the maturation of the Art Institute as a major force in the museum world. While the New York press venomously speculated whether the paintings would be led in triumphal procession to the museum's portals "in huge floats drawn by teams of milk white Berksheir hogs," Hutchinson cheerfully responded that the canvases were "corkers, every one of them."[22]

His approach to art was utterly idealistic, and fundamentally democratic. "Art awakens the imagination and quickens the conscience," he explained. "It increase(s) the satisfaction and joys of life for the great masses of the people."[23] It "is a universal language"; "art speaks alike to every man of every tongue; to bound and free alike .... Ideas of grace, beauty and power, eternal ideas can be set before the people to move their sensibilities and arouse the soul .... The minds of the masses are susceptible to the influence of art."[24] In Hutchinson's opinion, knowledge and culture went hand in hand, uplifting the community and enhancing public enjoyment. "Art is not destined for a small or privileged group," he emphatically noted. "It is of the people, and for the people."[25] It had to be available to everyone.[26] As Hutchinson explained, "We have built this institution for the public, not for the few." Vowing to make it a "three-ring circus" instead of a "mausoleum," he helped to institute a series of innovations, including public lectures, concerts, a broadly based art school, and free admission on Sundays.[27]

Attempting to unite the interests of art lovers, architects, and professional artists, the institute sponsored lectures by rising local figures like Louis Sullivan and Lorado Taft, while encouraging their contemporaries to contribute to the American Artist's show, held annually after 1888. "Drawn from all classes," enrollment in the art school grew by leaps and bounds, numbering three hundred in 1888, and six hundred in 1890.[28] Students ran the gamut from schoolchildren, who attended on Saturday afternoons, to professional artists and craftsmen who filled the evening classes. By 1890, courses in lithography, frescoing, mosaics, and stained-glass work were being offered along with more traditional fields like painting and sculpture.

Like the Atheneum, the Art Institute was located amid a nest of transportation lines, in order to insure accessibility to all parts of the city. As the trustees explained, "In several American cities art has, as it were, set itself apart, and the Art Museum has been placed in a remote park where comparatively few of the people can visit it." They chose a central location instead, despite the high cost of the land, because "proximity to the heart of the city" would benefit "the great masses of the people, to whom convenience of access is essential."[29] In 1882, the new museum opened its doors in a building formerly occupied by a tombstone factory, in the heart of the central business district at Michigan and Van Buren Streets.

By 1888, the trustees had initiated the practice of free admissions on Sundays as well. As Hutchinson explained, they were determined to "make our fine collections a source of pure and refreshing divertisment and refining instruction of the masses," whose only free day was the Sabbath.[30] Although the initial resistance of a few Sabbatarian board members prevented the program from being implemented sooner, when it was finally instituted it was immediately lauded by press and public. "Sunday is the only day of recreation and rest which the working classes have," commented the *Chicago Tribune*, "and it is but natural for them to seek entertainment . . . . The Devil has plenty of allurements for [them] . . . . Why should not the art institutes, the museums, the libraries, and the lecture rooms set up a competition?"[31] "Rich people and poor, from city, village, farm, and ranch" attended.[32] The first free day attracted seven hundred visitors; by the 1890s between two and six thousand regularly appeared each Sunday.

Newspapers continually commented on the size and composition of the crowd, which included "every class of society. Workmen go stumping over the mosaic floor with their hob-nailed boots, and women, with no head covering but a shawl, stare respectfully at rare Old Masters."[33] One regular visitor was a Polish laborer who faithfully trekked the two miles from his home in the stockyards district every Sunday, rain or shine. Many were "men in rough garments with unmistakable evidences of a life of manual labor about them."[34] Equally common was the "tall, lank, cadaverous individual" who had developed a taste for art in his native land. According to one observant reporter: "To listen to the remarks of this critic as he poses before some painting or group of statuary is in itself a lesson in art . . . . Surely, if there is anyone in Chicago . . . capable of distinguishing true from counterfeit art, it is our friend of the long hair, lean face, smudged collar, and the inevitable toothpick between his nervous lips."[35] Artisans, blue- and white-collar workers, visitors from the country, and wealthy art patrons all appeared in the museum's halls, a fact which delighted Hutchinson, who made daily visits and constantly kept tabs on attendance records. With his usual ebullience, he declared that the

Art Institute was overactive, overhospitable, overcrowded with passing exhibitions and students, but at least it was alive.

The Art Institute, like the Atheneum, offered something for everyone. In a society torn by strikes and empassioned clashes between capital and labor, the institute provided a neutral territory where representatives of both factions could meet and pursue common goals. Rather than citadels of imported values to which the rich could withdraw in times of strife, cultural institutions such as these embodied one of the few visible manifestations of communal effort and collective sentiment. Men like Hutchinson used these organizations to create institutional focuses for community sentiment and good will as the larger earmarks of communal life dissolved into a scenario of privatization, poverty, and strife.

This goal was shared by the creators of the city's first manual training schools. Few organizations were as widely supported in the 1880s and 1890s. From the Chicago Manual Training School, the first private venture of its kind in the United States, to the elaborate Armour Institute, to the public school courses started by men like Richard Teller Crane, the cause of technical, manual education was enthusiastically embraced by many of the city's wealthiest and most powerful men.

The idea itself was not a Gilded Age innovation. Antebellum educators enthusiastically endorsed the use of handwork as a means of promoting industry among students, programs frequently incorporated into asylum routines. The movement achieved renewed interest at the Philadelphia Centennial Exposition, where the techniques perfected by Victor Della Vos of the Imperial School at Moscow demonstrated how new mechanical skills could be quickly and easily inculcated by reducing them to their component parts, which students then emulated with ease. The idea was simple. Literary subjects like reading, writing, and history would be augmented with physical work, training boys in the arts of mechanical drawing and shopwork. In the process, the "whole boy" would be educated, his hands, eyes, and mind trained in concert.

Enthusiasm for Della Vos's system meshed with a growing dissatisfaction with traditional curricula. Rote memorization and the "drowsy effect of abstract speculation" were viewed as deadening to the intellect and irrelevant to the realities of an industrializing society.[36] Chicago's businessmen vociferously attacked the process of memorizing such "rubbish," "rules, rules, rules, to be memorized until the student has become a mere parrot."[37] Manual training promised to render the learning process more popular, efficient, and scientific.

It seemed to offer a substitute for apprenticeship, and promised to strengthen native mechanical skills in an era when American businessmen feared they were yielding industrial dominance to foreign competitors. The traditional method of educating the young, apprenticeship had fulfilled a variety of functions, producing a cheap source of labor, reducing idleness, and providing an informal system of poor relief by training youngsters within the context of the family. Colonial masters had been legally bound to teach their charges to read, fear God, and conform to the law, strictures repeated in the Illinois apprenticeship laws. Although legally sanctioned, by the mid-nineteenth century the practice was falling into disuse. As technological innovations made the craftsmanship of the elder generation obsolete, the demand for skilled labor and a thorough knowledge of the entire production process declined, and juvenile laborers no longer lived with their masters. The breakdown of apprenticeship paved the way for child labor and all its attendant ills. Children of impoverished parents now left school early to take jobs in "blind alley trades," with little hope for future advancement. Unskilled, untutored, with little parental supervision to restrain them, they posed a threat to the future of the democratic state.[38]

Education was viewed as a means of curbing pauperism and crime. Since shopwork would be more interesting to children than learning by rote, it was reasoned that they would stay in school longer, learn more, and become better citizens. Practical training would also inculcate skills which would serve as a hedge against unemployment in later life, thereby thinning the ranks of the next generation of vagrants and paupers. Having learned a deep respect and love of manual labor, graduates of such courses would be more content in their work and less inclined to rebel. Thus, manual training was embraced as the panacea for a welter of pressing social ills.[39]

It was particularly appealing to men who had made their fortunes without the benefit of a classical education. Of the nine men who founded and served as officers of the Chicago Manual Training School (1882), only one had a college degree, and two graduated from academies. The rest had primary school educations or less. Nevertheless, the board was drawn from the cream of the city's economic elite, including Pullman, Field, Crane, and N. K. Fairbank. All were members of the prestigious Commercial Club, which launched the undertaking with a hefty $100,000 endowment, including a $20,000 gift from the usually tight-fisted Field. Five were industrialists, four businessmen, and all were Yankees, born in New England, New York, or New Jersey in the 1820s and 1830s, arriving in Chicago in the 1850s (with the exception of latecomer John Crerar, who arrived in 1867). At least six were millionaires. Seven sat on the board of the Art Institute, five were officers of the CRA, and all held overlapping directorates in two or more organizations. In sum, they were the leaders of Chicago's Gilded Age social and economic aristocracy.

Many, like Field, Pullman, and Crane, regarded themselves as self-made men. Born in Patterson, New Jersey, in 1832, Richard Teller Crane was the son of a moderately well-to-do builder who lost most of his fortune in the panic of 1837. As a result, R. T. was put to work in a cotton mill at the tender age of nine. He changed jobs two years later, working in a tobacco factory until he was fifteen. Next, he was apprenticed to work in his uncle's brass foundry in Brooklyn. When the boy finally reached his maturity, he set out for Chicago, setting up his own small brass foundry in the mill yard of another uncle, wealthy lumberman Martin Ryerson, in 1855. This small parcel of land was apparently all he received from Ryerson, for until profits began to soar during the Civil War Crane both lived and worked in his tiny factory, reinvesting every spare cent in the company. The years of frugality and struggle quickly bore fruit for the enterprising young foundrymaster. In 1862, Crane added an iron foundry to his holdings, five years later he was manufacturing elevators, and soon he would add bathroom fittings as well, heading a company with nationwide factories and outlets.

He was a complex man, utterly paternalistic and authoritarian, yet admired by his men. Although neither particularly religious nor sociable, Crane was possessed of a keen social conscience and sense of civic duty. He was one of the first to introduce the eight-hour day in his factories, initiating a five-cent lunch program with hot coffee and soup for his men, providing free medical care for his workers and their families, and developing liberal profit sharing and pension plans long before other employers even considered such ideas. One of his major bequests was a $1,000,000 addition to the company's pension fund, with another $1,000,000 for workers' widows and children. Nevertheless, he vehemently resisted any attempts at unionization within his plants.

Crane never forgot his early struggles, and for the rest of his life he harbored a venomous disdain for the college education which was denied him. "I have made my way with my hands and head with little of the learning of books," he belligerently pointed out to all who would listen.[40] Crane's heroes were the "real builders," the inventors, mechanics, and businessmen who had directly benefited society through their native skill. The foundrymaster regarded manual training, with its practical emphasis on facts and work, as the ideal crucible for the development of such latter-day yeomen. College, on the other hand, was too theoretically oriented, breeding contempt for physical labor and those who had made their way without the benefit of a baccalaureate degree. Perhaps thinking of his own sons, or those of his friends, Crane sharply observed that "the whole tendency of the so-called 'higher education' is to puff the young man up with vanity, causing him to look with contempt upon labor, and even to despise his parents; their suggestions that he should work for a living are resented by him, since he expects to live by his wits."[41] Pointing to his own example, Crane asked, "If I, taking up the world's work at nine years old, could become a millionaire manufacturer, what's the use of education beyond the three R's, if a boy is going into business?"[42]

His fellow trustees apparently concurred, for several sent their sons to the Chicago Manual Training School (CMTS) between 1884 and 1900. The school was a good deal more than a mere training ground for factory workers, as has often been supposed. Entrance requirements were high and academic standards strict. Applicants were required to pass comprehensive entrance examinations covering reading, spelling, writing, geography, English composition, and mathematics, and had to bring written testimonials certifying to their moral character. "Impurity in act or words, disregard of school regulations, lack of interest in school duties, or failure to maintain a good standard of scholarship" were grounds for immediate dismissal.[43]

Once admitted, students followed a curriculum "substantially the same as that of the city public high schools," but augmented by one hour of drawing per day and two of shopwork, including carpentry, casting, forging, and machine tool work.[44] Those who completed the courses could look forward to profitable careers. Of the first three hundred graduates (1886–93), twenty-two became engineers, nineteen building and machine construction superintendents, sixty-five foremen, designers and draughtsmen, and fifty-eight salesmen, bookkeepers, architects, lawyers, and teachers. Some came from the poorer sections of Chicago, some from outlying cities like Peoria and Aurora, some from Prairie Avenue. Included among the graduates were Charles Blatchford, son of the president of the board, R. T. Crane, Jr.,

Elbridge Keith, Ferd Peck, Jr., Stanley Farwell, Edward E. Brown (future president of the First National Bank), and Charles Hutchinson's nephew, Noble B. Judah, who later served as the American ambassador to Cuba.[45]

Crane took his ideas a step farther, implementing a manual training program in the city's public schools in 1891, an experiment which ultimately cost him over $80,000. "Practically all educators appear to be aiming to do something for society at the top instead of at the bottom," carped Crane.[46] Even the CMTS had set its sights too high in his opinion. According to Crane's reasoning, "As the great bulk of our boys and girls get all their formal education in the grammar grades, it follows that here should be concentrated our most earnest efforts toward realizing the fundamental purposes of all school training," which, in his opinion, consisted of shaping conscientious citizens and providing them with the skills for self-support.[47] Nor was Crane the only CMTS trustee to initiate his own program. Millionaire industrialist George Pullman disinherited his twin sons and used the money ($1,200,000 of his $7,600,000 estate) to bequeath a manual training school to the citizens of his model company town. For men like Crane and Pullman, the notion of manual training exercised a powerful appeal.[48]

Their interest was shared by the legendary meat packer, Philip D. Armour. Like Crane, Armour's education had been interrupted. Expelled from Cazenovia (New York) Academy in 1849, he left his parents' farm and headed west in the California gold rush. Although nearly lynched en route, Armour managed to mine enough gold for a small stake, which he later invested in a Milwaukee packing firm. Wartime speculations parlayed his modest nest egg into a fortune, and by the time he settled in Chicago in 1875, he was a wealthy man. Arrogant, crude, opinionated, and yet surprisingly generous, Armour used to hand out $5 bills to passing strangers who looked down-at-the-heels, and he frequently surprised his clerks with unanticipated gifts. His aphorisms and pithy wit were legendary, his love of children large and genuine. As he stated in his inimitable prose, "I like to turn bristles, blood, bones, and the insides and outsides of pigs and bullocks into revenue now, for I can turn the revenue into these boys and girls, and they will go on forever."[49]

P. D.'s first important undertaking was his $100,000 matching grant for a mission at Plymouth Congregational Church, augmenting his brother Joseph's bequest. By 1890, he had invested almost a million dollars in the enterprise. Not a religious man himself, Armour used the money to subsidize manual training classes for boys, domestic courses for girls, a library, a dispensary, and a variety of other nonsectarian projects. And, as an endowment, he built Armour Flats, a block of 144 apartments surrounding the 31st Street mission, renting them to Armour Company executives.[50]

But the industrialist was best known for the Armour Institute of Technology, which began as a manual training school and quickly matured into one of the city's leading agencies of higher education. According to tradition, the idea for the institute was inspired by Rev. Frank W. Gunsaulus's sermon on "What I Would Do If I Had a Million Dollars." This initial encounter blossomed into a deep and lasting friendship, with Gunsaulus acting as the first president when the institute opened five years later, in 1893. When the plan was still in the formative stages, Armour and Gunsaulus toured the east coast, visiting the Pratt Institute, MIT, the Drexel Institute, and Cooper Union. Armour personally corresponded with Drexel, Pratt, and George W. Childs, and "collected data upon, and carefully inquired into the workings of all the philanthropic institutions both in this country and Europe."[51]

The end result was a prep school with a heavy emphasis on shopwork, mathematics, science, engineering, and drawing. College courses were soon added as well as classes in domestic science and library work. Although headed by a clergyman, the venture was strictly nondenominational. "The religion of Armour Institute will be sixteen ounces to the pound," growled Armour, "and it makes no difference to me whether its converts are baptized in a soup bowl, a pond, or the Chicago River."[52]

Like the Art Institute, it was open to everyone. Public lectures, recitals, art shows, and a circulating library were initiated for both students and neighborhood residents. A program of home libraries was also created, circulating books in many of the city's less affluent neighborhoods. As Gunsaulus explained, "it is hoped that its benefits may reach all classes. It is not intended for the poor or the rich, as sections of society, but for any and all who are earnestly seeking practical education."[53] For the very poorest, fees were waived. One source, describing the domestic classes, noted that "women who wish to learn how to know whether the servant's work is properly done" studied side by side with the girls who would one day be in their employ.[54] Maintaining a proper economic mix was a source of constant concern to Armour, who complained to Gunsaulus that "I am not exactly clear in my mind whether we are really hitting the object I had in mind by letting in so many rich people's sons and daughters."[55]

Instead of dealing directly with the problems of slum life, Gilded Age millionaires like Armour sought to provide the "ladders" on which the aspiring poor could rise, accompanied by the sons and daughters of the rich who would be humanized by their presence. Educational and cultural institutions were their solutions to the nagging problems of the "social gulf." As the *Chicago Tribune* explained, the Armour Institute of Technology represented

> an endeavor to furnish a clew [*sic*] to the solution of the social problem. It is an effort to do some leveling up and some leveling down, to help rub out the line between the laboring classes and the wealthy classes, between employees and employer, to show youth on the one hand how it may reach a self-respecting independence that need be overshadowed by no man's wealth, and on the other hand show the son or daughter of wealth how much there is more regal than the mere aristocracy that has only wealth for a foundation . . . . the millionaire's son and the workingman's son, or more wonderful still, the millionaire's daughter and my lady's dressmaker or laundrywoman, are already standing here, shoulder to shoulder, learning to see things from the same point of view.[56]

Unlike the patrons of the antebellum years, with their inward-turning cliques cemented by mutual interest and taste, men of Armour's ilk used their great wealth, their administrative ability, and the well-traveled expertise which was the badge of their class to forge institutional bonds between themselves and the rest of society. Extraordinarily rich, powerful, and ambitious, they organized their cultural undertakings as they did their business empires, on a grand scale, serving heterogeneous constituencies, and firmly implanted under their own control. The fire helped them to consolidate their ascendancy over culture and charities alike. During the ensuing decades they fashioned a dual system of private agencies, providing minimal aid and incarceration for the permanently poor, and the means of self-culture for the "fit," much as Carnegie had recommended. In the process, Chicago's self-made magnates served their city and themselves, celebrating their own distinctive vision of community in lasting monuments of mortar and stone.

Ironically, many of their solutions were ultimately rejected by their daughters and sons. Pointing to the CRA and Gilded Age temples of learning and art, critics of the Progressive Era argued that such centralized, institutional ventures were inadequate and inappropriate to the city's needs, palliatives rather than cures for endemic urban ills. Shifting their gaze from the central city to outlying neighborhoods, these younger stewards formulated different guidelines for serving the dispossessed, guidelines which often ran directly counter to their parents' mores, hopes, and dreams.

# PART TWO
## 1889-1929

Nettie Fowler McCormick and Anita McCormick Blaine. Courtesy of State Historical Society of Wisconsin.

# 5
# THE PROGRESSIVE REASSESSMENT 1889-1915

The men and women who matured in the 1890s were a generation of iconoclasts. Vocally denouncing the brick and mortar mentality of their predecessors, they set about reforging a network of personal ties with the poor. For those too immobilized by their poverty, for recent arrivals too timid to venture beyond the confines of their neighborhood, Progressive Era benefactors counterpointed the centrally located institutions of the Gilded Age, creating neighborhood outposts offering the same services. In art, in charity, and in medicine, the progressives[1] labored to decentralize and democratize the amenities of urban life.

The excesses of the Gilded Age brought the very notion of noblesse oblige, and the elitism it embodied, into question. Even as Carnegie was formulating his Gospel of Wealth, social critics were beginning to reassess the meaning of charity and benevolence in a democratic state. In the process, a new definition of civic stewardship was posited, stressing decentralization, research rather than impulse, flexibility, a working partnership between donors and professionals, and deinstitutionalization. In effect, the progressive reassessment represented a throughgoing rejection of the institutional ideal of the Gilded Age elite.

Although the wealthy were still urged to honor their responsibilities, the critics' injunctions were frankly tinged with the implied threat that, if the rich failed to bestow, the poor would rise up and take what was rightfully theirs. "The day has gone by when a rich man may keep his money to himself, or leave the whole of it to relatives at his death," the *Nation* solemnly warned.[2]

Their forebodings were generated by the repeated shock waves of urban violence which swept the nation's cities during the Gilded Age. As cities became increasingly industrialized after the Civil War, labor (and laborers) became a commodity, employer/employee relationships were depersonalized, and workers' bargaining power declined. Thousands of men vied for monotonous jobs, working ten to fourteen hours a day for meager sums which made saving an impossibility. Without workmen's compensation programs to insure them, men worn out by the industrial system faced the dismal prospect of fending for their families and themselves, aided only by tightfisted relief societies. Fanned by grievances, the decades between 1870 and 1900 periodically erupted into strikes and industrial violence. In 1877, the nationwide railroad strike left ten Chicago rioters and nineteen policemen dead. In 1886, a strike and lockout at the McCormick Reaper Works triggered the notorious Haymarket riot, in which over one hundred perished. The Pullman riot, too, left a legacy of bitterness and destruction.

George Pullman built his model suburb as an antidote to the problems of industrial unrest, on the theory that pleasant surroundings and good housing would produce contented workers. Employees continually chafed under his paternalism. As one embittered resident pointed out, "We are born in a Pullman house, fed from the Pullman shop, taught in the Pullman school, catechized in the Pullman church, and when we die we shall be buried in the Pullman cemetery and go to the Pullman hell."[3] During the depression of 1893, the company dropped wages but refused to correspondingly lower rents in a move to keep dividends up, forcing many workers to live without adequate food or fuel. Caught in an economic vise, they struck in early summer (1894). The ensuing riot and the tragic failure of Pullman's paternalism helped to touch off a basic reappraisal of plutocratic beneficence.

In one of the most telling commentaries, Chicago settlement worker Jane Addams labeled the industrialist "A Modern Lear." Like Shakespeare's King Lear, Pullman assumed a "dictatorial relation" to his employees. "The president assumed that he himself knew the needs of his men, and so far from wishing them to express their needs he denied to them the simple rights of trade organization."[4] Both performed "so many good deeds that they lost the power of recognizing good in beneficiaries."[5] Cut off from his workers' lives by his wealth, their needs and aspirations had developed outside Pullman's ken. He "cultivated the great and noble impulses of the benefactor, until the power of attaining a simple human relationship with his employes, that of frank equality with them, was gone from him." Separated by status and wealth, "he and his employes had no mutual interest in a common cause."[6]

Unable to recognize any other virtue but the individualism learned in his youth, Pullman had grown apart from the people and the social realities of his time. In the process, he fell prey to many of the ills of the philanthropist. Reveling in the pride, power, and public approbation which his experiment rendered, he gradually "ceased to measure its usefulness by the standard of the men's needs."[7] Although he provided a beautiful town for his men, he did so without their consent and without a full comprehension of their most pressing needs. As Addams explained:

> Lack of perception is the besetting danger of the egoist . . . [and] philanthropists are more exposed to this danger than any other class of people within the community. Partly because their efforts are overestimated . . . and partly because they are the exponents of a large amount of altruistic feeling with which the community has become equipped and which has not yet found adequate expression, they are therefore easily idealized. Long ago Hawthorne called our attention to the fact that "philanthropy ruins, or is fearfully apt to ruin, the heart." . . . One might add to this observation that the muscles of this same heart may be stretched and strained until they lose the rhythm of the common heart-beat of the rest of the world.[8]

Pullman failed because he sought to set himself above his fellowmen, to bestow, rather than to comprehend. "In so far as philanthropists are cut off from the influence of the *Zeit-Geist*, from the code of ethics which rule the body of men . . . so long as they are 'good to people' rather than 'with them' they are bound to accomplish a large amount of harm," Addams declared.[9]

"It sometimes seems as if the shocking experiences of that summer, the barbaric instinct to kill, roused on both sides, . . . can only be endured if we learn from it all a great ethical lesson," she concluded.[10] During the Progressive Era, a new generation of Americans attempted to do just that, reassessing the programs and gains of the Gilded Age, and positing new guidelines for benevolent effort. The Progressive movement marked an attempt by middle-class urbanites to restore democracy, morality, and civic purity to the American city. Many of the leaders, as Jane Addams had been, were born of old American families, the gentry that had traditionally been among the nation's intellectual and political leaders. But they had been dispossessed by the rise of a new breed of professional politician and Gilded Age wealth. Now, caught between predatory wealth above and poverty below, they sought to reassert their claim to authority, creating a better, more pure world.

Under their piercing scrutiny, the self-made man of the Gilded Age was revealed with all his flaws. By the nineties, wealth was no longer automatically associated with virtue. As Social Darwinism gave way to social conscience, the public grew increasingly suspicious of its erstwhile heroes. Formerly "it was believed . . . that the prosperous man was the righteous man," commented Jane Addams, but "we have learned since that time to measure by other standards, and have ceased to accord the money-earning capacity exclusive respect."[11] Muckrakers and Populists added their voices to the swelling chorus of criticism, assiduously laboring to dispel any lingering notions of the moral superiority of wealth. Between 1890 and 1900, a spate of highly critical works were published, detailing the corruption of the very rich. As Ignatius Donnelly explained, "A thousand men in a community worth $10,000 or $50,000, or even $100,000 each may be a benefit . . . but one man worth fifty or one hundred millions . . . is a threat against the safety and happiness of every man in the world."[12]

In the face of cyclical depressions and soaring industrial unemployment, the ideology of self-help and the self-made man lost much of its former credibility. "Nothing is more fallacious than an argument based upon a personal experience of thirty years ago. Since then an industrial revolution [has] taken place," mused Jane Addams.[13] William Stead's indictments were more pointed, more scathing. Labeling Field, Armour, and Pullman the Hannibals and Napoleons of the midwest, Stead concluded that "they loom up before the eyes of their fellow men because they have succeeded in ascending a pyramid largely composed of human bones."[14]

"If Christ came to Chicago would these men of many talents be able to show a good account of their stewardship?" Stead queried.[15] His answer, like that of many of his contemporaries, was a resounding "NO." Critics abhorred the big houses, fancy balls, and impressive trinkets which the wealthy lavished on themselves. Charity balls received particularly vehement censure. As Dr. D. W. Pierce of the Lincoln Street Methodist Church explained, "Any form of benevolence . . . that removes us away from the unfortunate rather than identifying us more closely with them, or that draws attention to our own ease, gain, or accumulation, as against the unrest, loss, or poverty of those we seek to benefit, is a charity which feeds our pride rather than hungry orphans."[16] "Jesus never instituted a charity ball where amid the voluptuous swell of the dance, the rustle of silks, the sparkle of diamonds, the stimulus of wine and women dressed decolleté, He could dissipate His love for the lowly," sneered another indignant cleric.[17]

Would-be benefactors were often portrayed in extremely unflattering terms. Patronage, and particularly institutional endowment, was depicted as a self-serving means of seeking notoriety, undertaken by donors contriving to "cover their nakedness with the mantle of respectability," and win unmerited praise.[18] Pointing an accusing finger at Armour, Stead disdainfully remarked that Armour Institute was the packer's "toy, his plaything."[19] Addams complained that many gifts cast "a certain glamor over all the earlier acts of a man, and make it difficult for the community to see possible wrongs committed against it, in the accumulation of wealth so beneficently used."[20] As one writer tersely noted, "To pay out money . . . to carve a family name on a gold brick, is not efficient giving."[21]

Critics insisted that the millionaires' motives were questionable, their wealth unmerited, their money tainted. Washington Gladden launched the tainted money debate in 1895, with the charge that nonprofit organizations had no right to grow fat off the millionaire's ill-gotten gains, enjoining them to refuse such suspect gifts out-of-hand. Sociologists, clergymen, and reformers quickly jumped on the bandwagon, vociferously decrying the practice of accepting conscience money from the corrupt. Calling such gifts "the Great White Plague [of] the rich man's university," and "the germ of moral tuberculosis," commentators asserted that "with one hand, the owner of such wealth thrusts his competitors into the abyss of commercial ruin, or grinds the faces of the poor; with the other, he hands the resultant gain to the Christian institutions of the land, which gratefully accept it, and rise to chant the paen of democracy triumphant."[22]

A few of the more moderate commentators pointed out the difficulty of distinguishing between saint and sinner, tainted money and clean. As Chicago settlement worker Graham Taylor remarked, "The pedigree of the penny, as well as the lineage of the dollar, would prove to be a very equivocal heritage from a very mixed ancestry if the income of every institution were subjected to a strict genealogical test."[23] Henry S. Pritchett, president of MIT, held that the conditions attached to the gift should figure more importantly than the reputation of the giver when determining whether or not it would be accepted. Others viewed the acceptance of such beneficence as a manifestation of Christlike absolution, advising their fellows to "take it from the Unspeakable Turk; take it from the Devil himself. Above all, take it from a bad man, a gambler, a thief . . . . Let the taint in some of his money be cleansed."[24]

Significantly, the loudest critics were the groups which were in the process of challenging the businessmen's centrality in local and national policymaking. Couching their bid for power in highly moralistic terms, women, clergymen, and educators—groups which had been excluded from the mainstream of urban decision making during the Gilded Age—asserted their right to a central role in shaping the future of city and nation alike. "Tainted money" was both a war cry and a symbol of their solidarity. By illuminating the corruption of the business world, they underscored their own moral qualifications and freedom from the taint of the money-getting process.

They were guaranteed a hearing because their arguments touched a deeper chord in the American psyche. Their charge that the rich were buying up the primary media of free thought—newspapers, universities, and the pulpit—smacked of Old World patronage and royalism. Indeed, the terminology used to describe Gilded Age magnates frequently incorporated royal metaphors. Businessmen were dubbed "robber barons," their wives "society queens," and their undertakings "feudalistic." Americans feared that the clergy, educators, and the poor were becoming the "creatures" of a hereditary class of idle rich, a concept antithetical to the Enlightenment ideals upon which the nation was founded.

Drawing upon the works of Harringtonian philosophers, the men of the Revolution believed that property conferred freedom. Dependency was viewed as a potential source of corruption. Seventeenth-century English philosopher James Harrington warned of the powers which the propertied man might exert over his impoverished brother: "Where a people cannot live upon their own, the government is either monarchy or aristocracy; where a people can live upon their own, the government may be democracy."[25]

Hence the appeal of the cherished ideal of the Jeffersonian yeoman: if Americans subsisted on their own labors, they would be independent, and the republic would be secure. Let them accept another man's gifts, and the threat of spiritual bondage and standing armies of sycophants and "creatures" commanded by the rich became a reality. Jefferson succinctly stated the problem when he observed that "dependence begets subservience and veniality, suffocates the germ of virtue, and prepares fit tools for the designs of ambition."[26] The debtor, the urban laborer dependent upon the goodwill of his customers, and the recipient of charity were all the antithesis of Jefferson's independent yeoman. Incapable of defending liberty, they had the power to subvert it. As historian Edmund Morgan notes, "An ambitious adventurer could buy them with bread, and arm them to attack the liberty of the rest."[27] Both steward and recipient were viewed with suspicion in the new republic.

Writing in the first half of the nineteenth century, the Transcendentalists echoed Jefferson's misgivings. "Do not tell me of my obligation to put all poor men in good situation," thundered Emerson. "Are they MY poor? I tell thee, thou foolish philanthropist, that I grudge the dollar, the dime, the cent I give to such men as do not belong to me and to whom I do not belong."[28] Thoreau concurred, charging that "he who bestows the largest amount of time and money on the needy may be doing the most by his mode of life to produce the misery which he strives in vain to relieve."[29] Emerson concluded simply, "I like to see that we cannot be bought and sold."[30]

Charity, and the obligations which it engendered were antithetical to the ideal of the "American Adam": a pristine and virtuous republic, devoid of anachronistic European social and intellectual institutions. The act of giving embodies a mutual relationship which entails an obligation on the part of both giver and recipient. Although the poor may not be able to render material recompense, they can give their loyalty to their benefactor and the social order which he represents. In the ancient city, this exchange was embodied in the patron-client relationship: the rich provided doles, feasts, and public amenities, and in return the poor gave "honor" in the form of social and political allegiance to their benefactors. Similarly, the early feudal lord initially held sway over his demesne by virtue of the services he rendered to his vassals and serfs. The master/slave relationship which this implied was incompatible with republican ideals.

Gilded Age excesses drew storms of criticism as businessmen became "barons" and social experimentation was translated into the "benevolent feudalism" of Pullman. Charity was suspect, "for poverty is the concomitant shadow of slavery—the premonition of it in every age and nation."[31] Hospitals, asylums, and missions, it was asserted, "are free in name only. . . . They foster dependence on the one hand and condescension on the other, thus emphasizing class-distinctions."[32] Decrying the practice of almsgiving as "distributing favors . . . a gift from success to failure, from superiority to apparent inferiority," commentators advised that America must not "allow itself to form the bad habit of leaning upon the large private donor."[33]

Aside from the inherent threat to democracy implied in such largesse, commentators underscored the pauperizing nature of such gifts, both to individuals and institutions. "Careless giving actually increases physical suffering and distress," by sapping the recipient's initiative and by perpetuating the conditions which initially engendered his poverty.[34] "It is always imperfect and temporary, a medicine which indicates social disease rather than a preventive of it."[35] Charity was a palliative which mitigated symptoms but afforded "no great increase of happiness and little sense of peace."[36] Ill-considered endowments, on the other hand, dampened institutional initiative and rendered the recipients insensitive to changing conditions, insulating them from public scrutiny and accountability, making them self-satisfied, and perpetuating their existence long after their purpose had been served.

In lieu of charity and plutocratic largesse, progressive spokesmen demanded social justice. "The world to-day is in far greater need of JUSTICE between man and man than of any charity offered as a sop for wrongdoing," they argued.[37] In order to achieve a more equitable distribution of life's benefits, progressive spokesmen advocated the enactment of social and industrial legislation "for the purpose of checking the stewards in their injurious methods of employing working people."[38] Rather than helping the few, social justice would improve the urban environment as a whole, even over the objection of the plutocratic steward. Rather than constructing eternal monuments, the new philanthropy was to be "of a disappearing nature," experimenting with untried techniques, promoting the passage of socially oriented laws, and subsequently moving on to new causes.

Progressives sought to extend controls over the manner in which gifts were given and the uses to which they were put. Rather than allowing the philanthropist to make decisions of his own accord, reformers insisted that he work in tandem with experts who had observed conditions firsthand and had the scientific training to interpret them correctly. As Rabbi Emil Hirsch explained, "Only one guided by expert knowledge and fortified by delicately tempered elasticity of experimental wisdom, may hope to be of use to himself and to others."[39] Experts were, in effect, to serve as liaisons between donor and recipient, interpreting the needs and capabilities of both for the benefit of society as a whole, permitting the isolated rich to view society through the prism of their perceptions.

Prevention was the keynote of the campaign for social justice, and facts its primary tools. Social research by experts devoting their full attention to the task would reveal the extent of the problem and educate the public about the city's needs. This entailed constant observation of the poor in their own habitats rather than simply manning centrally located services. After the turn of the century, sociologists and social workers embarked on a major campaign to publicize how the "other half" lived. Through articles, speeches, and courses given under the auspices of clubs, they labored tirelessly to sensitize potential donors to new areas of endeavor.

Decentralization was another key progressive concept. Living and laboring in the city's neighborhoods, reformers argued that centrally located services were not meeting the city's needs. Many slum dwellers, uninformed, impoverished, and frightened by the language and customs of a foreign land, lived and died without ever venturing beyond the familiar confines of their neighborhoods. In order to genuinely democratize the amenities of urban life, progressive spokesmen lobbied for the creation of neighborhood-based charitable, cultural, and public health organizations.

Espoused from pulpit and press, these ideas were carried into practice in Chicago by a small coterie of committed reformers. Although participation at the fringes of the movement was large, a tiny nucleus of dedicated adherents appeared behind every good cause, whether cultural, scientific, charitable, or reform. They came from a variety of backgrounds and, although many of their efforts centered around Hull-House, they were conscripted by a variety of means.

As a group, Chicago's progressives do not conform to the standard Progressive portrait: college educated, born in a small town, of an old American family, moving to the city to open a small business or enlist in the ranks of professionalism. For example, only two of the nine men and women who served as founders or officers in four or more progressive-oriented ventures between 1905 and 1915, when the Progressive impulse was at high tide, were professional social workers. Two were doctors, two belonged to industrialists' families, one was a banker, one the wife of a banker, and one the head of a national mercantile empire. Four were related to established Chicago families which had accrued sizable fortunes in the Gilded Age. All were approximately the same age, born between 1854 and 1866, and most hailed from the midwest. Two were born in small towns in Illinois, two in Wisconsin, and one in Iowa. But three were also born in Chicago, and a fourth was born in New England while his Chicago family was vacationing there. Nor were they uniformly well-educated. Although the four professionals held college degrees, their wealthy backers did not, graduating instead from finishing schools and the public school system.

Perhaps the best known was Jane Addams. Addams was born in Cedarville, Illinois, in 1860, the daughter of a well-to-do businessman. A member of the first generation of college women, she earned a baccalaureate degree from Rockford Female Seminary in 1882. Seven years later she opened Hull-House, Chicago's pioneer settlement, and one of the first in the nation. From a modest beginning the experiment quickly gained national recognition, serving as a fountainhead for a spate of humanitarian undertakings and Progressive reforms.

For Addams, humanitarianism was a "subjective necessity." Like many young alumnae, she complained of being well-educated, afforded every advantage, and then denied a proper outlet for her skills. Traditional fields of feminine endeavor—marriage, missionary work, teaching—did not seem to provide an adequate challenge to a woman with a college degree. Addams was particularly critical of parents who urged their daughters to acknowledge suffering and misery, inspired them to be self-sacrificing, and then blocked their every attempt to achieve a meaningful career. Caught between personal ideals and family claims, they achieved nothing. "Their uselessness hangs about them heavily," she recalled.[40]

"Weary of myself and sick of asking what I am and what I ought to be," Addams embraced Presbyterianism, briefly matriculated at the Woman's Medical College of Pennsylvania, withdrew for reasons of poor health, and ultimately drifted to Europe for a second grand tour in 1887, accompanied by her former classmate, Ellen Gates Starr.[41] The voyage marked a turning point in her career. Although she had dabbled in charity before, the work failed to sustain her interest. Her visit to London's Toynbee Hall, the pathbreaking university settlement in London's Whitechapel slum district, was a revelation. Rather than merely doling out material aid, settlement residents sought to understand the poor and placed a heavy emphasis on cultural uplift. Addams suddenly realized that by aiding the downtrodden she might save herself as well.

The women returned to Chicago in January 1889, determined to initiate a similar program in an American slum. After months of campaigning for support before women's groups, church organizations, and the boards of established charities, their plan became a reality. Launched in a dilapidated antebellum mansion in the middle of one of the city's worst slums, the notorious nineteenth ward, Hull-House opened its doors to the public in September 1889. Addams, Starr, and a constantly changing cast of residents lived there, extending their clubs, classes, and civic undertakings to rich and poor alike. All were welcome. Their watchwords were pragmatism, informality, and flexibility. Residents constantly ferreted out new needs, developing novel programs as outmoded or unsuccessful projects were discarded. The end result was "a department store of humanitarianism," offering a variety of programs geared to the changing aspirations of the city it served.[42]

Daily contact with the poor gave Addams and her co-workers a unique perspective on urban problems. "Longing to construct the world anew and conform it to their own ideals," they began to reassess the meaning of democracy in the industrial city.[43] Hull-House soon became the base for dozens of "small but careful investigations," in which the perils of slum life were charted, mapped, and graphically portrayed.[44] By publicizing the plight of the poor, Addams hoped to evoke a keener, more scientifically based understanding between the classes, bridging the social gulf with facts, figures, and vignettes. She also took the lead in a welter of social justice campaigns. Improved race relations, the decentralization of urban amenities, the anti–child labor movement, woman suffrage, and the crusades for better wages, working conditions, and public health all found an articulate spokesman in Miss Addams. Under her direction, Hull-House became the focus of an ever-widening circle of reform, wielding considerable influence in local, state, and national affairs. By 1912, Jane Addams had become the conscience of the nation.

People from all stations of life flocked to Hull-House. According to one observer, "Every one brings what he can to this charitable league—merchants, doctors, teachers, professors, students, clergymen, and mothers who are glad to give at least a few moments to the day nursery which helps so many other mothers."[45] Some served briefly, then left. Others lingered to become dedicated converts to the progressive cause.

Many of Julius Rosenwald's programs were shaped by his friendship with Miss Addams. The fabulously wealthy head of Sears Roebuck, the Chicago-based mail-order house, Rosenwald was born in Springfield, Illinois, in 1862, the son of German Jewish immigrants. After a brief two-year stint in high school, the boy was apprenticed to an uncle in the clothing business, arriving in Chicago in 1885. Rosenwald literally stumbled into his fortune, signing over a small loan to the partners at a crucial moment, a gesture which netted him the vice-presidency of what was to become one of the nation's largest and most successful mercantile concerns. "No one was more surprised at my sudden landing in the midst of America's multimillionaire class than I was myself," he modestly admitted.[46] A generous man with a deep and abiding sense of civic stewardship, he never lost sight of the fact that he owed his adopted city a debt of both money and time.

His purse strings were always open for every worthy cause. Estimates placed the amount of his gifts between $60,000,000 and $70,000,000. Over the years, Rosenwald developed some very definite ideas about the nature of giving. As he explained, "It is nearly always easier to make $1,000,000 honestly than to dispose of it wisely."[47] Prevention, deinstitutionalization, and flexibility were the watchwords of his philanthropic credo. Impulsive giving, "launched without scientific inquiry, without regard to existing institutions," was anathema to him.[48] In his opinion, charity was best when "propounded jointly by men of affairs and social experts."[49] He even refused to act as a sole donor, because he felt the role "too autocratic," proffering matching grants instead.[50]

Rosenwald saved his heaviest fire for perpetual endowments, arguing that they prolonged the life of institutions long after the need for them had passed. "Human conditions are changing so rapidly that a project which today is entirely commendable may be not only useless but vicious tomorrow," he noted.[51] Rather than building personal monuments to last the ages, the philanthropist should constantly be on the qui vive for new necessities, blazing a trail with his gifts. Future generations should be allowed to deal with their problems themselves. Putting his ideas into practice, he created the self-liquidating Rosenwald Fund. Capitalized with millions of dollars, the foundation was legally bound to spend both interest and principal within twenty-five years.

Rosenwald met Addams through their mutual friend, Juvenile Court Judge Julian Mack. He began contributing money to Hull-House in 1902, and by 1912 had joined the tiny board of trustees. He was also a major backer of the Chicago School of Civics and Philanthropy, United Charities, the city's many Jewish charities, and the University of Chicago. But race relations were the field which interested him the most. Rosenwald had his own "subjective necessity" for helping the blacks. His Jewish heritage made him fully aware of the legacy of persecution, sharpening his empathy with the dispossessed. As he explained, Jewish citizens could not afford to be too complaisant or to allow other groups to suffer prejudice and persecution: "The Jew must be a pillar of civic well-being and moral capacity. . . . If he falls short of this standard, he will himself have brought into being the monster which will one day destroy him and unseat him from his position of safety in America."[52] Accordingly, he underwrote black YMCAs throughout the nation, became a major backer of Chicago's Provident Hospital, and launched the Rosenwald Fund. He also tried to enlist other local philanthropists in the cause, chartering a special train to Tuskegee, and offering interested friends an expense-free trip to observe Booker T. Washington's work firsthand.

Louise de Koven Bowen was another wealthy Chicagoan drawn into the orbit of Hull-House by her charitable interests. Bowen, who proudly traced her ancestry back to the pioneer settlers at Fort Dearborn, was raised with a keen sense of stewardship. As she explained, "I had been brought up with the idea that some day I would inherit a fortune, and I was always taught that the responsibility of money was great, and that God would hold me accountable for the manner in which I used my talents."[53] As a young woman still in finishing school, she taught Sunday school and sewing classes at the family's Episcopal parish. Later, she hired a Swedish widow to assist her on her charitable rounds, investigating families and determining the depth of their needs. During this period, Bowen initiated a Kitchen Garden, joined several hospital boards, and continued with her church work, but she longed for something more.

Addams gave form and focus to Bowen's charitable proclivities. The women met when one of Bowen's friends, a society woman "tired of social life," decided to take up residence at the settlement. Intrigued by her tales of life among the poor, Bowen went to visit her, met Addams, and was invited to stay to help with the woman's club, thus beginning a life-long partnership. Bowen contributed two clubhouses, a "country club" for slum children, and after Addams's death played a major role in the management of Hull-House. "My whole acquaintance with Hull-House opened for me a new door into life," she later recalled: "I met many prominent people there, because anyone who came to Chicago always wanted to visit the House . . . and on the other hand I have made many good friends among working people and have come in contact with problems and situations about which I would otherwise have known nothing."[54]

Charles Hutchinson, the only member of the Gilded Age elite to make the transition to the progressive view, gravitated toward cultural reforms. Ever the democrat, he labored to decentralize the city's intellectual resources, bringing art to the neighborhoods and shaping programs in which everyone might participate. When the settlement opened a gallery in the nineties, Hutchinson was one of the first to volunteer to lend it paintings from his own collection. As a South Park commissioner, he was instrumental in bringing about the construction of neighborhood-based field houses which, after 1909, were graced by traveling loan exhibitions donated by the Art Institute. Similarly, he backed the Public School Art Society (1893), founded to amass a circulating collection of artwork for the city's public schools. When lumberman Benjamin F. Ferguson bequeathed $1,000,000 to the Art Institute for the erection of statuary and monuments throughout the city, Hutchinson was appointed one of the fund's trustees. Even in the 1880s, the banker had embraced the cause of public art. As he explained, "I would that at every turn were statue or monument or building, rich in artistic design, which would set forth ideas of beauty, grace or power, or speak of some noble soul whose life was far above that of his fellows."[55]

He believed that music, too, was capable of easing urban tensions and promoting understanding among the city's various ethnic groups. Hutchinson was one of the earliest and most enthusiastic backers of the Civic Music Association, founded in 1914 to provide "musical entertainment and instruction gratuitously or at little expense, in the small parks and playgrounds and other civic centers."[56] As one of the trustees explained, "Every social center should have its own choral club, orchestra, children's chorus and series of artist concerts. Every factory should have its choral club, orchestra and band."[57] Mammoth summertime concerts, music festivals, and community sings were among the organization's many programs, reaching into every neighborhood with affiliates like the Dvorak Park Bohemian Singing Society. Through agencies like the Civic Music Association, decentralizers like Hutchinson implemented their vision of a city in which cultural amenities would be available to all.

Hutchinson, Bowen, Anita McCormick Blaine, and Charles R. Crane were scions of some of Chicago's wealthiest families. Contemporary critics were quick to point out that the child of wealthy parents was in constant "danger of becoming a degenerate, a parasite, a creature who lives on the labor of others, whose powers ultimately atrophy from disuse."[58] Despite these claims, or perhaps because of them, many wealthy families reared their youngsters with a severity which seems excessive by the permissive standards of today. "Oh, to know how to raise them!" Nettie Fowler McCormick privately agonized in the pages of her diary. "Not their bodies alone, but what impressions to make upon their minds." Comparing her tiny brood to clay, she sternly reminded herself that "the vessel may be molded for honor or dishonor."[59] The McCormicks and the Cranes kept their children on a tight rein, emphasizing duty and instilling a considerable respect for the power of money. Allowances, when given, were small, and the children were encouraged to consign them to the poor rather than wasting them on personal embellishments. Both families labored to inculcate a sharp sense of noblesse oblige.

The McCormicks represented old money by Chicago standards. Daughter of the legendary "reaper king," by the time Anita McCormick Blaine was born in 1866, her father was a millionaire several times over. The McCormicks were deeply religious Presbyterians and committed philanthropists. Sociologists have noted that some clans develop "family images" by which they define their own activities and measure their success. Certainly this was the case with the McCormicks. After Cyrus Sr.'s death in 1884, Nettie dedicated herself to the bestowal of public benefactions. As her biographer points out, "Philanthropy was more than an avocation in life. It became life itself."[60] In a complex interaction of motives, Nettie's deep sense of Christian stewardship mingled with an urgent desire to achieve a lasting reputation as a great benefactress, an example which she encouraged her children to emulate.

Nettie was determined that each of her five children should leave legacies of McCormick generosity. Her task was made more difficult when two of them, Stanley and Virginia, suffered mental breakdowns from which they never recovered. Undeterred, the family donated funds in Virginia's name, and Nettie continued to fund the social settlements in which Stanley had been involved before his illness. Recalling his early interest in the Gads Hill Settlement, she informed the trustees that if they would care to permanently memorialize his activities by naming one of the club rooms in his honor, she would make a generous contribution to the building fund. While encouraging her children to develop philanthropic interests of their own, she expected them to continue their allegiance to her projects as well. Speaking of the McCormick Theological Seminary which her husband had helped to found in the 1850s, she remarked that she could not "contemplate a time, in however distant a future, when the great-grandchildren and great-great-grandchildren of this family would not feel a fostering interest in the Institution which their ancestor had founded."[61] For Nettie, the primary goal was to make the McCormick name synonymous with Christian benevolence.

Reared in an atmosphere of heightened social consciousness, Anita was painfully aware of the poverty which surrounded her wealthy family. As was the custom of the time, she was carefully educated by tutors, private schools, and European travel, rather than in one of the new women's colleges, and flowered into one of the town's most sought-after debutantes. Despite her social triumphs, she shared Addams's nagging sense of isolation and restlessness. At one point, she confided to her governess: "I have been lonely . . . for you know a thousand things make me sad. The trouble is that when I get depressed . . . my thoughts turn to myself. . . . My better self tries to assert itself, but it is a continuing battle between Christian resignation and wicked discontent—between true disinterested love and selfish complaining."[62] For Anita, the problem of selfishness was the key to personal self-discipline and happiness.

Her ennui seemed to vanish with her betrothal to Harvard Law School graduate Emmons Blaine, son of politician James G. Blaine. The couple was married in 1889, one week after the opening of Hull-House, and the following year they had a son. Then, suddenly, her contented world collapsed. Emmons died of blood poisoning in 1892, leaving Anita to care for their infant son. "I couldn't believe it true. I have lost a great deal out of my life. More than you can realize," she wrote constrainedly to her mother-in-law.[63] Only her fragmentary personal notes, scrawled on bits of paper and carefully preserved, reveal the depths of her grief. For the next two years she continually recorded her baby's reaction to the loss of his father, thereby displacing and acknowledging her own anguish: "This morning the baby in my arms looking over the mantlepiece . . . took down the silver frames. I put him in a chair and put them in his lap—saying nothing. He began to take apart the little silver frame, and put it back—then tried the other, but said 'at picture not come out'—then he took it up and looked thoughtfully at it and said, 'Want see Dadaa.'"[64] For Blaine, as for so many other women, benevolence became a means of working through her grief and carving a new role out of her widowhood.

Education was a natural choice for the young widow. Desiring the very best for her son, she began to investigate the curricula of several area schools. By 1894, her inquiries brought her into contact with two of the period's outstanding educational reformers: Colonel Francis Wayland Parker and John Dewey. Parker intrigued her the most. In 1898, Blaine offered to build him a private school, where he would be free from the political constraints which had hampered his work at the Cook County Normal School and which would serve as a model for the public school system.

Parker's emphasis on personal freedom, creativity, individualization and self-control, his rejection of grading systems which fostered competitiveness among children, his endorsement of nature study, and his vision of the school as an ideal community all struck a responsive chord in his benefactress. Blaine had chafed at the restraints of the classroom as a child, and through Parker her childhood dream was fulfilled. Schoolroom routine, she complained, "makes the daily life a regular treadmill never leaving any change or variety. The weeks are like a never-ending wheel which turns round and round, whose spokes are all the same."[65]

Teachers struck the young heiress as unduly authoritarian. Thus, she curtly noted, the schoolgirl "is never expected to have a mind of her own—must always defer to her teachers for their superior judgment, must never argue a point, for that would be unbecoming."[66] Even as a child, she abhorred the scramble for grades, for "here we see selfish ambition and rivalry."[67] As she explained, "The poorest education of the mind, but which teaches self-control, would be far better than an education which stores the mind with knowledge but does not teach this means of happiness and contentment."[68] Prophetically, she declared, "I am sure that if I ever survive it—which is very doubtful—I shall give countenance to those who murmur under their yoke and testify that their complaints are just."[69]

Although still only a child when she voiced these views, Blaine remained true to her word, ultimately subsidizing the very men who sought to overturn the conventional educational system which she had so despised. Initially she planned to finance two schools for Parker, one for the rich, and one for the poor to "take children from the streets—and make a little heaven for them."[70] Only the best teachers were to be hired for both. Ideally, the poor would taste the joys of learning, the rich would be taught a badly needed lesson in social responsibility, and all children would be helped as the model was adopted into the public school system. As Blaine pointed out, "The question for every pupil at every turn was not, how much can I get ahead of my brother, but, how much can I do to help my brother to do also."[71] Collectivism was to replace the outworn individualistic ethos of the Gilded Age.

Jane Addams, Graham Taylor, and the University of Chicago president, William Rainey Harper were all consulted about possible locations. The academic imperialist par excellence, Harper persuaded Blaine to incorporate her program into the university's school of education. On March 4, 1901, she transferred a million dollars' worth of property and assets to the university, setting aside another $90,000 to found a separate, less ambitious school for Parker alone on the north side. Her interest in the institution continued to grow after Parker's untimely death in 1902. By 1906, she had established an office there, devoting three days a week to overseeing the management of the school.

Blaine's educational enterprises brought her into contact with an ever-widening circle of experts, educators, and reformers. The date of her first meeting with Jane Addams is uncertain. Addams joined the McCormicks' congregation, the prestigious Fourth Presbyterian Church, shortly after her arrival in Chicago in 1889, but Anita was planning her wedding at the time and probably took little notice of the diminuitive woman from Cedarville. Mary Wilmarth invited her to a Hull-House reception for Prince Kropotkin in 1891, but once again there is no indication whether the invitation was accepted. It is possible that she may have been supporting a manual training program at Hull-House in 1898, and it is certain that she knew both Addams and Taylor in 1899 when they spoke before the trustees of the Parker school.

Blaine had begun to branch out into new fields by that time. In 1899, she sat on the executive committee of the Chicago Bureau of Charities, eventually donating over $100,000 to this organization and its successor, United Charities. Two years later her friend, Ethel Sturges Dummer, persuaded her to join the University Settlement Association, and she was one of a handful of trustees who saw the Chicago School of Civics and Philanthropy through its infancy. Blaine also chaired the executive committee of the City Homes Association, which she helped to found with Addams in 1900, listing Bowen, Hutchinson, and her sister-in-law, Edith Rockefeller McCormick (daughter of the oil king, John D. Rockefeller) among her co-workers.

For Anita, as for Nettie, wealth was "a privilege and a trust" to be used to benefit "the race that creates it."[72] However, as she matured, the young widow gradually drifted away from her family's narrowly

Presbyterian stewardship, and in 1926 she severed her financial affiliation with the McCormick Theological Seminary. According to relatives, the step was not taken lightly and was an extremely painful decision for her. But times had changed.

While Blaine relinquished the stewardship of her parents' generation only after a great deal of anguish and soul-searching, many of her contemporaries openly rebelled against the values of their elders from the outset. The friction was sharpest between the Progressive Era generation and their Gilded Age parents. The men who matured in the Gilded Age displayed a deep reverence for their sires. The letters exchanged between George Pullman and his mother, for example, reveal a dedication so intense, so overt, as to make the modern reader slightly uncomfortable. This sense of reverence was lost with the children of the Progressive decades. Enveloped by strident exposés of their fathers' misdeeds, and better attuned to the demands of an increasingly technological society, their charitable and cultural choices frequently reflected disillusionment with the world their fathers had made. Many joined in a quiet but determined revolt against their parents' values and dreams.

The Crane family is a case in point. Richard Teller Crane was a brilliantly talented, pugnaciously opinionated autocrat. According to his daughter, he "never realized he could be wrong about anything."[73] He had a violent, quickfire temper, and, while his children respected him, they feared him as well. Crane had little taste for the frivolities of Society, and night after night his gentle, refined wife kept silent vigil as he played solitaire for hours on end, working through the business or civic problems of the day. Between his domineering personality, his immutable opinions, and his glowering domestic presence, R. T. was "literally a law unto himself."[74]

Yet, in his own way, Crane was far more committed to the demands of social justice than many of his peers. He detested his fellow philanthropist, Andrew Carnegie, whom he leeringly referred to as "the Dr. Jekyll of library building and the Mr. Hyde of Homestead rioting and destruction."[75] Out of the millions Carnegie made through his workers, he bestowed "paltry thousands" on libraries which his employees could neither see nor use, a practice incomprehensible to the paternalistic Crane. Nor did he approve of civic monuments which neglected the neighborhoods of the poor, whether initiated as cultural undertakings or as part of a city plan. He was particularly scornful of cultural philanthropists intent upon bringing "the curious in touch with curios." "These people . . . do not allow common sense to tell them the best thing to do with their surplus wealth," he growled. "For the saving of manhood and womanhood, . . . a hard wrung dollar here and there. For the gathering of curios and anthropological specimens, thousands of dollars just for the asking."[76]

Crane believed that surplus wealth should be used to enhance the lot of the poor. His motives were not entirely altruistic. As he explained, workers were "the ones we must reach and control if we would be sure of the permanency of our social institutions." Nevertheless, he candidly admitted that "in many cases the wealth of the rich has been wrung from the poor. They have been robbed of their just rights, and it is equivalent to a second robbery for society to accept the alms of the rich for any purpose other than that of directly improving the conditions of the poor or reclaiming the criminal." In his vision of the ideal city, the solutions of the Gilded Age and the Progressive Era were curiously intermingled, calling for "clean and comfortable homes and tenements," playgrounds, accessible libraries, decent streets, and asylums for worn-out workers and old folks. Most important was an adequate educational system "from the kindergarten right through the grammar grades with plenty of manual training."[77]

R. T. sought to enforce his ideas even in death. In a letter accompanying his will, he enjoined his children to work hard, eschew "disgusting" habits of extravagance (one wastrel son was disinherited), cleave to the family's far-flung industrial empire ("the grandest one ever built up by any person"), and to honor the obligations of wealth. Pointing out that his "idea of charity is to help the lowest strata almost exclusively," he urged them to "devote a liberal share of their spare time to the interests of charity." And he explicitly outlined the types of endeavor they were to undertake: "It is my hope that they will continue the work I have started; also that they will confine their charities solely to the lines which I have always supported, and never do anything in directions that I consider to be largely ornamental or artificial—such as higher education, higher music, or higher art."[78] Few words could have been more ironic.

Charles Crane's every endeavor marked a "quiet but nevertheless determined revolt" against his father's dreams.[79] Although all of the Crane children had "a spotty sort of education," Charles's was the most incomplete.[80] According to his father's wishes, the boy began his apprenticeship in the family factory at the age of ten, working full time after graduation from grammar school. Later he briefly enrolled in the Stevens Institute, a school for mechanical engineering, and Rush Medical School, working in the factory after class. In both instances,

Charles had to withdraw due to recurring bouts of malaria. Like Hutchinson, he was denied the college education he yearned for but managed to acquire a good deal of learning on his own. A voracious reader, he devoured books about music, art, higher education, and languages in between his duties at the plant. The early years of overwork eventually proved to be his salvation from the industrial treadmill. As his health declined, R. T. reluctantly agreed to the physicians' prescription of travel and rest.

Touring extensively in Europe, the Middle East, and Asia, the younger Crane matured into a "student, a traveler, an observer of world movements, but at heart not a manufacturer or merchant."[81] Tall and extremely handsome, he had an amazing facility for winning friends among people of all stations in life, from kings to peasants. In one instance, the townsmen in a small Russian village in Central Asia tried to persuade him to remain there permanently by offering him "a booth in the bazaar where he could support himself by selling the American medicines in his travel kit."[82] Through his travels, he became fluent in Chinese, Russian, and Arabic, and was soon tapped for diplomatic missions, serving as an emissary to Russia during World War I, and later briefly serving as minister to China under Wilson. In a move that would have horrified his father, Charles sold his interests in the family business in 1914 in order to devote his full time to the pursuit of his international concerns.

Crane translated his love of the exotic into new programs for Chicago. One of William Rainey Harper's few close friends, he journeyed to Russia with the college president in 1900, escorting Harper to the homes of princes and artists. After such an original introduction, Harper was easily persuaded to implement a Russian Studies program at the University of Chicago, underwritten by Crane. Charles also generously subsidized the Marine Biological Laboratory at Wood's Hole, Massachusetts, where many of the university's scientists summered.[83]

Carl Sandburg called him "the best of the Chicago plutes."[84] Charles Crane was as openhanded as he was eclectic. As his friend, Harold Ickes, noted, "He was the one in a million who would contribute to a cause that he believed in even if he knew that it was hopeless."[85] His circle of friends included President Wilson, Justice Brandeis, Harvard President Charles W. Eliot, and all of Chicago's progressive philanthropists, among whom he was affectionately respected. Frank Billings caught something of his spirit when he described a meeting of several of the city's richest men, including

Rosenwald, Samuel Insull, John G. Shedd, and Cyrus McCormick, Jr. According to Billings, Rosenwald announced, "We five are probably the richest men in Chicago at the present time. It may be that in the future some of us or all may lose a part or all of our wealth and thereby the opportunity to do great things for Chicago. I propose that each of us put $5 million in a jack-pot and agree to spend it in the course of 5 or 10 years for various philanthropies." McCormick chuckled, Shedd scowled, and Insull pleaded that he was already overextended. Only Crane cheerfully agreed that "that's a swell idea; I will put my share in the jack-pot."[86]

He was also generous with his time, serving on the board of Chicago Commons, the executive committee of the Child Welfare Exhibit, and the Chicago Bureau of Efficiency. A firm believer in good government, he donated $50,000 to the unsuccessful mayoral bid of University of Chicago political scientist Charles Merriam. He was one of the handful of financial backers who guided the School of Civics and Philanthropy through its first years, and when he moved to New York he donated his house to the school, providing permanent quarters. When two of his nephews died in the Iroquois Theater fire of 1903, he underwrote an investigation which resulted in more stringent fire laws. He even persuaded his father to donate $100,000 to Hull-House for a nursery, as a memorial to his mother. Any cause connected with better government, more efficient charity, and democratic humanitarianism won Charles Crane's support.

Wealthy Chicagoans like Crane, Blaine, Bowen, and Hutchinson were conscripted and advised by a variety of professionals, ranging from clergymen and settlement workers to charity agency directors and family physicians. Three of the most important were Sherman Kingsley, Dr. Henry Baird Favill, and Dr. Frank Billings.

Kingsley was an inveterate modernizer. One of the new breed of social workers dedicated to the dissemination of progressive goals, he worked his way up the professional hierarchy through a string of appointments in New York and Chicago. In 1904, he was hired to head the Chicago Relief and Aid Society after Trusdell finally passed from the scene. Eight years later, he resigned to head the Elizabeth McCormick Memorial Fund. The fund had begun operations rather aimlessly, bestowing random doles on a variety of local agencies. Some of its first gifts included $5,000 for braces for the Home for Destitute and Crippled Children, and $50.00 for coal for the poor. Sensing the futility of such efforts, the McCormicks polled a variety of local leaders for fresh ideas. Drawing upon his ample experience,

Kingsley advised the subsidization of pilot projects for visiting housekeepers, tuberculosis prevention, or infant welfare. Impressed, the McCormicks invited him to become the fund's director. With Kingsley at the helm, the organization embarked on an elaborate program of pioneering, legislative reform, publicity, and investigation. Kingsley's years with the McCormick fund revealed his skills in promoting the newer ideals. Fashioning the previously unstructured foundation along progressive lines, he quickly transformed it into one of the nation's recognized leaders in the child welfare field.

Favill led the fight against tuberculosis. As president of the City Club, the Chicago Tuberculosis Institute, and a member of the boards of United Charities, the Municipal Voters League, and the Chicago School of Civics and Philanthropy, the Wisconsin-born doctor was a model of the socially minded physician who came to the fore after the turn of the century. His colleague, Frank Billings, was more of an institution builder than a volunteer. President of the American Medical Association (1902–4), and a fine bacteriologist in his own right, Billings was one of the most respected doctors in the city, numbering many of Chicago's wealthiest families among his patients. Harper schooled him in the art of fund raising, training him to use his abundant wit and charm to the best advantage. Tapping his professional relationships for civic ends, Billings persuaded Thomas Murdock and Philip D. Armour to donate $50,000 each to the Presbyterian Hospital, raised over $2,000,000 for Provident Hospital, and was instrumental in the creation of the McCormick Institute for Infectious Diseases (1902) and the O.S.A. Sprague Memorial Institute (1909) for medical research.

Kingsley, Billings, Favill, Addams, Bowen, Hutchinson, Rosenwald, Blaine, and Crane were the leaders of a subculture dedicated to reshaping the contours of the city's charitable and cultural organizations. Bound by shared values, mores, sanctions, and social relationships, they spearheaded the crusade for modernization on a variety of fronts. Friendship was the social currency which united them. Dining at Hull-House, socializing in clubs, serving on the same boards, they came into constant contact. Some even entered business ventures together, as when Crane and Rosenwald purchased *Harpers Weekly* with Cleveland Dodge and George Porter.

Each spread the progressive gospel in his own fashion. Socially minded physicians like Billings and Favill served as liaisons, mediating between the medical community, well-to-do patients, and nascent community needs. Wealthy reformers personally conscripted friends and clubmates into the causes they espoused. Professional social workers researched, lectured, and published copiously, ultimately training an entire generation to view urban ills through the filter of their perceptions.

Together, they cast aside the mandates of the Gilded Age and joined forces to democratize and decentralize the city's amenities. Flexibility, experimentation, pragmatism, careful study, and expert advice formed the cornerstones of their programs, translating the muckrakers' critiques into concrete reforms. No longer content to exercise their stewardship within the controlled setting of museum, hospital, and Home, they reached into the city's neighborhoods, studying the needs of those they sought to aid. In the process, Chicago's progressives reiterated their commitment to the community ideal and the obligations of noblesse oblige in an idiom that was uniquely their own.

Infant Welfare Society nurse with mother and children (ca. 1911). Courtesy of the Chicago Historical Society.

# 6
# THE NEW TITHINGMEN

"Home life is the highest and finest product of civilization," began the progressive manifesto which rocked many of Chicago's more established charities to their very foundations.[1] Announced at the 1909 White House Conference on the Care of Dependent Children, the declaration was a milestone, for it both legitimized the anti-institutional forces which had been gathering momentum for decades and split Chicago's charities into two camps. The progressives emphasized the need to rehabilitate the natural family within its own habitat and sought to achieve individual adjustment through social observation, research, and scientific expertise. Asylum advocates, on the other hand, continued to endorse individual rehabilitation through claustration from the temptations and maladies of city life. In the process, local traditions and national innovations collided head-on.

Friendly visiting, visiting nurses, infant welfare societies, and foster home care were among the many programs implemented during the Progressive Era to shore up the natural family and keep it intact. Urbanization and industrialization drained the family of many of its former educational and economic functions, leaving its future in doubt. After 1870, divorce rates began to rise while birthrates simultaneously dropped, raising the specter of race suicide. While the average American household contained 5.5 members in 1870, the number dipped to 4.5 in 1910. Armed with statistics from charity organization societies, settlements, housing reformers, and the National Divorce Reform League, critics argued that hotels and boarding houses, increasing opportunities for feminine education and employment, commercialized recreation and vice, the moral and physical maladies of tenement life, and a spate of other ills were destroying the foundation of home life in America.[2]

In the Progressive scramble for panaceas, the home emerged triumphant. Through constant supervision by visitors of all varieties, it was hoped that the family could be saved, cured, and improved. One historian has labeled them "the new tithingmen," and, indeed, the comparison is apropos.[3] Like their colonial prototypes, "visitors" were to insure family stability through intervention and ongoing supervision.

Children, especially, played a central role in their efforts. In a marvelously evocative sculpture entitled "The Blind," Lorado Taft depicted "a world groping toward the light through the guidance of the child," in much the same fashion as *Godey's Lady's Book* had shown transcendent motherhood in the lead half a century before.[4] With Rousseauian optimism, progressives looked to the child as the saviour of the race. More malleable than adults, youngsters could be easily molded into healthy, upstanding citizens.

They could also provide the perfect opening wedge into troubled families bent upon preserving their privacy. Day nurseries constantly asserted that by aiding their tiny charges they Americanized mothers as well. Visiting teachers, nurses, charity workers, and infant welfare representatives all gained access to the family through the child. Probation officers and moral reformers marveled at the ease with which recalcitrant parents could be cured of antisocial pastimes simply by threatening to deprive them of their offspring.

Children also figured largely in the popular crusade for human conservation. Comparing the urban labor force to the nation's natural resources, critics argued that workers were being ravaged and scrapped as maliciously and as wastefully as the trees and water supplies, pawns in the scramble for wealth. Industrialists overworked their employees, confined them in unhealthy, unsafe factories and slums, and then cast them out to fend for themselves when injured, ill, or worn-out. While social justice advocates sought to achieve a more realistic distribution of material benefits, conservationists demanded better health care. As one source sternly queried, "We are conserving our forests, our mines, our water power, what are we doing to conserve human life, our greatest national asset?"[5]

Rescue began in the crib. Saving babies was deemed the optimum means of conserving manpower. Reformers were fascinated by the malleability of the child and looked to him as the solution of the nation's ills. Even a level-headed technician like Herbert Hoover predicted, "If we could grapple with the whole child situation for one generation, our public health, our economic deficiency, the moral character, sanity and stability of our people would advance three generations in one."[6] Healthy children were less likely to think that the world owed them a living because it had denied them a chance, less likely to become tramps, less likely to be paupers. Conversely, United Charities spokesmen solemnly warned, "You cannot make an efficient citizen out of a blighted baby."[7]

Few could deny that Chicago's infants were being blighted at an appalling rate. Tainted milk and summer diarrheal diseases continued to carry off unconscionable numbers of infants each year. The first organization to deal directly with the problem was the Infant Welfare Society, an outgrowth of the Children's Hospital Society (1903).

The Hospital Society had a dramatic beginning. Chicago had few facilities for the care of contagious diseases. To operate effectively, an isolation hospital would have had to have been located within the city's limits, near the population it was designed to serve. But few property owners would tolerate the presence of such an institution, despite repeated assurances by the medical profession that modern scientific techniques would contain the contagion within the wards. The human implications of this inadequacy were poignantly illustrated on a frigid Thanksgiving night in 1902, when a desperate father frantically carried his dying child from private doctors to hospitals to City Hall, imploring the authorities to shelter and aid the infant. None accepted diphtheria cases, and the child died unaided. The plight of "little Baby Maloney" touched the city's conscience. Enlisting the aid of leading physicians like Frank Billings, the Chicago Woman's Club launched a campaign for improved facilities for contagious care.

Another issue which quickly elicited the group's attention was milk inspection. Bacteriological studies had proven that impure milk was an ideal medium for the transmission of a variety of childhood diseases. Some enterprising dairymen watered their products, or added chemicals to turn unpalatably bluish milk a creamier color. Others sold goods from tuberculous cows. Slum tenements, laden with flies and lacking facilities for the proper summer storage of dairy products, helped to further pollute the milk. These factors moved the founders of the Hospital Society to create the Chicago Milk Commission (1903), which investigated dairymen and distributed wholesome milk at reasonable prices. Led by a coalition of settlement workers, clubwomen, philanthropic businessmen like Charles Hutchinson, and reform-minded physicians, the Milk Commission drew together a group of interested citizens who would cooperate again and again in the creation of medical outreach programs. Aided by clean milk distributed through neighborhood "Pasteur Stations," the summer infant death rate dropped by 18% between 1903 and 1909.[8]

Still unsatisfied, the board concluded that the infant mortality problem transcended feeding alone. Changing its name to the Infant Welfare Society (IWS), they embarked upon the larger task of health care and maternal education. Aided by branch medical societies, Dr. William A. Evans districted the city and conducted a house-to-house survey of health needs. A spot map charting August infant deaths was drawn and baby tents established where the greatest number of dots converged. The results illustrated the interrelationship between overcrowding, inferior housing, poverty, and premature death. Within the first year, ten stations were put into operation in some of the city's worst slums. Modeled on the pioneer "fresh air stations for sick babies" established at the Northwestern University Settlement in 1905, each $250 tent was outfitted with beds and hammocks for ten to twenty infants, and staffed with two trained nurses.

Tents were deemed more useful than more substantial buildings for a variety of reasons. Their simple design ensured that they could be quickly and easily assembled near the homes of the poor, thus obviating the additional expense for transportation. Henry Booth House, Hull-House, Northwestern University Settlement, and Chicago Commons all hosted baby tents. Because they were conveniently located, mothers did not have to endure long walks or streetcar rides encumbered by their ailing infants. More important, because they were open and informal, many women who would not have dreamed of entrusting their babies to a hospital willingly brought them to the tents. Highly superstitious and leery of institutions, many foreign mothers were terrified by hospitals, where they feared their children might be used as clinical material, or subjected to unknown terrors like "the black bottle." The virtue of the tent was that it enabled mothers to keep their youngsters within sight at all times. In the process, they, too, were instructed, learning new techniques of feeding, bathing, and clothing their infants. "If you want to save a baby, you must save the mother also. The tent is in close touch with the mother and instructs her," explained IWS spokesmen.[9]

Through tent work, trained nurses, dietitians, and doctors were at the slum dweller's disposal. The Woman's City Club also sponsored sewing, cooking, and health classes at several tents, and in the early twenties child psychologists were added to their staffs. Two days a week mothers brought their infants in to be weighed, measured, and examined. During the interim, the nurses visited the clients' homes to ensure that the doctors' instructions were properly executed. They also inspected the sanitary conditions of the homes, and taught impoverished mothers how to keep their babies alive under urban conditions. Pointing out that the education of the mother was actually the society's most important mission, spokesmen declared, "Sentiment and love alone will not save a baby's life."[10] Mothers had to be trained to their task.

The work of the IWS was paralleled—and aided—by United Charities. Chicago was one of the last major American cities to embrace the cause of scientific charity on an enduring basis. Borrowed from British precedents, the Charity Organization Society (COS) movement was initiated in Buffalo, New York, in 1877, quickly spreading to other cities. Chicago's first COS was crushed by the rival CRA in 1887, before it had had time to implement its programs, or initiate a satisfactory friendly visiting movement. Later, it was revived as the Central Relief Organization, a stopgap agency created to cope with the emergency situation generated by the economic depression of 1893.

By the end of 1893, the city's charities were inundated, the poorhouse overflowing, and throngs of unemployed men loitered menacingly in the streets, ready tinder for demagogues and agitators. Spurred to action by the mounting crisis, the Civic Federation issued a call to representatives of all of Chicago's charities to meet and discuss the possibility of pooling their resources for the duration of the depression. CRA superintendent Charles G. Trusdell attended but stubbornly refused to recognize the proportions of the crisis, calmly insisting that his organization had amply provided for those in need. His actions unleashed a wave of vehement criticism from a variety of reformers who had long been frustrated by the agency's complacency. Charging that the CRA was "inadequate in extent and antiquated in method," they formed a rival Central Relief Association in January 1894.[11] Ironically, the CRA's hegemony was shattered by its own intransigence.

Later, the two agencies merged. Trusdell died in 1904, and many of the organization's Gilded Age trustees soon followed him to the grave. Pullman passed away in 1897, Field in 1906. Trusdell's successor, Sherman Kingsley, completely revamped the organization's policies. Drawing upon several years' experience in charities in Boston and New York, Kingsley introduced a range of new preventive programs, eagerly giving CRA backing to the antituberculosis campaign, the pure milk movement, fresh air stations, diet kitchens, and the City Homes Association. In a statement which would have astounded the postfire trustees, he announced, "The great task of this Society is keeping families together. On every hand children's institutions are crowded, mothers shrink from parting from their little ones, even temporarily.... More and more it seems to us that the only reason for breaking up a family ought to be moral unfitness of the parents or the absolute delinquency of the child."[12] Sensing an ally in this bright young man, and with an eye to the economic advantages as well, the trustees of the Chicago Bureau of Charities cheerfully endorsed the union between the two organizations, completed in 1909. As United Charities, they maintained COS techniques, and increasingly embarked on reform campaigns as well. The new board included some of Chicago's outstanding progressives—Jane Addams, Bowen, Blaine, Julius Rosenwald, Dr. Henry Baird Favill—and Kingsley, who was retained as superintendent.

The organization's aims ranged from fostering coordination and cooperation among existing charities, to surveying the extent of need through careful investigations and scrupulous record keeping on all applicants, finding jobs, and transporting habitual beggars to other towns. Under their guidance, the city was carved into districts, "so arranged that each contains a well-to-do community adjacent to a poor one." United Charities investigations clearly delineated the unique topography of poverty and human distress in Chicago.

The Central District, for example, was notable for its social pathologies: drug addiction, alcoholism, prostitution. Englewood was the antithesis, housing scores of temporarily disabled immigrant families who were "capable of being re-established by constructive effort." The Lower North District was overcrowded, and its residents most in need of remedial care: food, fuel, medical services. The Northern District, like Englewood, was filled with struggling families who could achieve permanent independence "through the attention of a friendly visitor or the watchful care of an office worker." The predominantly Polish Northwestern District was distinguished by poor housing, unsanitary living conditions, and high infant mortality rates. The tenements and rooming houses of the South Central District, on the other hand, were plagued primarily by tuberculosis, a condition which called "loudly for special inquiry as to housing conditions."[13]

And so the list continued. South Chicago was a city within a city, a wilderness of factories stalked by industrial accidents, disease, and casualized labor. The Bohemians on the southwest side were undernourished, overcrowded, and sickly. Woodlawn was the home of the genteel poor: educated, refined, and proud. Conversely, the nearby stockyards district was distinguished by every kind of inadequacy, sans recreational facilities, decent food, and sufficient medical care.

Girded by their precise territorial knowledge of the city's ills, the trustees had their work cut out for them. After 1910, United Charities launched a house-to-house survey of infant welfare problems, cooperated with the Chicago Tuberculosis Institute, created an exhibit of slum conditions, and joined the Illinois Committee on Social Legislation. Calling itself "a huge machine for family reconstruction," the agency lobbied for decent wages, protection against industrial accidents and disease, better working conditions for women and children, and upgraded community health and housing facilities.[14]

United Charities continually underscored the need for personal knowledge of the poor in their own homes. As they explained, "Workers [tried] to understand the situation of the poor family as a whole rather than the situation of merely one of its members."[15] Only through continual observation of the family within its natural habitat, it was argued, could problems be comprehended in all of their complexity.

The heart of the program was friendly visiting, corps of volunteers "seeing and knowing people in their homes, and trying, by means of personal influence and practical suggestion, to improve their condition."[16] Friendly visiting represented an attempt to recapture a sense of community cohesion—with a new twist. As late nineteenth-century cities jumped the confines of the traditional walking city, rich and poor, donor and recipient were drawn farther apart. As New York COS leader Josephine Shaw Lowell explained:

> In a country village, the mountain springs supply the water that is a necessity of life, and from the kind hearts of neighbors flows, also, a living stream of charity blessing those who receive it; but in the city, unhappily, we need reservoirs and pipes, ramifying through all the streets, and branching up into every house to bring us even the water we drink, while in like manner even our love to our neighbor must be guided through organized channels, or it will lose its life-giving powers and become a source of moral disease and death.[17]

Friendly visiting, properly practiced, was to restore right relations between the classes in America's distended cities.

The agency numbered two hundred friendly visitors in 1896, and over seven hundred by 1913. Most were middle- and upper-class women, moved by social feminist aims and a desire to play a meaningful role in solving society's problems within the framework of ladylike behavior. The visitor's first task was to gain the family's confidence, to befriend them, to "advise, to sympathise and to cheer." This in turn could be used as leverage to upgrade the behavioral norms of the clients. At its best, the relationship between the visitor and her charges acted "as a tonic, so that the family, in their desire to please and to show their gratitude, pull themselves together and rehabilitate themselves in a striking manner."[18] Ideally, both parties benefited, the poor receiving encouragement and aid, the visitor rehumanized by her contact with her less fortunate brethren. By restoring "neighborship" between the classes through tenuous ties of personal contact, spokesmen hoped to bridge the "social gulf," promoting enhanced understanding and circumventing the problems of anonymity, anomie and unrest.

Despite its simple outlines, there was nothing sentimental about friendly visiting. "Each case is to be RADICALLY dealt with," recommended Josephine Shaw Lowell. "Finding fellow beings in want and suffering, the cause of the want and suffering are to be removed if possible even if the process be as painful as plucking out an eye or cutting off a limb."[19] Visitors were to observe the minutest details of their family's existence, supplementing personal observation with records from the Bureau of Registration and interviews with relatives, former neighbors and employers, teachers and clergymen. They were advised to record the client's mental and physical condition, the manners of his children and the domestic skills of his wife, his salary, occupation, affiliations, debts, recreational tastes, and personal peccadillos. Once amassed, these facts served as the basis of social diagnosis; determining the root of the family's distress and devising a cure. Aid took a variety of forms. Some families received food and coal, ailing relatives were sent to hospitals and sanitoria, jobs were found, absconding husbands corraled and returned, child abusers hastened into court, and sloppy housekeepers indoctrinated in the subtle arts of domestic expertise. Sidestepping the traditional labels of "worthy and unworthy," visitors were continually reminded that the poverty and suffering they encountered was to be treated as "a transient and curable condition."[20]

The professional counterpart of the friendly visitor was the visiting nurse. Founded in 1889, after an abortive start six years earlier, Chicago's Visiting Nurse Association (VNA) was backed by a prestigious board of some of the city's wealthiest and most prominent women, including Addams, Bowen, and Florence Pullman. The association professed a triple goal: to aid the poor in their own homes, thus democratizing the best in medical care; to teach the proper care of the sick; and to spread the gospels of cleanliness and right living.

The board took a lively interest from the outset, doling out relief, helping with investigations, and tending the agency's headquarters. Some worked at the agency's office, others tagged along with the nurses on their rounds. Bowen recalled "interviewing and engaging nurses, talking to them of their duties, and trying to put a standard before them of what their work ought to be, urging upon them the patience, the sympathy, the kindness, and above all the tact, which they must use in every household which they visited."[21] However, as the service matured, board members were quickly weaned from day-to-day operations. By 1915, their efforts were confined to substation visits, and by the twenties fund raising accounted for most of their time.

The nurses' work, on the other hand, was rich and varied, covering many of the city's poorer districts. Nurses received their assignments at public telephone booths in neighborhood drugstores. Since Jane Addams was a charter member, the VNA maintained close ties to Hull-House, which served as a call station and put its diet kitchen facilities at their disposal. Nurses were instructed to limit their visits to forty minutes, for which they charged up to seventy-five cents. Conscientious in day-to-day operations, they rendered extraordinary service during emergencies, organizing and staffing an impromptu pesthouse during the smallpox epidemic of 1893, rushing to the scene of the Iroquois Theater fire in 1903, even delivering a baby on the seat of a streetcar. City-wide and flexible, telephones and transit lines enabled the VNA to quickly dispatch its nurses wherever they were needed most.

It is interesting to note how they managed their movements among the poor. Initially, the nurses wore white crosses on their uniforms, a symbol "which the most degraded dare not desecrate, [which had] been found to be a necessary protection."[22] While urged to observe home conditions, novices were cautioned to appear nonchalant, posing their inquiries casually, and never to record answers in the patient's presence. "Simple people dread formal questioning," Superintendent Foley explained.[23] The ultimate goal was to win their confidence, and "secure such a firm footing in each home that the inmates follow and acknowledge the nurses' advice without question."[24] That some resented their ministrations was clear. Foley noted that "To some people [the visiting nurse] is an angel of light; to just as many others she is an obnoxious meddler, much worse than a policeman, for he will sometimes mind his own affairs, but the Visiting Nurse is apt to take a 'childlike and bland' interest in everything, from the cleanliness of the refrigerator to the pay envelope of the entire family."[25] Like the social worker, she was there to observe as well as to cure.

Much of their work was with the chronically ill and incurables. Case histories revealed some of the horror of being seriously ill in an alien land. In one instance, a Swedish dressmaker was found in the last stages of consumption, using the remainder of her waning strength to fashion her own shroud. The nurse became "the only friend she had." Others begged their families to allow them to die in their filthy tenement homes, for "the thought of being brought before a clinic of students—the price one pays for becoming a charity patient—is not a pleasant one to any woman, and the separation from home and the fear of dying without a loved hand to cling to, as the cold waters of death creep up, is hardest of all, perhaps, to the so-called patient."[26] Although the prose is a little florid, this passage clearly reflected the nurses' compassion, and their conception of their own role in the battle against urban impersonality and anomie. The VNA prided itself on the fact that its services permitted families to remain intact, inculcating new skills within the natural home environment.

Adopting an antiinstitutional stance, VNA spokesmen pointed out that hospitals accomplished little lasting good by removing patients from their normal surroundings, cleaning them up, curing them, and then returning them to their filthy homes. "The one established principle of the work is to teach and to preach cleanliness and right living in the homes and to help the people bear the burden of caring for their own sick rather than shifting the responsibility to an INSTITUTION."[27] "It is by reaching the people in their own place, and teaching them there to utilize and make the best of what they have, that lasting good is best accomplished," they declared.[28]

Like friendly visitors, nurses were intent upon resocializing their patients to urban ways within the natural environment of the home. Their lessons embraced a variety of topics, from the proper care of convalescents to teaching a welfare mother to make do with niggardly grants from the county, and encouraging parents to raise their children as "good, intelligent, clean, honest, thrifty men and women."[29] Sewing, cooking, and child care all fell within their tutorial range. Sometimes they labored against incredible odds. One recalled the friendly greeting of a Bohemian mother who declined a bath for her daughter because she had "just sewed on all her clothes."[30] Laboring incessantly against the "dirt, the slovenly habits and the ignorance" of the poor, nurses sought to erase the habits of a lifetime, Americanizing immigrant women within the familiar confines of sickroom and kitchen.[31]

Facts culled from home visits served as the basis of new movements and needed laws. VNA president Mary Aldis likened their statistics to ammunition, "little black and white bullets, stubborn, hard-headed facts with which to batter down, wherever it is met, the opposing force of conservative ignorance or neglect."[32] The association lent its authority—and its statistics—to a variety of campaigns, ranging from pure milk and birth registration to sanitation and the call for better housing ("one of the vital things that touches almost every phase of a Visiting Nurse's work").[33]

The VNA bore a striking resemblance to all of the "visiting" programs of this period. Under the banner of charity and health, workers entered private homes and co-opted responsibility for a variety of family functions. While their observations served as an important source of data, their ongoing supervision served society by replacing the informal mutual aid of an earlier time with a network of formalized "friendships." In effect, the visiting movement reinstituted primary contact between the poor and the rest of society, and placed this previously spontaneous activity on a permanent, official basis.

Professionalization proceeded most quickly in the medical field because nurses were better organized, better trained, and backed by scientific considerations from the outset. Addressing potential candidates, VNA superintendent Harriet Fulmer warned that "none but the best-trained and well-paid people should go into the field" of public health nursing.[34] VNA representatives continually disparaged untrained nurses, describing one as an "old frump, doing things that would raise your hair."[35] By 1901, the Associated Alumnae of Trained Nurses claimed four thousand members, and the number of professional societies continued to proliferate during the ensuing decades. As they became increasingly professionalized, nurses' attitudes about untrained helpers became more rigid. As one source explained:

> When one goes merely as a visitor and not to be of service, there is a danger that one will not recognize the human being is the patient, that the study of character under adversity, remains a

> sealed book to the visitor; whereas to the nurse or social worker who goes into the home knowing why she is needed and what inherited economic or environmental difficulties required her presence there, sees first the person and then the dirty neglected surroundings.[36]

Clearly, the presence of the volunteer was no longer a wanted or necessary part of the nursing service.

Between 1900 and 1929 the forces of professionalization worked relentlessly to limit and redefine the role of the volunteer. By the 1910s, agencies began to report a dearth of volunteers. Many Chicagoans opted to devote their spare hours to a growing array of reform movements. At the same time, professional workers were quietly narrowing the options open to their lay colleagues. Reviving the critiques of the Civil War, untrained workers were "weighed in the balance and found wanting."[37] After 1910 the volunteer's star was rapidly eclipsed.

Even United Charities, the city's erstwhile promoter of friendly visiting, began to equivocate about the value of untrained workers. "There is a limit to the number of volunteers a society can safely absorb owing to the necessity of proper supervision, and direction of their work by trained persons," the agency's spokesmen explained.[38] By 1915, interested laymen were as likely to be consigned to a desk job as they were to be assigned to a family. Professionals were regarded as being better trained, more dependable, less emotional. Rather than relying wholly on the sporadic goodwill of benevolent housewives, organizations increasingly turned to the certified social worker.

Chicago's first school of social work, the Chicago School of Civics and Philanthropy (1903), was founded by Chicago Commons head resident Graham Taylor. Inspired by a similar venture developed by Prime Minister Gladstone's daughter at London's Women's University Settlement, its backers included a prestigious board of outstanding progressives like Addams, Blaine, Crane, Ethel Sturges Dummer, and Juvenile Court Judge Julian Mack.

From a modest beginning with two instructors, a borrowed classroom, and limited funding from the pocket of William Rainey Harper, the organization quickly grew to include hundreds of students tutored by some of the city's leading reformers, including Julia Lathrop, Robert Hunter, Charles R. Henderson, Edith Abbott, and Sophonisba Breckenridge. Lectures touched on every aspect of urban pathology, from family disorganization to the perils of tenement life. Great stress was placed on the cultivation of research skills, geared to "the prevention of evils, or to the improvement of conditions that promote or perpetuate them."[39] Under faculty supervision, students fanned out to the city's slums, charities, and settlements to master their newly acquired skills. Well on its way to becoming one of the nation's most important schools of social work, the institution received additional stature with its incorporation as the University of Chicago's School of Social Service Administration in 1920. Backed by the university's imprimatur, it lent considerable stature to its graduates' demands for recognition.

A second important bulwark of professionalization was the Chicago Council of Social Agencies (CCSA), founded in 1914 by a group of social workers intent upon centralizing, systematizing, and upgrading the city's agencies. Among the charter members were Sherman Kingsley, Minnie Low, and Wilfred Reynolds, all of whom were recognized leaders in the welfare field. The group was keenly aware that the city's social workers were not united, and they hoped that by providing a common forum they could arouse enough unanimity among their colleagues "to wield the practical influence in the affairs of common interest."[40] This entailed making surveys, serving in an advisory capacity, and using "its influence in every way possible to encourage the development of the right agencies at the right time and the adoption of right methods."[41]

Later, in order to assist in fund-raising efforts, the social workers nominated a number of progressive laymen favorable to the cause of professionalization to sit on the board. Included were Rosenwald, Albert W. Harris (founder of the Chicago Community Trust), and Louise de Koven Bowen. Under their joint control, the council quickly became an important force in the welfare community. Of particular significance were the numerous studies conducted under its auspices. In 1919, famed University of Chicago sociologist Ernest W. Burgess initiated a study of Chicago standard budgets which had a tremendous impact on the standardization of grants to the poor. In 1920, it assisted the Union League Club in a survey of boys' work. Two years later, the agency undertook a study of joint fund raising at the request of the prestigious Commercial Club. And it had a hand in several Child Welfare League studies of the city's established asylums. The results of these studies invariably emphasized the need for trained workers and casework techniques, making the CCSA a leader in the crusade for professionalization.

Like the physicians they aimed to emulate, social workers treated their clients individually, carefully observing the symptoms of each, followed by social diagnosis and prescription for cure. Rather than relying on outworn moralistic interpretations of poverty and deviancy, they sought to discover the roots of individual pathology through "scientific" means, to understand problems in all of their complexity. Because most cases required intensive study, social workers conducted "limitless investigations in the poorer districts of Chicago," carefully studying "the unfortunate in their favorite habitat as a student in engineering would examine a steam or electric plant."[42]

Students and agency personnel were instructed to subject every aspect of family life to close scrutiny. Illinois Children's Home and Aid Society agents were advised to note whether the housewife had

> a gentle voice, whether her manner is refined or coarse, whether she uses good English, whether she is a gossip.... While the housewife talks, you will observe the atmosphere of the house, the cleanliness of the windows, the rugs on the floor, the pictures on the wall. You will observe particularly the literature of the house. If you discover a "Police Gazette" or a "Day's Doings" anywhere in the house, you will reject the home. If you find trashy story papers, yellow-backed novels and detective stories, you will hesitate.... You will observe particularly the pantry; whether there are fresh papers on the shelves, how the food is put away; you will note particularly the quality of the bread.[43]

As experts of every variety and hue flooded into the homes of the poor, clients increasingly waived the right to privacy as the price for service and aid.

Casting about for a scientific base to legitimize their professional claims and break the traditional association between social work and charity, with all of its moralistic, class, and religious overtones, social workers increasingly embraced the cause of Freudianism and psychiatric treatment during the 1920s. By understanding the individual's psyche, it was reasoned, his behavior could be controlled and corrected, setting him on the road to social recovery. As the profession gravitated toward a scientific rationale for its ministrations, volunteers were increasingly relegated to the periphery of the helping process. Trained and experienced, the professional was in a better position to accurately interpret society's ills. And, because he was employed full time, he was enabled to serve as a permanent liaison between the poor, the growing number of services at their disposal, and the larger society.[44]

De-institutionalization was the logical concommitant of professionalization. The social workers' emphasis on family rehabilitation, social observation, and environmentalism generated a lively reassessment of the role of asylums in the twentieth-century welfare schema, opening a new page in a debate dating from Charles Loring Brace's pioneer placing-out activities in the 1850s. Although Brace's foster care programs were widely discredited, the issue took on new immediacy as social workers began to sing the paens of observation, diagnosis, and treatment of the poor in their own milieu.

They enlisted some formidable allies. The prestigious National Conference of Charities and Correction placed its weight in the family care corner in 1899, and the endorsement of the 1909 White House Conference seemed to accord the final seal of approval to the de-institutionalizers. Roosevelt himself had notified leading philanthropists and welfare workers of his earnest belief that dependent children should be cared for in family homes. In Chicago, prominent philanthropists like Julius Rosenwald echoed Roosevelt's sentiments, disdainfully labeling asylums "antiquated," "factorylike," and "prisonlike" vestiges of a less humane past. With the president, Rosenwald proclaimed that "it is the aim of discriminating charity today to make orphan asylums things of the past."[45]

The key issue was "institutionalism," the "combination of rote, routine, and dead levelism" which pervaded asylum life.[46] In a period when social workers were beginning to tout the virtues of individualized care, inmates were depicted as wandering "through the halls of the big institution with two or three hundred other children, looking and yearning for, but never finding that love and care which all fathers and mothers would like to have their children enjoy."[47] Critics argued that the mere presence of such agencies constituted a threat to family life, encouraging impoverished parents to rid themselves of unwanted youngsters. Herded together, disease spread rapidly among them and babies, especially, perished in devastating numbers. Those who survived were often placed sight unseen with new families, and could be scandalously misused. "Bound into slavery . . . without getting a cent in wages, they [were] forced to work from early morning until late at night."[48] Most observers concurred that "the shipped on approval plan is a bad one."[49] Coercive, spiritually deadening, and physically dangerous, asylums were viewed as little more than the outmoded remnants of "a system gone to seed."[50] De-institutionalization, family rehabilitation, and neighborhood reconstruction were part and parcel of the progressive welfare campaign which institutional care denied.

Not everyone agreed. Comparing asylums to the boarding schools of the rich, institutional proponents pointed out that inmates were optimally socialized through constant contact with their peers. They learned how to care for themselves at an early age, and developed regular habits (a fact few would deny). With a hint of some irony, spokesmen added that inmates received better ongoing psychological care within asylum walls, where they were subject to constant study and supervision by experts, than they could possibly obtain in the less structured milieu of the home. In the scientifically, technologically oriented society of twentieth-century America, this was their strongest and most viable rationale.

Impervious to the winds of change, Chicago's asylums flourished well into the 1920s. Just as the National Conference of Charities and Correction was in the process of denouncing them, Chicago's old settlers and Gilded Age moguls were placing the finishing touches on a new crop of enlarged Homes. During the 1890s, the Chicago Orphan Asylum moved to a $150,000 Georgian cottage complex at 5120 South Park Avenue, and the Chicago Home for the Friendless (CHFF) to a commanding English Gothic plant nearby. The Old People's Home joined the exodus to the south side, erecting a new facility near the CHFF, at 47th and Vincennes, in 1910. Only the Chicago Nursery and Half Orphan Asylum moved northward, building its four-cottage complex at Foster and California Avenues in 1900. All continued to receive substantial grants long after their new homes were built and paid for. One of the more interesting was the $8,757 given to the CHFF by Emma R. Singer in 1924 for the purchase and annual distribution of stockings and underwear for the inmates, a gift which had a thuddingly archaic ring by the 1920s.

Secure in their new surroundings, asylum trustees tenaciously guarded their autonomy, determinedly resisting the centralizing efforts of outside organizations like the Chicago Council of Social Agencies. The Chicago Orphan Asylum (COA) maintained a strained relationship with the Juvenile Court, which had been empowered to visit all of the institutions in which it placed dependents under its supervision. After refusing to accept three of the court's wards, the board's president snappishly reminded the court that since they were "receiving no money from the county, the Trustees feel at liberty to decide what children they will take."[51] COA board members rejected the Illinois Children's Home and Aid Society's offer to aid in investigations, resisted the inclusive overtures of the Council of Social Agencies, and grudgingly offered limited cooperation to its sister institution, the Home for the Friendless.

Nor did they employ caseworkers. The board continued to interview applicants themselves, just as their mothers had, excluding the superintendent from the interviewing process until 1926. Although their two hundred plus charges no longer wore uniforms, youngsters were still treated very much as charity cases who were "very lucky, very fortunate, to be in such a nice place and well cared for" well into the twentieth century.[52]

Superficially self-satisfied and self-contained, the COA was under siege by the 1920s. Applications were falling off, reduced by the immigration quotas, mother's pensions, and state aid to dependent families. Only 147 of its 250 beds were occupied in 1925. Outside pressures were becoming more formidable. The United States Children's Bureau called for inspection and licensing of all children's institutions in 1920. Shortly thereafter, a 1923 amendment to the Juvenile Court Act made public inspection mandatory, even for those agencies which were not under public subsidy.

The most formidable problem stemmed from its location. What had been a rural area, placidly removed from the bustle of city life in the 1890s, had become, by the 1920s, a hotbed of racial antagonism on the fringes of the city's swelling black belt. Welfare services for the city's burgeoning black population were pathetically inadequate. The Home for the Friendless was the only nonsectarian asylum to open its doors to Negroes of any age. Although the COA was founded by abolitionists, admitting blacks in an era when few institutions were willing to mix their populations, when impoverished blacks began to crowd into nearby housing and schools the asylum went lily-white. In 1907, there were still seven black inmates. After 1910, Negro applicants were pointedly referred elsewhere. In an era scarred by racial tensions, some of the animosity spilled over to the children. Several were accosted en route to school, causing the board to create its own classrooms for the younger inmates. The older children who remained in the public schools were continually besieged by neighborhood gangs. By 1929, the COA resembled an armed camp, bounded by window guards and a barbed-wire fence. Drawing attention to changing neighborhood conditions, the trustees began to ponder "the possibility of the next five years necessitating a change of location."[53]

While neighborhood relations steadily deteriorated, the composition and philosophy of the board also began to change. Led by president Ruth Lester, a group of younger women moved into control after 1926, wresting the institution from its antiquated practices and handing it over to professional social workers. The transition began when Lester, after auditing a speech by C. C. Carstens of the Child Welfare League, enlisted Chicago School of Civics and Philanthropy professor Sophonisba Breckenridge to survey the asylum's needs and chart its future course. Although some of the older board members resisted the innovations, the survey quickly ushered the COA into the twentieth century.

It urged that professionally trained workers be engaged and that the lay board submit to their expertise. Following its recommendations, the untrained matron was asked to resign and University of Chicago graduate student Eva Lou Longan was engaged in her stead. The first full-time social worker, hired in 1926, quickly assumed responsibility for investigations and admissions. Two years later a trained kindergartner and a recreation worker were added. By 1930, the organization had sponsored a lecture series for Chicago's other matrons, given by a psychiatric social worker, detailing optimum methods for dealing with inmate behavioral patterns, and had forged close ties to the University of Chicago, the Child Welfare League, and the CCSA.

In light of its longevity, the period between the survey and final de-institutionalization transpired with almost lightning speed. Under the caseworker's direction, the board began to experiment with paid boarding homes in 1927. Four years later, at the height of the depression, its Georgian Home was handed over to the Women's Municipal Shelter, enabling the COA to move to less imposing quarters at 4911 Lake Park Avenue. Many of the inmates were sent to three new cottage units in Austin, while the main office was refashioned into a receiving home. By this time the COA was directing its services toward troubled children "in need of highly individualized, experimental treatment and careful observation," rapidly evolving from orphanage to diagnostic center.[54] The metamorphosis was complete when the central receiving home was closed in 1936, ending eighty-seven years of institutional care.

The Chicago Home for the Friendless (CHFF) was also well on the road to de-institutionalization by the thirties. More of a catchall institution than the COA, it had cooperated more openly with other organizations, and had welcomed its black neighbors far more generously. By 1909, inmates were being accepted from a variety of agencies, including the Juvenile Court, United Charities, Travelers Aid, the police, and settlement houses. The board was also represented at the CCSA, the National Conference of Charities and Correction, and the Juvenile Court.

One of the reasons for its more catholic outlook may be traced to the board itself. CHFF directresses seem to have been far less insular than their peers at the COA, and a few of their representatives went on to become important reformers. One of the most outstanding was Lucy Flower, one of the originators of the Juvenile Court, and president of both the Chicago Woman's Club and United Charities. Flower may have been more attuned to the needs of the orphans and impoverished girls who passed into her care by the fact that she, herself, had been adopted. Through her activities in the Chicago Woman's Club, and her friendship with leading reformers like Addams and Bowen, she helped to link the CHFF to changing trends in child-care techniques.

Nevertheless, many of the board felt smugly superior to emerging social work practices. Because their organization was a total care institution, they congratulated themselves that their inmates could be isolated in "an environment wholesome and happy," rather than returning to sordid tenement homes, as settlement and charity patrons did.[55] They were also comforted by the fact that the children placed under CHFF auspices were protected from the "interference and unwise influence of [their] intemperate and altogether worthless parents."[56] Little reference was made in either minutes or annual reports of the antiinstitutional debate developing around them. Even as late as 1924, they still accepted many inmates on the basis of personal appeals, mixing unemployed women, deserted wives, aged ladies, and impoverished children within the asylum's walls. Priding themselves on their ability to extend immediate, temporary relief, the directresses noted, "Investigation has become a hobby of charity workers, and is certainly necessary, but we must not forget that it is often best to give a little timely help first."[57]

Many of their programs were frankly regressive. Youngsters were still indentured at the turn of the century. One child bitterly wrote to inform his mentors of the abuses he had suffered under the system. "All they cared for me was the work they got out of me .... As for sending boys out here my advice would be never to send them to this part of the country because it is just making it from bad to worse."[58] Inmates were taught to parrot patriotic songs and speeches in a weak attempt to Americanize them, daily religious observances lingered into the 1920s, and in the industrial school students still rose at 5:30

each morning in preparation for their tightly regimented days. Lacking adequate facilities for treatment and isolation, disease was rampant, as diphtheria, scarlet fever, and measles regularly thinned the populations under CHFF care.

Like the COA, the CHFF board was divided when younger women, fired with newer charitable ideals, began to replace older members after the turn of the century. By the twenties, the dominant younger faction was militating for a major overhaul of the asylum's programs. The turning point occurred in 1925, when they commissioned a Child Welfare League study to evaluate their programs. The findings advised that the board should be rigorously pruned, the number of committees reduced, social workers employed, and salaries correspondingly enlarged. It also emphasized the need for upgraded health care, the introduction of stringent record keeping and psychiatric examinations, recreational planning, the adoption of cottage care, and a new, less stigmatizing name. The study triggered a flurry of resignations, as the more conservative directresses, "reluctant to give up their personal contact with clients," defected to less forward-looking agencies.[59]

During the next seven years, most of the league's recommendations were realized. The Burr Mission was sold to its Chinese neighbors, and the industrial department closed. The newly acquired social worker quickly appropriated responsibility for admissions and investigations, a trained recreation worker and kindergartner were added, and, like the COA, the work increasingly shifted toward diagnostic lines. On the eve of the depression, CHFF spokesmen commented that "the boy or girl [now] enters the Home for the express purpose of being observed and studied."[60]

Following the lead of United Charities, the CHFF initiated a visiting housekeeper program in 1930. Housekeepers were deemed particularly well suited to care for problem-ridden families. Their weekly visits enabled them to compile detailed records, and observation quickly became "one of the most widely known phases of the housekeeping service."[61] In addition to social observation, their constant supervision was designed to help hold unstable families intact. This occasionally entailed the use of heroic measures: "In many cases where the father is out of the home or is unreliable she may assume the responsibility for all expenditures. Or, as in the case of the O'C. family, the housekeeper had, on occasion, to lock out the father's drunken friends and see that he was sobered up to get to work."[62] Under their authoritative gaze, new habits were inculcated, old ones amended, and children re-socialized under the conditions in which they normally lived.

The CHFF's de-institutionalization was hastened by the depression. In the years following the Armistice, rising consumer costs had begun to make inroads into the asylum's holdings. By 1930 the need for more economical management had reached crisis proportions. The housekeeping service was initiated as an economy measure, and by early 1932 children and old ladies were being placed in private families as well. Caught in a vise between rising applications and rapidly dwindling resources, the trustees finally began to consider the possibility of shutting down the Home. Thoroughly acclimated to social work techniques by this time, they insisted that the emphasis in "such a reorganization should be in accord with present day thought in child welfare," allotting larger sums for casework and less for custodial care. At a per capita cost of $2 per week, supervised foster home care was far more economical than institutionalization, and had the added sanction of modern casework techniques. Moreover, the CCSA was prodding them to abandon institutional services, arguing that "the present plant is (1) poorly located, (2) the school problem has become serious, (3) is expensive to operate, and (4) on account of congregate living arrangements is subject to quarantines which prolong the stay of children and make the service of the Home unavailable to the community for a considerable period each year."[63] At a meeting on June 7, 1932, the board voted to close the Home and turn exclusively to foster home and housekeeping care.

The initial response to the new program was one of mingled relief and pride. The next annual report outlined some of the benefits. Brothers and sisters could now be kept together in boarding homes, whereas before they would have been consigned to different areas of the building according to sex and age. Old ladies were enabled to select their own surroundings. After prospective foster homes were screened, the oldsters toured them, singling out the "foster mother" of their choice. "In every instance we find that our old people are happier with this type of care," noted the trustees.[64] And, of course, all would now be treated within the total environment of the supervised home.

In the process, the role of the board was fundamentally altered. The twenties and thirties were marked by an aggressive effort by social workers to harness and master the prerogatives of their boards. In the COA and CHFF studies, as well as in the one conducted by the CCSA for the Chicago Nursery and Half-Orphan Asylum (CNHOA), the entreaty to delegate increased authority to the staff was paramount. After enjoining CNHOA trustees to hire a professionally trained superintendent, the study candidly resolved that the institution's efficiency would be greatly improved "if responsibility for *all* matters of management of the institution could be centralized in the superintendent."[65] By the end of the thirties, observers had begun to remark that "some social work administrators seem to regard a lay board as a sort of vermiform appendage which may have had a function once when social work was starting under private auspices but which now is worse than useless."[66] With the scent of governmental subsidies filling the air, lay directresses and trustees were eyed as an unnecessary evil.

Some of the more ambitious professionals began to tinker with the composition of their boards, trying to strike an attractive balance between old and young, men and women, Catholics, Jews, and Protestants. Hereditary trusteeships, with their intransigent conservatism and imperious ways, were anathema to the new administrators. Social workers jealously guarded their newly won authority, condescendingly refusing to share information about complicated techniques with their employers, on the premise that mere laymen could not properly digest it. "As social work [became] more complex and scientific, debate [arose] as to the capacity of a lay board to settle policies which require expert knowledge."[67]

Moreover, when long-established asylums were swiftly transformed into social welfare agencies, directresses and trustees sometimes lost track of the work being performed under their auspices. "Each year since the beginning of this new program there has been a continual changing of policies and adjustment to community needs due to the chaos in the field of public social welfare," asserted CHFF spokesmen.[68] Confronted by bewildering programmatic maneuvers, the CHFF's beleaguered president announced with more than a note of frustration, "I have been told that our staff is so well organized that there is very little for our Board Members to do, but I am sure that there still remains much to be done and the work can be made very interesting."[69] One enterprising COA directress assembled a pamphlet outlining possible new functions, while another was sent as a delegate to an Institute for Board Members in the hope of gaining fresh insights.

How was the layman to visualize the work he was endorsing when it was being carried on in a hundred separate households? The CHFF scheduled periodic meetings between members, caseworkers, foster mothers, and housekeepers, in an effort to sensitize them to the implications of the new programs. At one point, they considered permitting directresses to tag along behind the social workers as they made their daily rounds. "Only in so doing can we get an actual picture of the work that is being done and can have a real part in the work of the Home," the board plaintively reasoned.[70] Caseworkers regularly read synopses of their work at board meetings. COA officers personally delivered Christmas presents to the orphans in their new homes. United Charities sent out periodic newsletters detailing particularly interesting case histories. Donors were also put in touch with the fruits of their beneficence through technological means. As organizations came increasingly to rely on professional service, the formats of annual reports changed. Heavily interlarded with photographs of grateful clients, and captioned in glib phrases designed to evoke just the right balance of sentiment and pride, reports and newsletters now became technological middlemen in the new, depersonalized medium of charitable exchange.

Under the exacting gaze of a freshly certified professional elite, boards were remodeled into fund-raising bodies and interpreters for the peripatetic workers they employed. By the thirties, social workers frequently moved about the country as they worked their way up the organizational hierarchy. By virtue of their roots within the community, it was reasoned, board members were in an ideal position to interpret the community's desires to incoming professionals, while similarly explaining the social worker's activities to the rest of the community. Social service had come full circle. While semiprofessional progressive settlement workers had designated themselves as mediators and interpreters between rich and poor, the rich were now expected to provide the same service for charity workers and the constituencies under their care.

The depression played a key role in reshaping extant organizations and forcing them to reorganize according to modern casework techniques. Although both the COA and the CHFF began the journey toward de-institutionalization before the crash of 1929, neither dispensed with its facilities until the depression was well under way. The economic crunch had devastating implications for agency budgets. Generous bequests of securities willed before the crisis became almost worthless as stock prices plummeted after October 1929. Casework was far less expensive than asylum care.

Demographic change was a second important factor in hastening the transition to noninstitutional care. While both the CHFF and the COA began to consider the benefits of alternative programs when the complexion of their neighborhood began to change, the CNHOA, located in a more stable area on the city's north side, remained tenaciously committed to asylum care through the 1930s, despite the inroads that the depression had made on its budget.

In 1923, Homer Folks proclaimed with unwarranted optimism, "The slums have gone. They now exist only in fiction and in the moving pictures."[71] America was dancing on the edge of a volcano. Less than a decade later, the entire nation was dotted with Hoovervilles, breadlines, and once proud laborers hawking apples on city streets. By the same token, progressive charitable notions far outdistanced the reality of the urban welfare system. Until the 1930s, the asylum, like the slum, remained a characteristic of city life. The combined effects of the depression and racial antipathies, rather than the call to social justice, made de-institutionalization a reality. As professional tithingmen fanned out into the city to enforce the moral rectitude of the poor and the dispossessed in their natural habitats, the role of the volunteer underwent a basic reassessment. Shorn of their traditional responsibilities, Chicago's indigenous elites were shifted to the periphery of the decision-making process, interpreters and handmaidens for a new army of professional middlemen.

"Milk Ladies"—Olive Farwell Boston, Marion Forgan Freeman, Dorothy Leslie Keith, Lucy McCormick Blair Linn (1917). Courtesy of the Chicago Historical Society.

# 7 THE DONOR GENERATION

"The man who enjoys the best position and the most considerations is not the man who is making money, but the man who is giving it away," advised Sue Bates in Henry Blake Fuller's Chicago novel, *With the Procession*. "THERE is an art to cultivate . . . give liberally and rightly, and nothing can bring you more credit."[1] And give they did. From a modest beginning in the 1850s, Chicago's generosity rose with each ensuing decade, climaxing in the 1920s with gifts totaling tens of millions of dollars. Public beneficence waxed strong precisely as the role of the volunteer waned. By the end of the twenties, Chicago's progressive activists had ceded stage center to a new group of fabulously wealthy patrons.

Nationally, as well as locally, American generosity assumed unprecedented proportions in the decades after the Spanish American War. In 1892, $29,000,000 was given nationwide for charitable and philanthropic purposes; by 1902, this figure had almost trebled, reaching $85,000,000. Three years later it had risen to $135,000,000 and the rate of growth continued until, on the eve of the Great Depression, American givers donated $2,330,600,000. The nation's increasing wealth, the maturation of post–Civil War fortunes, passage of income tax laws, inflation—all combined to inspire Americans to ever-increasing heights of generosity. In the words of one observant wit, "The passion to find some new cause to endow is sweeping over rich Americans like a whirlwind . . . . Like some of Shakespeare's characters, they have developed a habit of flinging purses at the least provocation and crying: 'Spend this for me!' "[2]

Everyone seemed to have a plan for its disposition. Richard T. Ely advocated tenement reform, education, and preventive medicine programs. Chicago's literary journal, the *Dial,* endorsed cultural undertakings. Washington Gladden, in a surprising article which antedated his "tainted money" crusade, recommended a string of Carnegie-like projects: libraries, gymnasia, public baths, manual training for the poor. In response to the question of what Mrs. Russell Sage should do with her millions, university president David Starr Jordan suggested academic research; a psychology professor nominated scientific undertakings; the chancellor of the University of Nebraska painted the virtues of an endowed agricultural college; sociologist Edward A. Ross advised the endowment of newspapers, to ensure that social critics would receive a fair hearing; and Columbia University professor Franklin H. Giddings advocated using the $80,000,000 to upgrade college teachers' salaries.

In Chicago, culture and education received the lion's share of public largesse. According to a Community Trust survey conducted in the early 1920s, $52,536,354 had been donated for use in these fields since the city's inception. Health work and hospitals ranked second, accumulating $11,263,750. Religious work and charities received $4,703,655, care for the aged drew $4,262,500, the Wieboldt Foundation was capitalized at $4,500,000, other general charity trusts comprised another $2,807,000, child care received $2,068,250, relief $1,378,000, and settlements $701,000, bringing the total to $84,220,509.[3]

If these statistics are broken down by intermittent decades, a clear pattern of ever-increasing generosity emerges. Omitting sectarian ventures, only three gifts of $5,000 or more were donated by Chicagoans in the 1850s, totaling $20,000: $10,000 (one) for charity, and $10,000 (two donors) for higher education. Antebellum largesse was limited because the city's adolescent economy would not permit the diversion of large amounts of cash into nonprofit ventures. Cash was scarce, volunteers plentiful. Socialized in a milieu which placed a high premium on personal service and individual beneficence, marshaled by pulpit and press, citizens assumed a large share of managing the city's charities and infant cultural ventures, keeping them alive despite the chronic lack of cash for salaries and endowments.[4]

During the 1880s, the tally rose to $5,885,000 from thirty donors. The largest gifts were two bequests, totaling $4,500,000 from Walter Loomis Newberry and John Crerar, for the creation of libraries in the city's north and south divisions.[5] Backed by their generosity, cultural endeavors took the lead, netting $4,575,000 from four donors. Hospitals and health organizations received $830,000 from fourteen citizens, educational enterprises $270,000 (6), charities $122,000 (4), and religiously oriented character-building organizations received $88,000 (6).[6] Antebellum Chicago had been a city of the young and the strong. The Newberry and Crerar bequests represented the fruits of a maturing economy, the passing of the first generation of leaders and the beginning of the demise of the second. Gifts to hospitals and health organizations represented an awakening interest in science and the healing arts, kindled by the path-breaking discoveries of Koch and Pasteur. Charitable donations, on the other hand, were limited by the apparent financial stability of the city's charities and asylums. Achieving a modicum of economic security through munificent fire relief grants, they were no longer begging for public support, hat in hand.

After the turn of the century, the pace accelerated. Between 1900 and 1909, Chicagoans' gifts topped the $10,000,000 mark, totaling $19,191,000 from eighty-eight donors, including $9,547,000 from twenty-eight bequests. Culture, again, led the way with $10,243,000 from twenty donors. Charities gained $4,122,000 (47 gifts), health and hospitals $2,669,000 (12), character-building undertakings $825,000 (14), and education $1,332,000 (16). Two bequests formed the backbone of the cultural sums, including $8,000,000 from Marshall Field for the Field Museum, and $1,000,000 from lumberman Benjamin Ferguson for municipal statuary. Other established institutions, like the Art Institute and the Chicago Symphony Orchestra, were just beginning to amass endowments at the turn of the century. The charitable sum was considerably raised by a single, $2,000,000 bequest from James King for the establishment of an old people's home. Most flowed into the coffers of asylums rather than noninstitutional charities, underscoring the donors' proclivity to finance tangible memorials. Only in the health field were large sums set aside for study and research as well as charitable ends. Both Cyrus McCormick, Jr., and his brother, Harold, established health-oriented foundations, reflecting the era's more progressive philanthropic ideals.

During the Jazz Age, Chicagoans' generosity reached unprecedented heights. During the five-year period from 1925 to 1929 an enormous sum, $44,545,000, was forwarded by 140 donors, including $13,979,000 from forty-nine bequests. Aided by the skilled guidance of the John Price Jones Corporation, education took the lead for the first time, gaining $21,660,000 from fifty-nine donors. Cultural organizations received $11,460,000 (52 donors), health agencies and hospitals $6,070,000 (30), charities $4,220,000 (26), and religious undertakings $1,135,000 (7). All benefited from postwar affluence and the expansionist psychology it engendered. Cultural organizations continued to prosper and multiply. As mechanization shortened the American workweek, patrons rushed to provide new amenities for leisure hours. Sons and grandsons of Gilded Age moguls endowed the monuments which bore their family's name, while major new institutions like the Shedd Aquarium, the Museum of Science and Industry, and the Adler Planetarium opened their doors to welcome throngs from the Century of Progress Fair. Although adequately endowed, charities did not fare as well, hampered by secularization and the public's optimism that immigration quotas and continued prosperity would erase the nagging problems of the poor.

Many of the largest gifts came from individual donors. Between 1849 and 1929, thirty-three Chicagoans signed over gifts of a million dollars or more to individual nonprofit organizations.[7] Most (31) were given in the twentieth century, eighteen of which were donated in the 1920s alone. Not surprisingly, education (14) and culture (9) received the bulk of their munificence, followed by charity (4), foundations (4), health (3), and the YMCA (1).[8] A composite portrait of these outstanding donors reveals a Protestant industrialist or businessman, born in the mid-nineteenth century, educated in public grammar and high schools, who, having earned his own fortune, gave away a sizable portion of it when he reached the age of sixty-five. Their place of birth depended upon the timing of their gifts. Nineteenth-century donors were transplanted easterners, from New England and the Middle Atlantic states, while their twentieth-century counterparts included Chicagoans, midwesterners, and immigrants. Six of the eight scions of wealthy families were born in Chicago. Most began their business careers as teenagers, precluding college educations. Only three earned baccalaureate degrees, while four others matriculated but failed to complete their courses. Of the five women, only one, Helen Culver, was single, and a businesswoman in her own right, and none held college degrees.

On the whole, women gave less than men, and often for different reasons. Departing from the larger, general trends, feminine donors gave smaller sums for culture and education, more for health. The first significant gift from a woman was Eliza Garrett's $100,000 grant for a theological seminary in the 1850s, the decade's only major feminine donation. In the 1880s, twelve benefactresses gave $795,000, the bulk of which was consigned to hospitals and health care facilities. Between 1900 and 1909 the figure rose to a respectable $1,380,000, with charities leading at $632,000. Culture received $431,000, followed by education ($232,000), and health ($69,000). During the last period, 1925 through 1929, thirty-eight women donated $11,460,000, or about one-fourth of the total sum, favoring education over the most traditional fields for the first time. Universities netted $5,960,000, health $2,270,000, culture $1,800,000, and charities $1,430,000.

Helen Culver was the first Chicago woman to donate a million dollars for philanthropic ends. She was an amazing lady. Born in an era when few spinsters had the heart to attempt a single career, Culver mastered four: teaching school as a girl, commanding a military hospital during the Civil War, becoming a formidable businesswoman in the aftermath (she was also the first female notary public in Illinois), and ending her life as one of the city's leading philanthropists.

Born in upstate New York in 1832, Culver moved to Chicago in the fifties, becoming the business assistant of her cousin, millionaire realtor Charles J. Hull, a decade later. When Hull died in 1889, leaving her the sole mistress of his multimillion-dollar estate, Culver began to shop around for a suitable monument to his largesse. To Jane Addams she leased, and later gave Hull-House, the family's dilapidated west side mansion. And to the University of Chicago, where Hull had once been a trustee, she donated $1,000,000 for scientific research laboratories in 1895. Undoubtedly influenced by her wartime experiences as a Sanitary Commission nurse, she stipulated that part of the money was to be set aside for west side university extension lectures on science, sanitation, and hygiene, to make "lives more sound and wholesome." As she explained, "I have believed that moral evils would grow less as knowledge of their relation to physical life prevails—and that science, which is knowing—knowing the truth—is a foundation of pure religion."[9] Later, she augmented this gift with a $968,000 bequest to the university in 1923.

Religious beliefs played a significant role in eliciting gifts from men and women alike. Recalling his days at Dwight Moody's Sunday school as a youth, Victor Lawson declared, "The religious instruction and other aids to character building that I received there were of the greatest possible value to me."[10] Mindful of the lessons he learned at Moody's knee, the editor bequeathed $1,000,000 for a north side YMCA in 1926. Grief played an important role in generating million-dollar monuments, as did tribalism. McCormicks subsidized the

McCormick Theological Seminary, Fields backed the Field Museum, and J. Ogden Armour assumed the helm of the Armour Institute after his father's death in 1901, donating over $6,000,000 by 1920.

Others were inspired by avocations, travel, and fairs. John Crerar and Walter Newberry, both well read and extremely fond of books, bequeathed libraries to the city. Travel reinforced benevolent impulses, registering vivid models for new undertakings. When Chicago lumberman Benjamin Ferguson visited Europe for the first time, he was dazzled by the civic statuary which he beheld at every turn. Upon his return, he drew up a will bequeathing $1,000,000 for the commissioning of municipal monuments. Similarly, the idea for the Museum of Science and Industry, launched with a $2,000,000 grant from Julius Rosenwald in 1925, was first conceived during Rosenwald's visit to Munich's Deutsches Museum, which served as its model.

The spoils of the Columbian Exposition goaded Marshall Field into parting with his first million-dollar gift in 1893. The richest man in Chicago, Field had been relentlessly stalked by a variety of ambitious fund raisers, but without result. Only when his friend, Edward E. Ayer, made it clear to him that "a tremendous amount of material from different countries as well as from all parts of America . . . could be secured at a minimum price at the end of the exposition" did the tightfisted merchant agree to endow the museum bearing his name.[11]

During the 1920s, the prospect of the upcoming Century of Progress Exposition generated a second crop of well-endowed cultural institutions, including the Museum of Science and Industry, the Shedd Aquarium, and the Adler Planetarium. In addition to serving as lasting monuments to their creators, cultural amenities helped to mitigate the city's decidedly unsavory reputation as the home of pig stickers, "clown Mayor" William Hale Thompson, and the notorious "Scarface" Al Capone. As one journalist defensively pointed out:

> In Chicago, infamous, cruel, degraded place that it is, 11,000,000 books are taken out of the public library in a year; about a million people visit the Art Institute, and another million the Field Museum; and nearly 150,000 attend the concerts of the Chicago Symphony Orchestra. In Chicago, where Youth is supposed to be going to its doom, you will find music schools and art schools in such numbers that no one has recently counted them. . . . In Chicago, the ignorant and barbarian, two great non-sectarian universities attract 20,000 students a year, and are centers of research and instruction better known in Europe than at

> home.... The ordinary man...even knows the names of some of their scientists as well as he knows the names of some of our most celebrated assassins.[12]

Donors touted their gifts in quantitative terms, emphasizing that each was the first, biggest, or best. The Adler Planetarium was the first in the Western Hemisphere; the Shedd Aquarium the largest in the world; the Museum of Science and Industry the first in the nation. Suitably embellished by museums and universities, patrons hoped to make Chicago, once again, the Athens of the West.

Ironically, the cultural arena was the only area in which the individual donor could still exercise a free hand, unfettered by the mandates of professionals. Rosenwald and Shedd both commissioned studies of similar European ventures before publicly pledging their gifts, augmenting the investigators' findings with personal observations of their own. While cultural organizations grew fat with public largesse, many charities starved. "We are poor as poverty,"[13] carped Juvenile Protective Association president Louise de Koven Bowen: "We need the support of our old friends now very much. A good many older ones have died and subscriptions have lapsed; unfortunately, the coming generation does not seem to be as generously disposed as their parents and grandparents."[14] Hedged in by professional strictures, traditional charities lost much of their appeal.

Between 1900 and 1929, the forces of professionalization worked relentlessly to limit and redefine the role of both donor and volunteer. The course of professionalization was most rapid and complete in the field of medicine, where trained nurses and physicians quickly relegated the layman to an inferior role, doing busywork safely removed from the actual task of healing. There was as little place for the dilettante in the diagnostic center as there was in the operating room. Based on the subsidization of intangible undertakings and anticipated results, medical and scientific charity became an act of faith.

The professionalization of social work proceeded at a more erratic pace, rapidly eclipsing volunteer charitable work, but implemented far more slowly in institutional care. In this field, de-institutionalization and professionalization were synonymous. As the city outgrew the range and vision of individual private benevolence, armies of trained workers moved in to fill the communications gap formerly marshaled by the volunteer. The twentieth-century "back to the home" movement could not have been realized without the ready availability of corps of trained professionals to supervise, observe, and record on a full-time basis. Outstanding philanthropists like Julius Rosenwald willingly deferred to their expertise. Avowing that the problems of modern welfare were beyond the ken of the untutored layman, Rosenwald unhesitatingly conceded that "in this age of expert service, philanthropy is being reduced to a science administered by paid experts."[15]

Cultural endeavors followed suit more slowly, hampered by the absence of scientific techniques on which to base professional claims. Librarianship was the most markedly professionalized, led by innovators like William F. Poole, head librarian at the Chicago Public Library, and later the Newberry as well. By imposing a system of precise classification upon their massive holdings, Poole quickly helped to lift his calling to the status of a profession, disseminating his techniques through national organizations like the American Library Association.

The Association of American Museums continually sounded the call for improved curatorial standards and enhanced clout. Citing the growth of librarianship, one critic concluded that "the time has come when the go-as-you-please method of museum building and museum administration must settle down to something less vague, less whimsical, and more definite."[16] The first course for curatorial work, with a heavy emphasis on the management of trustees, was initiated at Harvard in 1923. By the end of the 1930s, spokesmen were unabashedly asserting that "running a museum is a technical job that calls for special training."[17]

The difference between fin-de-siècle curators and their twentieth-century successors was striking. Many Gilded Age directors were little more than the "hired hands" of their trustees. Frederick Skiff, the first director of the Field Museum, was engaged because his Colorado Exhibit at the Columbian Exposition was "one of the best, cleanest and [most] organized . . . and we thought that any man that could keep a collection in that condition and maintain it in that condition at the time of the exhibit would make a good Director."[18] W. M. R. French, the first director of the Art Institute, was a landscape gardener and engineer. Educated at Phillips Exeter Academy and Harvard, his closest tie to the art world was the success of his brother, sculptor Daniel Chester French.

Later, greater emphasis would be placed on training and administrative ability as the proper yardsticks for measuring museum officials. Walter Chute, the first director of the Shedd Aquarium, was the veteran of a lengthy apprenticeship as manager of the Boston Aquarium Society, and the former director of the Boston Aquarium. Similarly, Art Institute director Robert B. Harshe was the erstwhile director of the Oakland (California) public museum and the Department of Fine Arts of Pittsburgh's Carnegie Institute. Hired in 1921, he served an eight-year stint as president of the Association of Art Museum Directors, between 1927 and 1935.

Even in fund raising, local elites began to solicit and adhere to the dictates of outside professionals. During the 1920s, higher education shared the major portion of each donated dollar with the city's cultural institutions. Always popular with donors, Northwestern University and the University of Chicago boosted their portion of the profits with the aid of one of the nation's first and most successful professional fund raisers, John Price Jones.

Nineteenth-century fund drives were modestly conceived and limited in scope, based on personal appeals to the wealthy few. When the first University of Chicago collapsed under the weight of its own debts in the 1880s, John D. Rockefeller proffered a $600,000 matching grant to save it, contingent upon the trustees' ability to raise an additional $400,000. Responsibility for finding the money fell upon the reluctant shoulders of two Baptist clergymen, Frederick Taylor Gates and Thomas Wakefield Goodspeed. It was a year that neither would have cared to relive. "The discouragements were many and great," Goodspeed quietly admitted.[19] Less inclined to mince words, Gates hissed, it was "the most disagreeable, depressing, and anxious work of my life."[20]

Few of the city's Baptists were wealthy, and those who were had been bombarded for years with appeals to aid the faltering school. Having failed once, many felt that it would fail again, and were reluctant to fund a sinking ship. Undeterred, the clerics relentlessly pursued their quarry. Outlining their "Rules of Procedure," Gates sternly reminded himself to dress well, and "be cheerful, to the point, and indefatigable in stalking your 'victim.'" Tact, caution, and dogged perseverance were the backbone of their approach:

> If you find him big with gift, do not rush him too eagerly to the birth. Make him feel that he is making the gift, not that it is being taken from him with violence .... Appeal only to the highest motives. His own mind will suggest to him all the more selfish ones ... work continually, rapidly, and at a hot pace. If your work flags, you are gone .... Canvas everyday, all day, going rapidly from man to man, rain or shine.[21]

They succeeded, but barely, pushed over the top when Field consented to lend them the cachet of his support. Subsequent campaigns, based on these same "hand-to-hand and face-to-face" techniques, continued to net the university adequate, if not spectacular gains.[22]

Professional fund raisers completely revamped the process. The difference between the two approaches is striking. Initially, the university mapped out its 1924 drive as "an inside job," to be carried out "chiefly, if not wholly, by the Alumni, Trustees, and Members of the Faculty." Rather than "a wide reaching for small, or even moderate gifts," the trustees contemplated "the reaching of a few notable givers for very large sums," drawn from "a select, limited public."[23] Fortunately, Jones's success in aiding other universities proved too tempting to resist. After weeks of investigation and debate, the trustees reluctantly decided to seek professional aid. Commissioned late in 1924, the $12,000 John Price Jones report laid the groundwork for a $17,000,000 campaign.

Jones proposed nothing less than a total blitz of the community's resources. During a previous campaign, the university raised $4,300,000 from among sixty people. Jones wanted to multiply the number of donors tenfold. To achieve this, the agency split the board into a number of committees, adding an outside Citizen's Committee of one hundred, "calculated to impress the public with the importance and size of the undertaking," and a Special Gifts Committee of twenty-five very rich men to solicit large gifts from among their friends and acquaintances.[24] Next, he advised the university to undertake a major survey of the community's resources—population, commerce, transportation facilities, and projected growth—conducted jointly by students and local businessmen, "to find out how the University of Chicago can render greater service to the city, and show the status of the city, and of the University, on the city's centennial."[25]

This in turn was to serve as the basis of a major publicity campaign, initiated "to sell the University to the public in Chicago and throughout the country."[26] Citing Ivory Soap's successful slogan ("it floats"), several themes were suggested, most stressing the quest to make the school one of the great universities of the world. Alumni were tapped; faculty members conscripted for public lectures; magazines, newspapers, and radio stations inundated with news items; and a spate of pamphlets printed for popular consumption among a variety of audiences. Journalist Henry Justin Smith chaired the publicity campaign, communications executive Bernard E. Sunny chaired the drive as a whole, and steel magnate Edward L. Ryerson, Jr., headed the committee on special gifts.

Like social workers and scientists, professional fund raisers couched their claims in scientific terms, stressing their ability to compile data, analyze needs, and manipulate donors through subconscious suggestion. Writing to University of Chicago trustee Harold Swift, Jones commented, "I deem it important that you, who are new to the psychology of this work, should have an ideal situation and state of public mind toward which to strive." Urging Swift to understand the psychology of his donors, in order to train them to proper patterns of giving, Jones continued:

> First *sell* them on the necessity of having the money, next, on their obligation toward the University, and then make them see the part they had in establishing in the public mind the need for the money by being the first to give to the fund; by making them realize that unless they supported it liberally according to their financial ability, the University could not expect people of less wealth to give generously. Once you have this idea sold, then let them select the particular building or fund to which they wish to give.[27]

In the words of one of Jones's contemporaries, "The spirit of the age . . . has turned psychological."[28] Professional fund raising, like professional social work, was first legitimized in an era marked by a pervasive and uncritical acceptance of psychological theories. Freud revealed that man was not an entirely rational being, and Watson demonstrated how that irrationality could be manipulated by those properly skilled in scientific techniques. Behaviorism, which reduced all human reactions to stimulus and response, was enormously popular during the twenties. Admen and professional fund raisers continually labored to promote the notion that habits of giving, like habits of consumption, could be instilled, reinforced, and fashioned into a natural reflex by those who possessed the appropriate skills.[29]

Rather than doing the actual work itself, the Jones Corporation schooled the trustees in the finer points of the art of fund raising. Prospects were assiduously courted at a variety of luncheons, dinners, and lectures. Using the trustees to "emphasize this contact element," the agency skillfully exploited the nouveaux riches' craving for contact with the city's established families, offering aspiring social climbers a chance to rub shoulders with the rich and wellborn in return for hard cash.[30]

Next, they amassed an impressive list of prospects, ranging from Samuel Insull ("very simple and easily controlled in some things. Very shrewd in others")[31] to Mr. and Mrs. Robert McElwee ("terribly rich, and, according to reports, terribly tenacious").[32] One by one, the agency ticked off the human considerations and minor vices which motivated individual giving. Alumni were to be approached on the basis of loyalty and gratitude. Opportunities for perpetuating the family name at alma mater were to be dangled before their eyes. If this failed to evoke the desired response, tax benefits would be enumerated. After 1917, income tax laws permitted deductions for charitable gifts. Seizing upon this point, tax specialists pointed out that sizable gifts could net the donor "a saving in his current income tax . . . [and] cost him much less than the actual gift received by the University."[33] Inheritance and estate taxes could also be sidestepped through timely generosity.

In a tacit reference to the encroaching black belt, the agency suggested that Hyde Park residents could be successfully canvassed, "due to the great influence which the University has had in preserving real estate and other values in its vicinity."[34] Older businessmen, at the end of their careers, were to be approached as civic stewards, while ethnic citizens were to be permitted to make amends for the war. The German Division of the campaign isolated five projects for sponsorship by their countrymen, including a fund for Germanic studies, a German museum, a modern language building, scholarships, and a German library. Thus, the committee hoped to effect "a speedy restoration of German culture to its proper place in American civilization."[35]

Jones was particularly sensitive to the generative powers of grief: "There is always a strong appeal to erect some building, or series of buildings, to perpetuate a name. Such memorials are the most effective monuments a man can find today; fulfilling all the requirements of being useful, inspiring, visible and permanent."[36] Since many Chicago families had recently lost sons in World War I, the agency urged trustees to move quickly to capitalize on parental bereavement.

Much of the money was channeled into the medical school and scientific research. Led by men like Frank Billings and Abraham Flexner of the Rockefeller Foundation, the university was in the midst of a concerted crusade to upgrade the quality of medical care. Because they had been conducted strictly as profit-making ventures, nineteenth-century medical schools were rarely endowed, and most scientific breakthroughs emanated from European laboratories with their corps of professional researchers. Surveying America's 155 medical colleges in 1910, Flexner found a dismal collection of inferior schools, among which Chicago's were some of the worst. In order to remedy the problem, Flexner devised a plan for the reorganization of the training facilities at the University of Chicago, advising the consolidation of its teaching and clinical facilities on the campus, the implementation of a complete four-year course, and the merger of the city's diverse research organizations. Aided by Rosenwald and Rockefeller, Flexner managed to set a $5,000,000 development campaign in motion in 1916, culminating in the creation of Billings Hospital. As professors were compelled to devote more hours to research at the expense of their private practices, other donors were enjoined to subsidize the research, to enable the most talented scientists to pursue their investigations on a full-time basis.

Jones's aides carefully mapped out the strategy of the science endowment campaign. "Prominent in the appeal for the medical project, of course, will be the humanitarian theme, based on the broad principle of preventive medicine," agency spokesmen advised.[37] Elaborating upon this approach, trustee Harold Swift emphasized that "we want to show that pure research of the laboratory produces very practical results, such as the telephone, telegraph, radio, etc."[38] Faculty lectures, pamphlets, and radio programs spread his message to the public.

Girded by professional encouragement and advice, the campaign was a ringing success. In 1927, the clinical departments were opened in Billings Hospital and the new Max Epstein Clinic. Albert D. Lasker, former chairman of the United States Shipping Board, donated $1,000,000 for the Lasker Foundation, for the study, prevention, and cure of degenerative diseases. The resources of the Home for Destitute and Crippled Children were transferred to the university, housed in a new one-hundred-bed hospital built with a $300,000 gift from Mrs. Elizabeth McElwee. Pepsodent president Douglas Smith donated $1,000,000 for research, and Mr. and Mrs. John Roberts forwarded the same amount for a medical clinic to memorialize their son.

Citing the tendency to donate sums for specific purposes, Flexner testily remarked that "no one, be he private individual or an important official, possesses the wisdom and foresight that would justify such specific choices except in very rare instances."[39] Since scientists were constantly seeking new problems and solving old ones, the wisest benefactions were those with the fewest strings attached. Despite their limited roles, Chicagoans responded to the call of science with unstinting generosity, endowing work they could not see, with results they often did not comprehend, in the hope of enhancing the quality of community life.

The amassing of huge sums for what Harper termed "benevolent work at a distance" marked a sharp break with the practices of the Gilded Age.[40] Although some of the money was allocated for buildings, much was designated for investigation. Chicagoans had begun to subsidize intangibles. VNA spokesman Harriet Fulmer neatly summarized the inherent paradox in noninstitutional beneficence: "The laity have only a vague idea of what the work is; for we have nothing tangible to show the public who contribute to its support—no spacious hospitals surrounded by beautiful grounds . . . no beautifully furnished rooms in this or that institution."[41] "Nowadays we don't know who our neighbors are," complained another observer. "We have no personal information about the lame, the halt, and the blind unless they put themselves in front of us, at the street corner or in a doorway."[42]

The twentieth century witnessed a vigorous redefinition of the meaning and function of the gift. As the focus of public benevolence shifted from charity to enhancement of society as a whole, the individual donor receded into the background. Until about 1900, it was commonly accepted that donors had the right to specify how their gifts were to be used, and sometimes they rendered their offerings with amazing detail. Stephen Girard's bequest for his orphan college, for example, was accompanied by minutely detailed instructions for its implementation. Similarly, when Chicagoan A. C. Lewis willed the city $650,000 for the creation of a manual training school in 1877, he specified the curriculum, floor plan, and composition of the library. As D. K. Pearsons defiantly asserted, "If I choose to give away what I do not want, I rather think I have the right. I give where I have the largest satisfaction in the knowledge that it is doing good."[43]

A childless widower, Pearsons exclaimed, "I have the greatest joy in my colleges. They are my children. They are my only children . . . . No father was ever more proud of his family than I am of these colleges."[44] Nineteenth-century donors frequently used their gifts as leverage to compel existing organizations to reorganize along business lines more to their liking, or to wrest control from professional interests, clergymen, and entrepreneurs. They displayed a possessive sense of pride in their undertakings. Lucy Sprague Mitchell recalled that "the opening of the University was to Father a climax of his pride for the city he loved almost as a personal possession."[45] Monetary beneficence enabled them to monumentalize themselves, memorialize their families, and assert their gratitude to the community in tangible form.

During the twentieth century, however, a concerted effort was put in motion to separate the donor's personality from his gift. For outreach agencies like the Visiting Nurse Association or United Charities, this was inherent in the nature of the work itself. Other agencies had to resort to more overt means. "Benevolence today has become altogether too huge an undertaking to be conducted otherwise than on business lines," asserted Julius Rosenwald.[46] The activities of enlightened philanthropists like Rosenwald eloquently exemplified the movement away from specified gifts. Rosenwald helped to further curb the practice of restricted giving by calling for legislation to regulate bequests, and summoning his fellow philanthropists to the campaign for self-liquidating endowments. "Like the manna of the Bible, which melted at the close of each day, I believe that philanthropic enterprises should come to an end with the close of the philanthropist's life, or, at most, a single generation after his death."[47]

Community Trusts and Chests served to widen the gap between donor and gift. The Community Trust movement was devised as a means of providing for the flexible administration of bequests in keeping with changing community needs. Chicago's was the second in the nation. Following Cleveland's example, banker Norman Wait Harris and his son Albert started the organization in 1915 with a $600,000 endowment. Like Rosenwald, the Harrises stressed that urban problems were constantly in a state of flux and that each generation could best determine how the money should be spent. By eliminating mortmain, they insured that future generations of experts, rather than past generations of laymen, would control the destiny of the gift.

The progressive cry for social justice worked another fundamental change in the meaning of interpersonal exchange. In preindustrial cities, the act of exchange entailed a mutual obligation of services and deference. However, by equating charity with justice, making it a right rather than a bounty, progressive thinkers destroyed the element of mutuality. Bowen vividly recalled her "mortification one day, when I said, 'I have done everything in the world for that woman and she is not even grateful.' [Miss Addams] looked at me quizzically and said,

'Is that the reason you helped her, because you wanted gratitude?'"[48] Addams's implicit censure spoke volumes. As she was quick to admit, "Probably there is no relation in life which our democracy is changing more rapidly than the charitable relation—that relation which obtains between benefactor and beneficiary."[49] Steeped in moralistic idealism, the progressives demanded that giving be openhanded and rendered without expectation of thanks, a philosophy which lingers still.

The modern philanthropist was encouraged to fund programs for which he received no concrete return, and in which he was only a marginal participant. The question of administrative expenses took on a new significance in this milieu. If a donor subsidized a building, he could point to the physical proof that the money had been spent for the use for which it had been earmarked. But noninstitutional programs made giving an act of faith, and agency spokesmen spent a great deal of time assuring the public that "it costs money to find out the facts and to invent and apply preventive measures .... It is what we must pay to get the work done."[50]

This in turn entailed the slippery problem of keeping donors interested and informed without encouraging them to participate more directly. The twenties were a time of experimentation. Photographs, speeches, newsletters, publicity—all were sampled in an effort to achieve a satisfactory relationship between the public and the programs being conducted under their auspices.

The problem was heightened by the city's changing form. With the advent of the automobile, people began moving to the suburbs in ever-increasing numbers. Many turned their backs on the urban dilemmas they left behind. In light of these demographic trends, one of the key issues became maintaining the interest and patronage of the city's rapidly dispersing wealth. One method was to follow them out to suburbia with branch organizations and outreach programs. Shortly after the turn of the century, the movement to spread urban welfare services to nonurban areas began to gain momentum. Organized charity proponents launched a veritable missionary crusade after 1905, arguing that "hardly any community is now considered too small to organize its charitable resources even when to do so it becomes necessary to share with another community or with a whole county the services of a paid professional worker."[51] The spirit of messianic progressivism was even more apparent in the workings of the wartime Illinois Woman's Committee of the Council of National Defense, which bombarded tiny communities throughout the state with questionnaires designed to ascertain the charitable resources at their command. They then appointed chairmen in each of the 102 counties, and all the towns and townships, to oversee the implementation of welfare programs.

Similarly, infant welfare clinics began to appear in suburbs as diverse as Cicero and Winnetka, traveling tuberculosis clinics toured the countryside after 1916, and the visiting nurses vowed to station a nurse in every community. By 1915 there was a Highland Park Visiting Nurse Association, a Winnetka Relief and Aid Society, and chest clinics and dispensaries were on the drawing board for outlying hamlets like Arlington Heights and Lemont. Some provided their constituencies with services formerly available only in the city, decentralizing the benefits of health and social welfare services with none of the drawbacks.

Others were designed merely as liaisons between affluent suburbanites and urban needs. Many north shore Infant Welfare Society members, for example, raised funds, sponsored inner-city clinics, and occasionally visited their stations in order to keep in touch with the type of work being done. Some even sewed garments to be distributed to the poor through the society, in an atavistic attempt to participate more directly in the task of aiding the needy.

Chicago's suburbs were becoming increasingly insular in the twenties. No longer completely dependent upon the central city for goods and services, suburbanities were beginning to develop an autonomous self-identity, sharply opposed to the interests of the city. In contrast to contested urban neighborhoods where ethnic tensions were now heightened by racial antipathies, the suburbs of the well-to-do resembled nothing so much as tranquil, homogeneous New England towns. The growth of auxiliary charities, while keeping suburbanites apprised of new developments, also ensured that they could exercise the obligations of stewardship at a safe remove from the problems they were helping to solve.

When one enterprising University of Chicago sociologist sampled the opinions of Winnetkans in the twenties, he found them defensively complaisant in their peaceful isolation. One woman remarked that she did not know "of any women from Winnetka who go out in the field to do actual charity work in Chicago."[52] Another candidly admitted that "Dr. W. at the University of Chicago wanted me to go down there on the West Side where all those horrible slums are to see 'real life.' I wouldn't do it. They're too dirty and besides its too dangerous. I can't see how anyone could get a kick out of doing that.

Merely the idea of it is nauseating to me."[53] Weighing the evidence, he concluded that most suburbanites had an extremely inadequate comprehension of the actual needs being met by the agencies under their direction. "They are quite removed from scenes of want and destitution; moreover, many of them do not care much to know of these first-hand."[54] Few were willing to engage in field work.

Ironically, their contempt was shared by many of their peers who remained in Chicago. Arthur Meeker recalled that "during all the years of our early childhood we seldom went to the other parts of the city," and "the West Side I cannot recall ever seeing."[55] As the rich physically cut themselves off from the rest of the urbanscape, they became increasingly dependent on the perceptions of the professionals who served them. Moreover, as the pace of society quickened after the war, the Jazz Age generation abandoned the self-questioning of their progressive parents and adopted an itinerant existence of parties, travel, and aggressive socializing. Professionalization set the alternatives in bold relief. Since, in most fields, dilettantes were no longer welcome, one could devote one's life to a career of good works, or one could become a socialite. By the 1920s, the options of previous generations had considerably narrowed.

Eased from stage center by expanding armies of technocrats and their own reluctance to participate, lay Samaritans became increasingly irrelevant, their motives increasingly suspect. The traditional linkage between wealth and virtue was sundered by the muckraking jeremiads of the 1890s. Later, the popular media took up the cry, perpetuating the stereotype of the irresponsible rich even as they updated it to correspond with the professionalized milieu of the postwar years.

The celluloid philanthropist of the 1920s was an extremely unattractive character, ranging in moral fiber from hypocrite to imbecile. In *Blockade,* for example, the main character is a rumrunner who poses as a philanthropist, covering his misdeeds with a patina of respectability.[56] The hero of *The Prince of Pep* was more of a Robin Hood.[57] A wealthy young doctor who devoted most of his spare time to visiting ailing youngsters in hospital wards, he becomes "The Black Flash" after a severe head wound causes him to lose his memory and assume a new identity. As "the flash," he spends his nights robbing gamblers to subsidize his clinic. Lionel Barrymore, too, played a "philanthropical druggist" in *The Wrongdoers,* subsidizing his charities by robbing the rich.[58]

Other Samaritans were depicted setting up soup kitchens, homes for fallen women, and asylums: vestiges of an unenlightened age. If men, they were portrayed as gullible marks for sharp-eyed gold diggers. Women fared even worse, shown as uninformed, meddling busybodies who had little conception of the real nature of their work. In *The Foolish Age*, for example, the protagonist is Margie Carr, a young woman with an uncontrollable passion for aiding the poor.[59] Carr innocently hires a thug named Bubbs as her office aid. Bubbs, of course, then proceeds to act as a self-appointed bouncer, fending off prospective clients.

Echoing popular themes, social scientists began to note that experts, rather than elites, were managing the city's private agencies, while society leaders were content merely to lend the glamor of their names to worthy causes and "pet" charities. Harvey Zorbaugh's brilliant study of *The Gold Coast and the Slum* was as much a call for a renewed sense of civic stewardship as it was a survey of social distance. Zorbaugh graphically depicted the social customs of the insular world of the rich young men and women of the Gold Coast. According to his analysis, charitable giving and cultural patronage had been reduced to rungs in the social ladder, and the urge to do good inspired by the prospect of having one's good deeds immortalized in the society pages. In the absence of society leaders like Mrs. Potter Palmer, church and family counted for naught. One's cachet was determined by philanthropic, charitable, and club affiliations.[60]

The point that Zorbaugh missed, however, was that their aggressive socializing was perfectly adapted to their newly defined role within the philanthropic schema. As professionals increasingly assumed responsibility for day-to-day management within agencies, as well as the formation and implementation of innovations in purpose and technique, the function of boards was reduced to fund raising and interpreting agency goals to the rest of the community. In the course of their breakneck dance through rounds of parties, lectures, dinners, and bridge, Chicago's elites were continually forming new contacts to be tapped for funds. A typical day, outlined by one of Zorbaugh's wealthy respondents, included morning telephoning, afternoon interviews to raise money, followed by dinners and parties. In the process, news of their agencies' work was informally publicized through the network of gossip. The techniques of professional fund raisers like John Price Jones underscored the symbiotic relationship between Society and postwar benevolence. Enlisting the aid of prominent trustees, Jones set up a variety of informal luncheons, dinners, and lectures to snare gifts from social climbing prospects. In effect, for this brief moment, the demands of stewardship and the joys of society were one.

It was a highly tenuous relationship. Many prominent backers understood little of the actual work being conducted under their sponsorship. Some argued that their peers had not had conditions portrayed vividly enough to arouse any genuine interest on their part. As one respondent noted, "Organizations look after everything, and they give to them, so why think about it?"[61] Feeling that agencies were dealing with the problems for them, their "sense of individual responsibility [was] drugged."[62] One of Zorbaugh's interviews revealed with stunning clarity the extreme superficiality of the Gold Coaster's approach to civic affairs:

> One day the society woman dashes from party to party, in the latest and most luxurious styles; the next day she spends at a political meeting, working strenuously on the destinies of the state; the next she is sewing on belated ballet costumes until the small hours—this is as a friend of the opera; she may lunch the next day with Japs or Indians because she is a friend of foreign college students. Not only in Chicago, but in New York and Europe she grasps eagerly at variety in life.[63]

This kind of dabbling was a far cry from the earnest efforts of the women who built the city's asylums in the 1850s, their daughters who pioneered in the creation of new professions for women in the 1880s, and the semiprofessionals of the 1910s, like Anita McCormick Blaine and Jane Addams, who made community betterment the focus of their lives.

Chicago's Jazz Age elites lacked the first-hand experience of their parents in philanthropic management. When the depression struck, they quickly surrendered responsibility for maintenance of the city's welfare resources to outside control. In the process, the locus of decision making shifted from the local to the national level. The aggressive professionalization of the postwar years coupled with corresponding limitations on the role of the lay elite to pave the way for the new federalism. Ironically, men like Cyrus McCormick, Jr., bitterly resented the implications of the incursions of big government which their own philanthropic efforts had helped to set in motion. For McCormick, the government's "determined effort . . . to clip the wings of those who were able to give liberally to the causes which awakened their enthusiasm" represented a fundamental negation of the democratic ideal.[64]

The efforts of the donor generation marked the culmination of decades of professionalization, urbanization, and intensifying public skepticism. Although forwarding sums on a new scale, Chicago's Jazz Age elites exercised far less authority than their sires. Shunted into an inferior role by a rapidly professionalizing technical elite, stewards were asked to interpret, rather than instruct, to render gifts devoid of strings. Outreach organizations and publicity reinforced these trends, keeping sponsors informed and interested while effectively discouraging more direct means of participation. Popular prejudices, too, warned potential stewards that even the most well-intentioned individual efforts were apt to end in disaster and ridicule. Separated from the objects of their largesse by widening social and geographical gulfs, the city's elites retreated into pleasurable rounds of luncheons, fund raisers, and soirées. Stewardship and socializing were one, proclaimed the experts. Money, rather than service, was the bond between the Jazz Age steward and his fellow citizens. The cash nexus reigned supreme.

Jane Addams. Courtesy of University of Illinois Library at Chicago Circle Campus, Jane Addams Memorial Collection.

# 8
# CONCLUSION: A PLEA FOR THE VOLUNTEER

By 1929, the meaning of noblesse oblige had considerably narrowed, stripped of its functions by an aggressively professionalizing technical elite, and deprived of traditional sanctions by popular suspicion. Earlier generations had celebrated the urban steward, and urged him to his task. During the 1850s, when professions were weak, professionals few, and the funds to salary them only intermittently available, Chicago's volunteers played a vital part in creating and maintaining the city's charitable and cultural resources. Everyone was expected to participate. Churches, national evangelical societies, and domestic publicists continually admonished the lady of wealth and her less fortunate sister to organize charities and personally minister to the poor. Bibles in hand, Chicago's benevolent ladies combed the city's slums for inmates to fill their asylums. They gained as much as they gave. Charity work briefly liberated them from the monotony of domestic routine, enhanced their standing in the community, and gave them a modicum of power. Within the sanctuary of the asylum they were the decision makers. Their word was law.

While women fashioned asylums, men initiated charities and cultural undertakings. The counterpart of the benevolent lady was the Christian Gentleman. Generous, refined, and keenly conscious of his debt to the community, he was the model of republican virtue. Despite their lingering reputation for rapacious materialism, Chicago's wealthier citizens assumed the role of the Christian Gentleman as soon as their pocketbooks and business schedules would permit. Together, they founded relief and learned societies, hospitals and lyceums, laboring shoulder to shoulder with men of lesser means in the creation of necessary services.

Both men and women were urged to their task by clerical injunctions and the inexorable weight of public opinion. Hampered by a chronic lack of cash, they kept their fledgling organizations alive through dedicated personal service and modest gifts-in-kind. Yet there were significant differences between the asylums fashioned by women and the organizations dominated by men. Married women had little choice in the types of gifts they rendered. Restricted by discriminatory laws, they could neither own nor transfer property, a fact which prevented them from donating sums on a significant scale. The method of conscription also differed. While men were drawn into the voluntary arena by their hobbies, business considerations, political and religious interests, women were rallied solely by the church. Men rationalized their activities on a variety of grounds, embracing social, democratic, and business aims. Feminine activities, on the other hand, were invariably framed in the idiom of hearth and home.

Moreover, men could choose the types of activities they wished to sponsor. Cultural, medical, and charitable organizations all opened their doors hospitably wide to potential male trustees. Women could sew for the poor, nurse them, pray with them, or succor them in asylums—nothing more. Masculine efforts were designed to aid the city as a whole; women cared only for its victims. Even within the context of the asylum a noticeable division of labor appeared. While women aided society's flotsam, the innocent losers in life's race, public authorities prescribed "paternal" discipline for the more willful offenders treated at county expense.

Benevolent ladies were continually urged to ascend new heights of selflessness and self-sacrifice. Businessmen, on the other hand, were cautioned to act in their own best interest, preserving their character and mercantile integrity by guarding the public weal. The ultimate issue was one of power. The rhetoric of Jacksonian equality had genuine relevance for Chicago's Christian Gentlemen. As they carved their city out of the prairie wilderness, they assumed the steward's role as part of their larger economic, political, and civic duties. For women, charitable work was a means of achieving power rather than a manifestation of it. Excluded from the larger decision-making arena, asylum duties gave them enhanced mobility, a modicum of power, and public recognition. It permitted them to make decisions like a man, without transgressing the dictates of the cult of the lady. It was one of the few socially acceptable escape routes from the home.

The Civil War and the fire of 1871 ushered in a new era. Richer than their mothers, and hampered by fewer restraints, Chicago's Gilded

Age managers and patronesses moved beyond the narrow world of the asylum, joining clubs, founding art associations, and launching nursing schools. Newly enriched by the passage of the Illinois Married Woman's Property Act of 1861, wives could now afford to fund projects in lieu of staffing them, paying others to do the less appealing tasks. In the process, the older service ethic of the antebellum period fell by the wayside, sullied and invalidated by the experiences of the war and the perquisites of wealth.

While women pioneered new fields, their husbands fashioned institutional arenas for the controlled interaction of rich and poor. Determined to exercise their civic obligations apart from the sordid arena of the slum, they used the world's generosity, and later their own, to weave the city's formerly autonomous charities into an elaborate, private system of social control. Echoing the dictates of Carnegie's Gospel of Wealth, they afforded enhanced opportunities for the ambitious, and minimal monetary assistance and incarceration for the "unfit."

Although men's and women's activities drew closer together in the Gilded Age, significant differences still remained. Both groups were richer than their predecessors, and emphasized money and management to a greater degree. The growing influence of club activities was universal, as was the widening range of opportunities. While health and cultural agencies began to attract growing feminine constituencies, men assumed new stature in museums and charities, centralizing their authority over the length and breadth of the city's nonprofit resources. But while men labored to create a workable system, women were still slowly fighting to legitimize their participation beyond the tiny universe of the asylum and the home. Despite substantial gains, they remained segregated in women's organizations catering to carefully limited clienteles. By 1910, many of these differences had been equalized by growing career, educational, and leadership opportunities. But in 1890, the divisions were still sharp and clear.

Set apart by their wealth and elitist social codes, Chicago's Gilded Age stewards lost touch with the vibrant pulse of the city. Their progressive successors rejected their institutional solutions, calling for social justice to counterpoint plutocratic largesse. Self-help was inadequate, they proclaimed. Neighborhoods, not institutional Homes and Palaces of Culture, were now deemed the proper arenas for the steward's skills. Decentralization, de-institutionalization, research, pioneering, alliance with experts: these were the rallying cries of Chicago's progressives.

They were also the epitaph for the individualistic volunteer. As legions of visiting nurses, social workers, and housekeepers filtered into the city's homes to succor the needy and hold families intact, the untrained Samaritan was eased to the edges of the helping process. The pace was erratic, occurring more rapidly in some fields than others. Medical workers quickly demanded autonomy; social workers achieved recognition more slowly, and cultural workers lagged far behind. But steadily, persistently, the role of the citizen narrowed, his alternatives withdrawn.

Local initiative suffered as well. Never an isolated "island community," Chicago's early asylums, literary and relief societies, art-unions and hospitals were all built on borrowed precedents. Yet each was specifically tailored to fit local needs, a process aided by the informal manner in which institutional precedents were conveyed. The quality of local programs was closely linked to the quality of the communications network. In an era when human interaction and interurban contact were synonymous, news of novel undertakings spread slowly, borne by newspapers, correspondence, and the insights of travelers who had observed them at close range. Clergymen, settlers, and cosmopolitan civic stewards all became catalysts of change, liaisons between their cities and the world beyond. Since there was no centralized medium for the implementation and standardization of institutional practices, responsibility rested on the stewards' shoulders alone.

As transportation and communications innovations speeded the pace of information circulation, institutional development was lifted to a more sophisticated plane. Spurred by the quickening rate of domestic and international tourism, wealthy localites journeyed in ever-increasing numbers to observe new programs firsthand. Clubs simultaneously provided informal, national information networks, while telephones, photography, and improved printing techniques allowed information to be transmitted more quickly and precisely than ever before.

The rise of the mass media gradually eroded the hegemony of local elites, enabling middle-class reformers and technocrats to assume the role of national opinion makers and innovators. By the 1920s, cadres of technocrats had implanted themselves squarely between donor and recipient, controlling each. Psychiatric social workers, visiting teachers, and visiting nurses used their scientific expertise to engineer the behavior of the poor, while their control over the flow of publicity dictated the stewards' response as well.

As information became standardized, a new movement was set in motion to bring local practices more in line with national, professional rhetoric and goals. The de-institutionalization campaign is a case in point. Antebellum asylums had been in the vanguard of social welfare practices. After the turn of the century, however, reformers increasingly shifted the locus of social regeneration to the natural family and the slum. De-institutionalization and professionalization went hand in hand. As professional schools and associations began to lobby for the diffusion of casework techniques, asylums became the logical target for their reforms. With the growing emphasis on family rehabilitation, social observation and environmentalism, orphanages, and homes for the friendless came to be viewed as retrogressive bastions of unprofessional techniques, the vestiges of an unenlightened past. Professional pressures ultimately merged with demographic trends and the economic imperatives of the depression to effect the abandonment of institutional care. Local factors clashed, then combined, to draw Chicago's oldest charities into the mainstream of national social welfare trends.

The crusade for de-institutionalization and decentralization touched every aspect of urban life. Probation, outpatient care, and cultural outreach were all part of the campaign to democratize and professionalize urban services and upgrade the quality of life for the poor. Yet even as reformers posited their goals, countervailing forces were at work to revivify the institutional ideal. The same generation that closed the city's asylums and generously underwrote research also funded museums, hospitals, and universities on a new scale. The cross-pull between institutional and noninstitutional beneficence veered from the brick and mortar mentality of the Gilded Age to progressive decentralization, and then back to a more equitable position in the twenties, when donors supported both.

The relationship between donors and doers, professionals and volunteers evinced a similar ambivalence. The 1960s would witness a concerted campaign to revivify the role of the local volunteer. The Jazz Age, on the other hand, was the heyday of the technocrat. By 1929, many board members had become the servants of their staffs, raising funds for salaries, and interpreting community needs to peripatetic employees. Donors were asked to give, but not demand, rendering gifts devoid of strings. Technological middlemen further separated the donor from his gift, training citizens to respond to abstractions and well worded emotional appeals rather than visible needs.

Sponsoring projects they often could neither touch nor comprehend, Chicago's stewards equated salaries with service, signing checks with noblesse oblige.

Their generosity reached new levels in the late twenties, elicited in a growing stream of gold by skillful publicists and fund raisers. But something vital had been lost in the translation. As one concerned critic explained:

> Back in the country.... Relief was personal, direct, frank, and above board.... In the cities...the giver never sees the object of his bounty, nor is witness to the act of dispensing what he has provided.... Whether the recipient is made happy or is embittered by the gift, is unknown to him. Giving is impersonal, indirect, mechanized.... The process is as cold as the payment of taxes.... Under modern conditions, particularly in the cities, we must call upon our powers of imagination to help us obtain by proxy, so to speak, the emotional response that our nature requires.[1]

The mutuality of the gift had been sundered, the act of giving transformed into a bloodless operation requiring neither effort nor commitment. Rather than acting as a social bond, it had become a tedious obligation, elicited from anonymous donors, bestowed upon anonymous beneficiaries. The Progressive cry for social justice, the increasing prerogatives of professionals, and the geometrically mounting scale of urban needs shattered the traditional meaning of "the gift."

Professionalization diminished the administrative capabilities of Chicago's stewards, casting their efforts in an increasingly materialistic mold. Donors rather than decision makers, Jazz Age urbanites served as patrons, fund raisers, and agency liaisons. The depression further reduced their role, stripping potential donors of their financial resources. As America shifted to the "dimes and dollars" campaigns of the 1930s, individual stewards receded into the background. The combined forces of professionalization and economic duress undermined local autonomy, paving the way for the rise of the new federalism and the innovations of the New Deal.

Yet even as the opportunities narrowed, a few citizens posited a plea for the volunteer. "I hold that every man owes something besides his taxes to the community in which he lives," Samuel Insull asserted.

> The more he has been favored mentally and materially by fortune, the more he owes. In discharge of that debt, he is under obligation to do for the community something that he does not get paid for, something that he does not make money by. His obligation to do this is not just a once-in-a-while obligation, and what he does in discharge of it should be limited only by his abilities and opportunities.[2]

Insull's contemporary, Edward L. Ryerson, agreed, calling for new means of interesting "people to a point where they will know and understand their community's needs."[3] The course of twentieth-century charity and cultural patronage has been marked by continuing efforts to strike a suitable balance between the need for urban services, the prerogatives of the volunteer, and the fundamental necessity of maintaining a sense of collective commitment to community welfare. Although the rationale and the participants have changed over time, the concept of civic stewardship has endured, transposing the essence of the antebellum ideal onto the complex world of twentieth-century urban America.

# NOTES

## Preface

1. Harvey W. Zorbaugh, *The Gold Coast and the Slum: A Sociological Study of Chicago's Near North Side* (Chicago: University of Chicago Press, 1929); F. Scott Fitzgerald, *The Great Gatsby* (New York: Charles Scribner's Sons, 1925).
2. Michael Harrington, *The Other America: Poverty in the United States* (New York: Macmillan Co., 1962).
3. W. Lloyd Warner, J. O. Low, Paul S. Lunt, and Leo Srole, *Yankee City* (New Haven: Yale University Press, 1963); Sam Bass Warner, Jr., *The Private City: Philadelphia in Three Periods of Its Growth* (Philadelphia: University of Pennsylvania Press, 1968); E. Digby Baltzell, *Philadelphia Gentlemen: The Making of a National Upper Class* (Glencoe, Ill.: Free Press, 1958).
4. Allen F. Davis, *American Heroine: The Life and Legend of Jane Addams* (New York: Oxford University Press, 1973); Howard E. Wilson, *Mary McDowell, Neighbor* (Chicago: University of Chicago Press, 1928); Louise C. Wade, *Graham Taylor: Pioneer for Social Justice 1851–1938* (Chicago: University of Chicago Press, 1964); Joseph Frazier Wall, *Andrew Carnegie* (New York: Oxford University Press, 1970); M. R. Werner, *Julius Rosenwald: The Life of a Practical Humanitarian* (New York: Harper & Row, 1939).
5. Ben Whitaker, *The Foundations: An Anatomy of Philanthropy and Society* (London: Eyre Methuen, 1974); Frank D. Watson, *The Charity Organization Movement in the United States: A Study in American Philanthropy* (New York: Macmillan Co., 1922); David Rothman, *The Discovery of the Asylum: Social Order and Disorder in the New Republic* (Boston: Little, Brown & Co., 1971); Robert S. Pickett, *House of Refuge: Origins of Juvenile Reform in New York State, 1815–1857* (New York: Syracuse University Press, 1969); Foster Rhea Dulles, *The American Red Cross* (New York: Harper & Bros., 1950); Allen F. Davis, *Spearheads for Reform: The Social Settlements and the Progressive Movement, 1890–1914* (New York: Oxford University Press, 1967).
6. Roy Lubove, *The Professional Altruist: The Emergence of Social Work as a Career: 1880–1930* (Cambridge: Harvard University Press, 1965).
7. Walter I. Trattner, *From Poor Law to Welfare State: A History of Social Welfare in*

*America* (New York: Free Press, 1974); Roy Lubove, *The Struggle for Social Security, 1900–1935* (Cambridge: Harvard University Press, 1968); Harold L. Wilenski and Charles N. Lebeaux, *Industrial Society and Social Welfare* (New York: Russell Sage Foundation, 1958).

8. Robert H. Bremner, *American Philanthropy* (Chicago: University of Chicago Press, 1960); Robert Bremner, *From the Depths: The Discovery of Poverty in the United States* (New York: New York University Press, 1956); Scott M. Cutlip, *Fund Raising in the United States: Its Role in America's Philanthropy* (New Brunswick, N.J.: Rutgers University Press, 1965); Clifford S. Griffin, *Their Brothers' Keepers: Moral Stewardship in the United States, 1800–1865* (New York: H. Wolff, 1960).
9. Nathan I. Huggins, *Protestants against Poverty: Boston's Charities, 1870–1900* (Westport, Conn.: Greenwood Publishing Co., 1971); Raymond A. Mohl, *Poverty in New York, 1783–1825* (New York: Oxford University Press, 1971); Edward Pessen, *Riches, Class and Power before the Civil War* (Toronto: D. C. Heath & Co., 1973); Carroll Smith-Rosenberg, *Religion and the Rise of the American City: The New York Mission Movement, 1812–1870* (Ithaca: Cornell University Press, 1971); Helen Lefkowitz Horowitz, *Culture and the City: Cultural Philanthropy in Chicago from the 1880s to 1917* (Lexington: University of Kentucky Press, 1976).

## Chapter 1

1. Edward Pessen, *Riches, Class and Power before the Civil War* (Toronto: D. C. Heath & Co., 1973), p. 262; E. Digby Baltzell, *Philadelphia Gentlemen: The Making of a National Upper Class* (Glencoe, Ill.: Free Press, 1958).
2. Hobart Chatfield-Taylor, *Cities of Many Men* (Boston: Houghton Mifflin Co., 1925), p. 230.
3. Edward L. Peckham, "My Journey Out West," in *As Others See Chicago: Impressions of Visitors, 1673–1933,* by Bessie Louise Pierce (Chicago: University of Chicago Press, 1933), p. 167.
4. Raymond A. Mohl, *Poverty in New York, 1783–1825* (New York: Oxford University Press, 1971); John K. Alexander, "The City of Brotherly Fear: The Poor in Late-Eighteenth-Century Philadelphia," in *Cities in American History,* by Kenneth T. Jackson and Stanley K. Schultz (New York: Alfred A. Knopf, 1972), pp. 79–97; David J. Rothman, *The Discovery of the Asylum: Social Order and Disorder in the New Republic* (Boston: Little, Brown & Co., 1971); Robert H. Bremner, *From the Depths: The Discovery of Poverty in the United States* (New York: New York University Press, 1956).
5. Donald M. Scott, *From Office to Profession: The New England Ministry, 1750–1850* (Philadelphia: University of Pennsylvania Press, 1978); Joseph Kett, *The Formation of the American Medical Profession: The Role of Institutions, 1780–1860* (New Haven: Yale University Press, 1968); Richard Harrison Shryock, *Medicine and Society in America, 1660–1860* (New York: New York University Press, 1960); James G. Burrow, *AMA: Voice of American Medicine* (Baltimore: Johns Hopkins Press, 1963); Daniel H. Calhoun, *Professional Lives in America: Structure and Aspiration, 1750–1850* (Cambridge: Harvard University Press, 1965).
6. Joanna Bethune, *The Power of Faith, Exemplified in the Life and Writings of the Late Mrs. Isabella M. Graham* (New York: American Tract Society, 1843). See, also, Barbara J. Berg, *The Remembered Gate: Origins of American Feminism: The Woman and the City, 1800–1860* (New York: Oxford University Press, 1978).
7. *Chicago Daily Tribune,* July 8, 1857.

8. Chicago Erring Woman's Refuge, *Annual Report* (1865), p. 15.
9. Ruth Orton Camp, "The Chicago Orphan Asylum, 1849–1949" (unpublished MS, Chicago Historical Society [hereafter cited as CHS]), p. 16.
10. Newspaper interview with Mrs. Sanger (mother of Mrs. George Pullman), in "Scrapbooks Dealing with the Pullman Family," 1:63, CHS.
11. For a fuller discussion of the asylum's early operations, see Mamie Ruth Davis, "A History of Policies and Methods of Social Work in the Chicago Orphan Asylum" (Master's thesis, University of Chicago, 1927); and Clare L. McCausland, *Children of Circumstance: A History of the First 125 Years (1849–1975) of the Chicago Child Care Society* (Chicago: R. R. Donnelley & Sons, 1976).
12. Quoted in Camp, "The Chicago Orphan Asylum," p. 23.
13. Although it has been suggested that antebellum asylum discipline was universally severe, COA punishments consisted primarily of sending unruly children to bed without dinner, much as they might have been in a normal household. For a very different interpretation, see David J. Rothman, *The Discovery of the Asylum,* p. 228.
14. "Reference Book of the Asylum, 1849–1867," cited in Davis, "History of the Chicago Orphan Asylum," p. 24.
15. "Copy of Articles of Agreement," ibid., p. 134.
16. Chicago Home for the Friendless (hereafter cited as CHFF), *Annual Report* (1864), p. 8.
17. Report, October 1863, quoted in the "Annual Report of the Superintendent," Chicago Home for Girls, *Annual Report* (1928), p. 18.
18. *Jane C. Hoge, In Memoriam* (Privately printed, 1890), p. 76, CHS.
19. CHFF, *Annual Report* (1865), p. 23.
20. Mrs. N. B. Judd, quoted in Marion Barnett Smith, "History of the Chicago Home for the Friendless" (Master's thesis, University of Chicago, 1930), pp. 10–11.
21. Mrs. Wheeler, quoted in CHFF, *Twenty-seventh Annual Report* (1885), p. 11.
22. Mrs. N. B. Judd, "Reminiscences of the Organization and Early Days of the Home," copy in "Minutes (Original) of Board Meetings, January 1, 1858 to January 1, 1881, Chicago Home for the Friendless," in possession of Child and Family Services, Chicago.
23. CHFF, *Fortieth Annual Report* (1898), pp. 14–15.
24. CHFF, *Annual Report* (1860), p. 12.
25. CHFF, *Twenty-seventh Annual Report* (1885), p. 11.
26. CHFF, Minutes (June 13, 1861), p. 83.
27. W. W. Everts, *Christian Womanhood: Life of Mrs. M. K. Everts* (Chicago: Church & Goodman, 1867), p. 316.
28. Chicago Nursery and Half-Orphan Asylum, MSS, CHS, and *Annual Reports;* Chapin Hall, *One Hundred Years of Devotion to Children* (Chicago: Chapin Hall, 1960); Old Ladies' Home, *Annual Reports;* Erring Woman's Refuge of Chicago, *Annual Reports;* Helen Denton Haseltine, "A History of the Chicago Home for Girls, Founded in 1863 as the Erring Woman's Refuge for Reform" (Master's thesis, University of Chicago, 1934).
29. For an interesting comparison with an eastern organization, see Susan Porter Benson, "Business Heads and Sympathizing Hearts: The Women of the Providence Employment Society," *Journal of Social History* 11 (Fall 1978): 302–13.
30. Alexander Young, *The Beneficent Woman: A Discourse Occasioned by the Death of Mrs. Catharine G. Prescott* (Boston: John Wilson & Son, 1852), p. 7.

31. Everts, *Christian Womanhood*, p. 35. See, also, Barbara Welter, "The Feminization of American Religion," in *Clio's Consciousness Raised: New Perspectives on the History of Women*, ed. Mary S. Hartman and Lois Banner (New York: Harper & Row, 1974), pp. 137–57.
32. Timothy L. Smith, *Revivalism and Social Reform in Mid-Nineteenth-Century America* (New York: Abingdon Press, 1957), p. 168.
33. *Advocate of Moral Reform* 3 (August 15, 1837): 311, quoted in Robert Samuel Fletcher, *A History of Oberlin College from Its Foundation through the Civil War* (Oberlin, Ohio: Oberlin College, 1943), 1:298–99.
34. Flora L. Northrup, *The Record of a Century: 1834–1934* (New York: American Female Guardian Society and Home for the Friendless, 1934); Carroll Smith-Rosenberg, "Beauty, the Beast, and the Militant Woman: A Case Study in Sex Roles and Social Stress in Jacksonian America," *American Quarterly* 23 (1971): 562–84.
35. Mrs. Sarah R. Ingraham, *Walks of Usefulness, or Reminiscences of Mrs. Margaret Prior* (New York: American Female Moral Reform Society, 1844), p. 74.
36. "Eulogy of Reverend Eddy," in Everts, *Christian Womanhood*, p. 340.
37. Benjamin B. Wisner, *Memoirs of the Late Mrs. Susan Huntington* (Boston: Crocker & Brewster, 1826), p. 118.
38. Mary A. Livermore, *My Story of the War* (Hartford, Conn.: A. D. Worthington & Co., 1888), p. 170.
39. Catharine Beecher, *A Treatise on Domestic Economy* (New York: Marsh, Capen, Lyon & Webb, 1841), p. 162.
40. Everts, *Christian Womanhood*, pp. 47–48.
41. Ibid., p. 73.
42. Ibid., p. 265.
43. Ibid., p. 334.
44. Harriet Martineau, *Society in America* (New York: Saunders & Otley, 1837), 2:363.
45. Nancy F. Cott, *The Bonds of Womanhood: "Woman's Sphere" in New England, 1780–1835* (New Haven: Yale University Press, 1977), chap. 4.
46. Wisner, *Susan Huntington*, p. 167.
47. Catharine Beecher, "An Address to the Christian Women of America" (1871), in *The Oven Birds: American Women on Womanhood, 1820–1920*, ed. Gail Parker (New York: Doubleday & Co., 1972), p. 149.
48. Sarah Josepha Hale, "Editor's Table," *Godey's Lady's Book* 44 (March 1852): 228.
49. Lydia Maria Child, "Letters from New York (1852) in Parker, *Oven Birds*, p. 83.
50. Governor Bigler, quoted in *Godey's Lady's Book* 49 (August 1854): 175.
51. Dr. William A. Alcott, *The Gift Book for Young Ladies* (Buffalo: George H. Derby & Co., 1852), p. 243.
52. Mrs. Louisa C. Tuthill, *The Young Lady's Home* (New Haven: S. Babcock, 1839), p. 356.
53. Ibid.
54. Kathryn Kish Sklar, *Catharine Beecher: A Study in American Domesticity* (New Haven: Yale University Press, 1973).
55. Mrs. Garrett's donation was the only large gift from a woman during this period. The largest cash gift was Cyrus McCormick's $100,000 grant to the Presbyterian Assembly in 1859, proffered in order to persuade them to relocate their seminary in Chicago. The industrialist paid part of the promised sum but ultimately withheld an equal amount, diverting the final $25,000 installment to a rival school more in line

with his doctrinal preferences. Although large sums were audaciously pledged, promised gifts often failed to materialize.

56. George Rogers Taylor, *The Transportation Revolution, 1815–1860* (New York: Harper & Row, 1951), p. 312.
57. Abbe Farwell Ferry, *Reminiscences of John V. Farwell by his Elder Daughter* (Chicago: Ralph Fletcher Seymour, 1928), 2:120.
58. Thomas Wakefield Goodspeed, *A History of the University of Chicago: The First Quarter-Century* (Chicago: University of Chicago Press, 1972), p. 13 (originally published 1916).
59. Robert H. Bremner, *American Philanthropy* (Chicago: University of Chicago Press, 1960), p. 51.
60. Chicago Reform School, *Twelfth Annual Report* (1868), pp. 48, 49.
61. Chicago Reform School, *Third Annual Report* (1858), p. 25.
62. Chicago Reform School, *First Annual Report* (1856), p. 14.
63. "Matron's Report," CHFF, *Annual Report* (1864), p. 9.
64. *Jane C. Hoge, In Memoriam*, pp. 67, 69.
65. Mary A. Livermore, *The Story of My Life* (Hartford, Conn.: A. D. Worthington & Co., 1899), p. 91. For a fascinating discussion of Livermore's subsequent career as a domestic reformer, see Dolores Hayden, *The Grand Domestic Revolution: A History of Feminist Designs for American Homes, Neighborhoods, and Cities* (Cambridge: MIT Press, 1981), chap. 6.
66. For a more detailed discussion of the teaching profession, see Keith Melder, *Beginnings of Sisterhood: The American Women's Rights Movement, 1800–1850* (New York: Schocken Books, 1977), chap. 2.
67. Livermore, *My Life*, p. 457.
68. Melder, *Beginnings of Sisterhood;* Gerda Lerner, "The Lady and the Mill Girl: Changes in the Status of Women in the Age of Jackson," *Midcontinent American Studies Journal* 10 (Spring 1969): 5–15; Ann Douglas, *The Feminization of American Culture* (New York: Alfred A. Knopf, 1977), chap. 2.

## Chapter 2

1. Louise de Koven Bowen, *Growing Up with a City* (New York: Macmillan Co., 1926), p. 50. Most visiting was still done on an individual basis. Although a Charity Organization Society operated briefly in Chicago between 1883 and 1887, it ceased operations before its friendly visiting program could be adequately implemented.
2. Erving Goffman, "The Nature of Deference and Demeanor," *American Anthropologist* 58 (1956): 494. Jane Addams sensitively portrayed the perils of this "absolute clashing of two ethical standards" in *Democracy and Social Ethics* (1902). Pointing out that the poor often regarded the charity visitor's insistence on temperance and thrift as "different," and "agin' nature," she noted that "the difficulty of making clear one's own ethical standpoint is sometimes insurmountable." Christopher Lasch, ed., *The Social Thought of Jane Addams* (Indianapolis: Bobbs-Merrill Co., 1965), pp. 66, 68, 67.
3. Bowen, *Growing Up*, p. 61.
4. *The Chicago Chronicle*, June 1902, in Lucy Flower Scrapbook, Chicago Historical Society (hereafter cited as CHS), p. 38.
5. Barbara Stein Frankle's "The Genteel Family: High Victorian Conceptions of Domesticity and Good Behavior" (Ph.D. diss., University of Wisconsin, 1969) pro-

vides a fascinating overview of Victorian etiquette, the cult of domesticity, and the role of the lady.

6. However, it should be noted that not everyone approved of the social cast which charitable work had acquired. The most fashionable affair, the great charity ball sponsored annually by Mrs. Potter Palmer after 1887, was roundly condemned in some quarters. Even the participants were occasionally uneasy about the implications of their actions. "My conscience hurts me when I pay out two hundred dollars in order to earn ten dollars for the poor," shuddered a character in society writer Herma Naomi Clark's *The Elegant Eighties*. "We might better have refrained from getting out our fine feathers, stayed at home, and given the money to the poor." *The Elegant Eighties: When Chicago was Young* (Chicago: A. C. McClurg & Co., 1941), p. 224.
7. "An Act to Protect Married Women in their Separate Property," *The Public Laws of the State of Illinois Passed at the Twenty-second Session of the General Assembly* (Chicago: D. B. Cooke & Co., 1861), p. 140.
8. Sarah Josepha Hale, "A Life of Good Works," *Godey's Lady's Book* 62 (July 1870): 81.
9. Nettie Fowler McCormick to Cyrus McCormick, Jr., July 8, 1894, Cyrus McCormick, Jr., MSS, Wisconsin State Historical Society, Madison.
10. The 1883 Chicago telephone directory reveals that the majority of the relatively small number of telephones in operation belonged to leading businessmen, attorneys, physicians, businesses, and some nonprofit organizations.
11. George M. Fredrickson, *The Inner Civil War: Northern Intellectuals and the Crisis of the Union* (New York: Harper & Row, 1965).
12. Ann Douglas, *The Feminization of American Culture* (New York: Alfred A. Knopf, 1977), p. 327.
13. Frances Willard, quoted in Mary Earhart, *Frances Willard: From Prayers to Politics* (Chicago: University of Chicago Press, 1944), p. 184.
14. Six paintings were also displayed at the 1859 exhibit by feminine artists, including four by Eliza Allen Starr, aunt of Hull-House co-founder Ellen Gates Starr. See Chicago Exhibition of Fine Arts, *Catalogue* (1859).
15. "Charity," *Godey's Lady's Book*, vol. 52 (1856).
16. "1861," ibid., vol. 62 (1861). For the domestification of literature, see Douglas, *The Feminization of American Culture*.
17. Sarah Josepha Hale, "The Fine Arts at Home," *Godey's Lady's Book* 61 (December 1860): 566.
18. "Catalogue of Paintings, Statuary, etc., in the Art Department of the Great Northwestern Sanitary Fair" (June 1865); A. T. Andreas, *History of Chicago* (Chicago: A. T. Andreas Co., 1885), 2:557; Mary A. Livermore, *My Story of the War* (Hartford, Conn.: A. D. Worthington & Co., 1889), pp. 415, 441.
19. "Art Needlework," newsclipping dated April 12, 1876, in Mrs. Elizabeth E. Atwater, comp., *Scrapbook of Clippings from the Centennial*, CHS.
20. Amelia Gere Mason, *Memories of a Friend* (Chicago: Laurence C. Woodworth, 1918), p. 66.
21. On feminine employment alternatives, see Robert W. Smuts, *Women and Work in America* (New York: Schocken Books, 1971). According to Bessie Louise Pierce, the number of women in Chicago's labor force increased fivefold during the interim between 1870 and 1890. *A History of Chicago* (Chicago: University of Chicago Press, 1957), 3:237.

22. Chicago Society of Decorative Art, "Circular No. 4" (1889).
23. Ibid.
24. Addie Hibbard Gregory, *Reminiscences of Lydia Beekman Hibbard, by Her Eldest Daughter* (Chicago: Privately printed, 1929), p. 39.
25. Quoted in undated newsclipping, Chicago Society of Decorative Art *Scrapbook*, CHS, p. 4.
26. "President's Report," in Chicago Society of Decorative Art, *Constitution and By-Laws* (1886), pp. 19–20.
27. Ibid., p. 20.
28. For a more detailed account of the medical history of Chicago, see: Thomas N. Bonner, *Medicine in Chicago, 1850–1900* (Madison: American History Research Center, 1957); and James Nevins Hyde, *Early Medical Chicago* (Chicago: Fergus Printing Co., 1879).
29. For a description of proselytizing techniques in hospital wards, see William Welsh, ed., *Women Helpers in the Church: Their Sayings and Doings* (Philadelphia: J. B. Lippincott & Co., 1872), pp. 67–81.
30. "Hospital Directresses in Spain," *Godey's Lady's Book* 91 (October 1875): 376, 377.
31. *The Daily Democratic Press*, March 10, 1854, and May 1, 1855, quoted in Bessie Louise Pierce, *History of Chicago* (New York: Alfred A. Knopf, 1941), 2:451.
32. Livermore, *My Story of the War*, p. 188. Wartime casualties were enormous. Antiseptics were virtually unknown, and gangrene flourished in the unhealthy atmosphere of the wards. The wounded rarely survived more than a few days, and those who did were often carried off by the epidemics which periodically ravaged the camps. An estimated 110,000 Union soldiers died of wounds, while another 250,000 perished from disease. Richard Shryock, "A Medical Perspective on the Civil War," *American Quarterly* 14 (Summer 1962): 161–72.
33. Laura Houghteling Reynolds, "Reminiscences of the War of Rebellion" (typescript MS [1890], Chicago Historical Society), p. 28. For an extremely perceptive treatment of women's role in the Sanitary Commission, see Ann Douglas Wood, "The War within a War: Women Nurses in the Union Army," *Civil War History* 18, no. 3 (September 1972): 197–212.
34. On international medical developments, see Richard Shryock, *The Development of Modern Medicine: An Interpretation of the Social and Scientific Factors Involved* (Philadelphia: University of Pennsylvania Press, 1936).
35. Illinois Training School for Nurses, "Women Physicians and Training-Schools for Nurses in Illinois" (1893), p. 2.
36. Florence Nightingale, *Notes on Nursing: What It Is, and What It Is Not* (London: Harrison & Son, 1860).
37. For a more detailed account of the development of American nursing schools, see Mary M. Roberts, *American Nursing: History and Interpretation* (New York: Macmillan Co., 1954); and Lavinia L. Dock and Isabel Maitland Stewart, *A Short History of Nursing from the Earliest Times to the Present Day* (New York: G. P. Putnam's Sons, 1920).
38. Grace Fay Shryver, *A History of the Illinois Training School for Nurses, 1880–1929* (Chicago: Board of Directors of the Illinois Training School for Nurses, 1930), p.1.
39. Mrs. J. N. Flower, "The Illinois Training School for Nurses," in *The Reporter of Organized Charity*, November 1887, Lucy Flower Scrapbook, CHS, p. 54.
40. "Trained Nurses," undated newsclipping, Illinois Training School for Nurses *Scrapbook*, CHS, p. 16.

41. Mrs. Galusha Anderson, *The Story of Aunt Lizzie Aiken* (Chicago: Jensen, McClurg & Co., 1880), p. 146.
42. Illinois Training School for Nurses, "Women Physicians," p. 2.
43. "It Is a Noble Calling," undated newsclipping, Lucy Flower Scrapbook, CHS, 2:17.
44. Undated letter, Mrs. C. B. Lawrence to N. K. Fairbank, Illinois Training School for Nurses MSS, folder 1, CHS.
45. Quoted in Shryver, *Illinois Training School for Nurses*, p. 31.
46. "Preparatory Draft of Third Annual Report," Illinois Training School for Nurses MSS, CHS. Lawrence repeated the same theme in her private fund-raising letters. Lawrence to Levi Leiter (n.d., ca. 1883), Illinois Training School for Nurses MSS, folder 1.
47. Illinois Training School for Nurses, *First Annual Report* (1881), p. 9.
48. Franklin H. North, "A New Profession for Women," *Century Magazine* 25, n.s. 3 (November 1882): 41.
49. Dr. Sarah Hackett Stevenson, quoted in undated newsclipping, Lucy Flower Scrapbook (ca. 1885), 5:49.
50. "Woe for the Wardens," undated newsclipping, ibid., pp. 41, 44–46.
51. Illinois Training School for Nurses, *Second Annual Report* (1882), quoted in Shryver, p. 142.
52. Commissioner Stewart, quoted in "Worsted by Women," newspaper clipping dated October 28, 1887, Lucy Flower Scrapbook, 2:5.
53. The schools included: Women's Hospital Training School for Nurses (1885), Women's and Children's Hospital Nursing School (1885), St. Luke's Training School for Nurses (1889), Lincoln Park Sanitarium Training School for Nurses (1889), and the Bethesda Nursing School (1889).
54. Unfortunately, Newberry's bequest was never received, for her mother successfully challenged the grant in court, claiming her right to inherit the entirety of her daughter's $110,000 estate, Charles Harpel, comp., "Miss Newberry's Estate," *Obituary Scrapbook* 10 (1885): 5.
55. Undated *Chicago Daily News* newsclipping (ca. 1888), Chapin Hall MSS, CHS, Box 13.
56. Ibid.
57. Quoted in Ishbel Ross, *Silhouette in Diamonds: The Life of Mrs. Potter Palmer* (New York: Harper & Bros., 1960), p. 159.
58. Statistics for board members based on city directories, random biographical data, and the 1880 MS census reports. Unfortunately, membership lists for the Chicago Woman's Club were not available, although it is likely that most of the women belonged to this group as well. The Fortnightly was the more exclusive of the two.
59. Cornelia Gray Lunt, *Sketches of Childhood and Girlhood: Chicago, 1847–1864* (Evanston, Ill.: Privately printed, 1925), p. 80.
60. Bowen, *Growing Up*, p. 19.
61. Harriette Greenbaum Frank and Amalie Hofer Jerome, *Annals of the Chicago Woman's Club, 1876–1916* (Chicago: Chicago Woman's Club, 1916).
62. See, e.g., William L. O'Neill, *Everyone Was Brave: A History of Feminism in America* (Chicago: Quadrangle Books, 1971), pp. 85, 89.
63. Frank and Jerome, *Annals*, p. 21.
64. Ibid., p. 9.
65. Chicago Woman's Club, "Columbian Souvenir Edition" (n.p., 1893), CHS.
66. Frank and Jerome, *Annals*, p. 36.

67. Chicago Woman's Club, Minutes, December 5, 1883, p. 1, Chicago Woman's Club MSS, Box 1, CHS.
68. "Resolution," ibid., December 12, 1883, p. 2.
69. Quoted in Wallace Evan Davies, *Patriotism on Parade: The Story of Veterans' and Hereditary Organizations in America, 1783–1900* (Cambridge: Harvard University Press, 1955), p. 59.

## Chapter 3

1. William B. Ogden, letter to A. Bushnell, November 24, 1940. Letter Press Book III, Ogden MSS, Chicago Historical Society (hereafter cited as CHS), p. 25.
2. For a more detailed account of governmental relief programs, see James Brown, *The History of Public Assistance in Chicago, 1833 to 1893* (Chicago: University of Chicago Press, 1941).
3. Chicago Relief Society, *Constitution and Directory of the Chicago Relief Society* (1851), p. 7.
4. Ibid., p. 8.
5. New York Association for the Improvement of the Condition of the Poor, *First Annual Report* (1845), p. 28.
6. Ibid., pp. 26–27.
7. For a fuller discussion of these trends, see Seymour J. Mandelbaum, *Boss Tweed's New York* (New York: John Wiley & Sons, 1965).
8. Chicago Relief and Aid Society, *Annual Report*, reprinted in the *Chicago Daily Democrat*, November 17, 1857, p. 3.
9. Isaac N. Arnold, "William B. Ogden and Early Days in Chicago" (paper read at the Chicago Historical Society, December 20, 1881) (Chicago: Fergus Printing Co., 1882), p. 24.
10. As Perry Miller points out, these obligations were taken quite seriously by antebellum Americans: "A man could no more safely, in America of 1820, publicly come out against benevolence, or announce that men were so constituted as to derive happiness not from benevolent dispositions as from the selfish calculations of Hobbes and Mandeville, than he could advocate sexual promiscuity." *The Life of the Mind in America* (New York: Harcourt, Brace & World, 1965), p. 78.
11. Mrs. L. G. Abell, *A Woman in Her Various Relations* (New York, 1851), quoted in Carl Bode, *Midcentury America: Life in the 1850s* (Carbondale: Southern Illinois University Press, 1972), p. 78.
12. William H. McGuffey, *McGuffey's New Fifth Eclectic Reader* (New York: Wilson, Hinkle & Co., 1857), p. 75.
13. Donald M. Scott, *From Office to Profession: The New England Ministry, 1750–1850* (Philadelphia: University of Pennsylvania Press, 1978).
14. Paul Goodman, "Ethics and Enterprise: The Values of a Boston Elite, 1800–1860," *American Quarterly* 18 (Fall 1966): 447.
15. Ibid., p. 438.
16. Freeman Hunt, *Lives of American Merchants* (New York: Hunt's Merchants' Magazine, 1856), 1:276.
17. Freeman Hunt, *Worth and Wealth: A Collection of Maxims, Morals, and Miscellanies for Merchants and Men of Business* (New York: Stringer & Townsend, 1856), p. 468.
18. Ibid. Wilbur K. Jordan, *Philanthropy in England, 1480–1660: A Study of the Changing Pattern of English Social Aspirations* (London: George Allen & Unwin,

Ltd., 1959). For an interesting treatment of American obituaries, see Sigmund Diamond, *The Reputation of the American Businessman* (Cambridge: Harvard University Press, 1955).

19. William Graham Sumner, *What Social Classes Owe to Each Other* (New York: Harper & Bros., 1883), p. 25. For a fuller account of the effects of the Civil War in discrediting sentimental benevolence, see George M. Fredrickson, *The Inner Civil War: Northern Intellectuals and the Crisis of the Union* (New York: Harper & Row, 1965), chap. 7.
20. Recent scholarship has done much to discredit the notion that the millionaires of the Gilded Age were genuinely "self-made," i.e., that they had made their fortunes primarily through their own efforts, rising from relative poverty to great wealth. As it is used in this study, the term "self-made" refers to the mind set of the generation which rose to power and wealth in the decades immediately following the Civil War rather than the financial careers of specific individuals.
21. Andrew Carnegie, *The Gospel of Wealth and Other Timely Essays,* ed. Edward C. Kirkland (Cambridge: Harvard University Press, Belknap Press, 1962), p. 7.
22. Ibid., p. 26.
23. Ibid., p. 31. As Carnegie's biographer points out, "Not knowing failure himself, Carnegie would always be insensitive to the feelings of those who had failed." Joseph Frazier Wall, *Andrew Carnegie* (New York: Oxford University Press, 1970), p. 105.
24. Carnegie, *Gospel of Wealth,* p. 14.
25. Ibid., p. 28.
26. Mrs. Aurelia King, letter dated October 21, 1871, quoted in Paul M. Angle, ed., *The Great Chicago Fire* (Chicago: Chicago Historical Society, 1971), pp. 21–22.
27. Elias Colbert and Everett Chamberlin, *Chicago and the Great Conflagration* (New York: C. F. Vent, 1871), pp. 266–67.
28. Ibid., p. 445. For a list of donations, see Chicago Relief and Aid Society, *Fifteenth Annual Report* (1872).
29. Ezra B. McCagg to Charles Hutchinson, March 17, 1885, p. 2. Charles L. Hutchinson MSS, Box 2, Newberry Library.
30. Marshall Field, *Elements of Success* (Chicago: Lakeside Press, 1896), p. 5.
31. Ibid., pp. 9–10.
32. Stanley Buder, *Pullman: An Experiment in Industrial Order and Community Planning, 1880–1930* (New York: Oxford University Press, 1967).
33. As Carnegie's biographer Joseph Wall points out, many of the men of this generation remained firmly committed to their belief in the openness of the system, even after industrialization began to alter the chances for rapid social mobility. *Andrew Carnegie,* p. 379. This is particularly true of men like Field. See, e.g., his *Elements of Success.*
34. Chicago Relief and Aid Society, *Second Annual Report* (1869), p. 5.
35. Charles G. Trusdell, "The History of Public and Private Outdoor Relief," National Conference of Charities and Correction, *Proceedings of the Twentieth Annual Session* (Chicago, 1893), p. 104.
36. Charles G. Trusdell, "Organized Charities," National Conference of Charities and Correction, *Proceedings of the Twelfth Annual Session* (Washington, D.C., 1885), p. 335.
37. "Report of the Special Committee on Charitable Institutions," Chicago Relief and Aid Society, *Eighteenth Annual Report* (1875), pp. 13–19; and *Report of the Dis-*

*bursement of Contributions for the Sufferers by the Chicago Fire* (Chicago, 1874). The final tallies were: Old People's Home, $63,185; Chicago Home for the Friendless, $47,300; Mercy Hospital, $40,000; St. Joseph's Orphan Asylum, $37,906; Chicago Nursery and Half-Orphan Asylum, $30,615; St. Joseph's Hospital, $30,000; House of the Good Shepherd, $27,000; Deaconesses Hospital, $25,000; Women's and Children's Hospital, $25,000; St. Luke's Hospital, $28,000; Western Seamen's Friend Society, $25,000; Uhlich Orphan Asylum, $21,350; Illinois Charitable Eye and Ear Infirmary, $20,000; Newsboy's and Bootblack's Association, $18,173; Alexian Brothers Hospital, $18,200; Western Seaman's Bethel Union, $15,000; North Star Dispensary, $15,000; Hahnemann Hospital, $15,000; and Chicago Orphan Asylum, $12,050.

38. David Macrae, *The Americans at Home: Pen-and-Ink Sketches of American Men, Manners, and Institutions* (Edinburgh: Edmonston & Douglas, 1870), 2:202.
39. St. Luke's Hospital, *Fourth, Fifth, and Sixth Annual Reports* (1869), pp. 6, 11.
40. St. Luke's Hospital, *Seventh and Eighth Annual Reports, 1869–1871* (1872), p. 7.
41. Chicago Relief and Aid Society, *Report of Disbursement of Contributions*, p. 286.
42. Old People's Home, "Agreement," March 21, 1873, reprinted in *Twenty-ninth Annual Report* (1902), p. 25.
43. Laura Houghteling Reynolds, "Reminiscences of the War of the Rebellion" (typescript MS [1890]), CHS, p. 3. Reynolds, a directress of the CNHOA, vainly traveled to the east in search of subscriptions after the fire.
44. For the CRA and the Jewish Hospital, see Patrick McCallig and Raymon Solomon, "A History of Michael Reese Hospital and Medical Center" (MS, Michael Reese Hospital), p. 11.
45. Lucy Sprague Mitchell, *Two Lives: The Story of Wesley Clair Mitchell and Myself* (New York: Simon & Schuster, 1953), p. 63.
46. Ezra B. McCagg, "The Charities of Chicago," *Proceedings of the Sixth Annual Conference of Charities* (Chicago, 1879), p. 147. On the mob which stormed the CRA, see the *Chicago Tribune*, December 24 and 27, 1873; and W. Alexander Johnson, *Adventures in Social Welfare Being Reminiscences of Things, Thoughts, and Folks during Forty Years of Social Work* (Ft. Wayne, Ind.: n.p., 1923), p. 62.
47. Chicago Relief and Aid Society, *Twenty-seventh Annual Report* (1884), p. 8. (Their emphasis.) For a highly critical report of the merger, see Johnson, *Adventures*, pp. 76–78.

## Chapter 4

1. Isaac N. Arnold, *Address Delivered at the Annual Meeting of the Chicago Historical Society* (Chicago: Fergus Printing Co., 1877), p. 16.
2. For a more complete discussion of these trends, see chapter 2.
3. Jacqueline Peterson, " 'Wild' Chicago: The Formation and Destruction of a Multiracial Community on the Midwestern Frontier, 1816–1837," in *The Ethnic Frontier: Essays on the History of Group Survival in Chicago and the Midwest*, by Melvin G. Holli and Peter d'A. Jones (Grand Rapids, Mich.: William B. Eerdmans Publishing Co., 1977), p. 52.
4. Irvin G. Wyllie, *The Self-Made Man in America: The Myth of Rags to Riches* (Glencoe, Ill.: Free Press, 1954), p. 73.
5. Carl Bode, *The American Lyceum: Town Meeting of the Mind* (Carbondale: Southern Illinois University Press, 1956), p. 32.
6. For a more detailed discussion of these trends, see Bode, *The American Lyceum;*

Sidney Ditzion, *Arsenals of a Democratic Culture: A Social History of the American Library Movement in New England and the Middle States from 1850 to 1900* (Chicago: American Library Association, 1947); Neil Harris, *The Artist in American Society: The Formative Years, 1790–1860* (New York: Simon & Schuster, 1966); Richard C. Wade, *The Urban Frontier: Pioneer Life in Early Pittsburgh, Cincinnati, Lexington, Louisville, and St. Louis* (Chicago: University of Chicago Press, 1959).

7. Colleges have not been included in the following overview, because Chicago's first universities were initiated as sectarian ventures in the 1850s (Northwestern was Methodist, Lake Forest Presbyterian, and the University of Chicago Baptist), and therefore are beyond the scope of this study.
8. A. T. Andreas, *History of Chicago* (Chicago: A. T. Andreas Co., 1885), 2:556.
9. *Biographical Sketches of the Leading Men of Chicago* (Chicago: Wilson & St. Clair, 1868), pp. 32–33.
10. Harlow N. Higinbotham, *The Making of a Merchant* (Chicago: Forbes & Co., 1906), p. 29.
11. Marshall Field, *Elements of Success* (Chicago: Lakeside Press, 1896), pp. 3–4.
12. Chicago Atheneum, *Twelfth Annual Report* (1882), p. 7.
13. Chicago Atheneum, *Fifth Annual Report* (1875–76), p. 7.
14. Chicago Atheneum, *Sixth Annual Report* (1877), p. 6.
15. W. T. Baker, quoted in undated newsclipping, Art Institute *Scrapbook*, Art Institute of Chicago, 1:4.
16. Charles L. Hutchinson, quoted in undated newsclipping, ibid., p. 3.
17. Most (10) of the nineteen officers and founders were businessmen: 2 were lawyers, 2 listed themselves as "capitalists," 1 was a manufacturer, 1 a banker, and 1 a doctor. Data were unavailable for two others.
18. Wayne Andrews, *Battle for Chicago* (New York: Harcourt, Brace & Co., 1946), p. 157.
19. Undated newsclipping (ca. 1899), Charles L. Hutchinson *Scrapbook*, Box 3, Hutchinson MSS, Newberry Library.
20. Charles L. Hutchinson, "Art, Its Influence and Excellence in Modern Times" (lecture delivered before the Art Institute, reprinted in the *Saturday Evening Herald*, March 31, 1888).
21. Diary, May 18, 1890, Hutchinson MSS, Box 1, Newberry Library.
22. *New York Press*, July 4, 1890.
23. Hutchinson, quoted in the *Inter-Ocean*, June 24, 1891.
24. Hutchinson, "Art, Its Influence and Excellence."
25. Hutchinson, "Notebook, with Special Reference to the Art Institute," p. 4, Hutchinson MSS, Newberry Library.
26. For a contrasting interpretation, see Helen Lefkowitz Horowitz, *Culture and the City: Cultural Philanthropy in Chicago from the 1880s to 1917* (Lexington: University of Kentucky Press, 1976), p. 105.
27. Hutchinson, quoted in the *Chicago Herald*, November 20, 1887; and Russell Lynes, *The Tastemakers* (New York: Harper & Bros., 1949), p. 149.
28. Lucy B. Monroe, "Art in Chicago," *New England Magazine*, n.s. 6 (June 1892), p. 416.
29. Art Institute of Chicago, *Annual Report* (1888), p. 8.
30. Hutchinson, quoted in the *Morning News*, October 27, 1888.

31. *Chicago Tribune*, November 27, 1888.
32. Ernest Poole, "Art and Democracy: How the Chicago Art Institute Reaches the People," *Outlook* 85 (March 23, 1907): 666.
33. Undated newsclipping, Art Institute *Scrapbook* 5 (ca. 1895): 33.
34. *Chicago Tribune*, November 26, 1888.
35. *Chicago Chronicle*, May 19, 1896.
36. Charles H. Ham, "Manual Training," *Harper's Magazine* 72 (February 1886): 406.
37. Citizen's Association of Chicago, "Report of the Committee on Education" (Chicago, 1881), pp. 6, 7.
38. For a more detailed discussion of manual training and the breakdown of apprenticeship, see Paul H. Douglas, *American Apprenticeship and Industrial Education* (New York: Columbia University Press, 1921); and Charles A. Bennett, *History of Manual and Industrial Education*, 2 vols. (Peoria: Manual Arts Press, 1926, 1937).
39. Charles H. Ham, *Manual Training: The Solution of Social and Industrial Problems* (New York: Harper & Bros., 1886).
40. Quoted in the *Chicago Tribune*, June 9, 1907.
41. Richard Teller Crane, *The Utility of All Kinds of Higher Schooling* (Chicago: Privately printed, 1909), p. 103. Something of a fanatic in his dislike of higher education, Crane at one point hired a detective to investigate the moral fiber of Ivy League underclassmen and graduates. The results, according to R. T., were "too disgusting to be published" (p. 128).
42. *Chicago Tribune*, June 9, 1907.
43. Chicago Manual Training School, *Fifth Annual Catalog* (1887–88), p. 8.
44. Ham, "Manual Training," p. 409.
45. Chicago Manual Training School, *Souvenir* (1893).
46. "Richard Teller Crane: A Real Friend of Education," *Valve World* 8 (April 1912): 21.
47. Crane, *Utility*, p. 258.
48. Pullman's will stated that he disinherited the boys because "neither of my sons has developed such a sense of responsibility as in my judgement is requisite for the wise use of large properties and considerable sums of money." *New York Journal*, October 26, 1897. Crane also disinherited one of his sons for being a wastrel and too much of a playboy.
49. Quoted in the *Dictionary of American Biography* (New York: Charles Scribner's Sons, 1929), 1:349.
50. Harper Leech and John Charles Carroll, *Armour and His Times* (New York: D. Appleton-Century Co., 1938), p. 211.
51. *Chicago Tribune*, December 13, 1892. Armour, with his straightforward, sometimes profane manner, and the cultured, flowerly Reverend Gunsaulus made a strange pair. Except when fighting for fiscal measures, Gunsaulus tried to manage his brusque mentor with praise and flattery. In one instance he wrote to Armour (one assumes with no sense of irony): "I rejoice that nothing has been done in this Institution which places it below anything else which has the Armour brand upon it. I would hate to be connected with an institution founded upon the Armour Star Ham and the Armour Bacon which was not just as good in its way as these are" (undated letter, Armour Institute of Technology MSS, John Crerar Library, Illinois Institute of Technology).
52. P. D. Armour, quoted in Andrews, *Battle for Chicago*, p. 194. Armour had a natural

affinity for the concepts embodied in manual training programs. As he explained, "I have always had a great respect for facts. If there were fewer theorists in the world, there would be more success." Ibid., pp. 87–88.

53. Frank W. Gunsaulus, "Armour Institute," pamphlet in the Armour Institute of Technology MSS, Crerar Library, Illinois Institute of Technology.
54. Clifford L. Snowden, "The Armour Institute of Technology," *New England Magazine,* n.s. 16 (May 1897), p. 369.
55. P. D. Armour to Frank W. Gunsaulus, December 5, 1893, Armour Institute of Technology MSS.
56. *Chicago Tribune,* October 15, 1893.

## Chapter 5

1. The "progressive" civic stewards were not necessarily Progressive reformers (although many were). I have used the uncapitalized "progressive" to indicate those who espoused the newer philanthropic and charitable ideals.
2. "The Justification of Wealth," *Nation* 70 (January 25, 1900): 66.
3. Quoted in Ray Ginger, *Altgeld's America: The Lincoln Ideal versus Changing Realities* (Chicago: Quadrangle Paperbacks, 1958), p. 149. For a fuller account of the town and the strike, see Stanley Buder, *Pullman: An Experiment in Industrial Order and Community Planning, 1880–1930* (New York: Oxford University Press, 1967); and Almont Lindsey, *The Pullman Strike* (Chicago: University of Chicago Press, 1942).
4. Jane Addams, "A Modern Lear," *Survey* 29 (November 2, 1912): 131–37, reprinted in Christopher Lasch, ed., *The Social Thought of Jane Addams* (Indianapolis: Bobbs-Merrill Co., 1965), p. 111.
5. Ibid., p. 113.
6. Ibid., pp. 112–13.
7. Ibid., p. 112.
8. Ibid., p. 118.
9. Ibid., p. 119.
10. Ibid., p. 107.
11. Jane Addams, *Democracy and Social Ethics* (New York: Macmillan Co., 1902), pp. 14–15.
12. Ignatius Donnelly, *Caesar's Column: A Story of the Twentieth Century* (Cambridge: Harvard University Press, Belknap Press, 1960), p. 104 (originally published 1890).
13. Jane Addams, "Child Labor and Pauperism," *Charities* 11 (October 3, 1903): 302.
14. William T. Stead, *If Christ Came to Chicago!* (Chicago: Laird & Lee, 1894), p. 75.
15. Ibid., p. 90.
16. *Chicago Tribune,* January 16, 1905.
17. Rev. Harry C. Vrooman, "Charity, Old and New," *Arena* 11 (January 1895): 274.
18. Edward Alsworth Ross, "Philanthropy with Strings," *Atlantic Monthly* 114 (September 1914): 290.
19. Stead, *If Christ Came to Chicago!* p. 83.
20. Addams, *Democracy,* p. 160.
21. William H. Allen, "Efficiency in Making Bequests," *Atlantic Monthly* 99 (March 1907): 329.
22. G. W. Alger, "Generosity and Corruption," *Atlantic Monthly* 95 (June 1905): 783;

Vida D. Scudder, "Ill-Gotten Gifts to Colleges," *Atlantic Monthly* 86 (November 1900): 675.

23. Graham Taylor, "Shall the Dollar's Pedigree Defeat Its Destiny?" *American Review of Reviews* 32 (October 1905): 472.
24. "Tainted Money," *Independent* 58 (April 6, 1905): 790.
25. Quoted in J. G. A. Pocock, "Machiavelli, Harrington, and English Political Ideologies in the Eighteenth Century," *William and Mary Quarterly* 23, no. 4 (October 1965): 555.
26. Thomas Jefferson, *Papers,* ed. Julia Boyd (Princeton: Princeton University Press, 1950), 8:426.
27. Edmund Morgan, *American Slavery, American Freedom: The Ordeal of Colonial Virginia* (New York: W. W. Norton & Co., 1975), p. 383.
28. Ralph Waldo Emerson, "Self Reliance," in *The Literature of the United States,* ed. Walter Blair (Glenview, Ill.: Scott, Foresman & Co., 1969), 1:403.
29. Henry David Thoreau, quoted in Robert H. Bremner, *American Philanthropy* (Chicago: University of Chicago Press, 1960), p. 44.
30. Ralph Waldo Emerson, "Gifts," in *Essays and English Traits* (New York: P. F. Collier & Sons Corp., 1937), p. 222.
31. John Clark Ridpath, "The Cry of the Poor," *Arena* 18 (September 1897): 408.
32. Bolton Hall, "Giving and Getting," *Forum* 42 (November 1909): 457.
33. John G. Brooks, "The Future Problem of Charity and the Unemployed," *Annals of the American Academy of Political and Social Science* 5 (June 1894): 15; Ross, "Philanthropy with Strings," p. 294.
34. Josephine Shaw Lowell, "The True Aim of Charity Organization Societies," *Forum* 21 (June 1896): 499.
35. Francis G. Peabody, "How Should a City Care for Its Poor?" *Forum* 14 (December 1892): 490.
36. "The Failure of Philanthropy," *Living Age* 209 (April 25, 1896): 232.
37. Charles Brodie Patterson, "Organized Charity," *Arena* 25 (March 1901): 281.
38. Florence Kelley, "Socialism and Charity," *Charities* 18 (July 6, 1907): 398.
39. Emil O. Hirsch, "The Place of the Individual in Organized Charity," in *First National Conference of Jewish Charities* (Chicago, 1900), pp. 146–47.
40. Jane Addams, *Twenty Years at Hull-House* (New York: New American Library, 1960), p. 94 (originally published 1910).
41. Ibid., p. 68. The literature on Addams is voluminous. In addition to her autobiography, some of the better studies include: Allen F. Davis, *American Heroine: The Life and Legend of Jane Addams* (New York: Oxford University Press, 1973); James Weber Linn, *Jane Addams: A Biography* (New York: D. Appleton-Century Co., 1935); and John C. Farrell, *Beloved Lady: A History of Jane Addams' Ideas on Reform and Peace* (Baltimore: Johns Hopkins Press, 1967).
42. Perry Duis, *Chicago: Creating New Traditions* (Chicago: Chicago Historical Society, 1976), p. 61.
43. Addams, *Twenty Years,* p. 74.
44. Ibid., p. 213.
45. Madame Blanc, *The Condition of Women in the United States* (Boston: Roberts Bros., 1895), p. 75.
46. Julius Rosenwald, "The Burden of Wealth," *Saturday Evening Post* 201 (January 5, 1929): 12.

47. Ibid., p. 13.
48. Julius Rosenwald, "Undated Speech to the American Jewish Committee," Rosenwald MSS, University of Chicago, Box 5, folder 5.
49. Julius Rosenwald, "Charity," *Harpers Weekly* 60 (May 29, 1915): 522.
50. M. R. Werner, *Julius Rosenwald: The Life of a Practical Humanitarian* (New York: Harper & Row, 1939), p. 106.
51. Rosenwald, "Burden," p. 12.
52. Julius Rosenwald, untitled speech (May 20, 1912), Rosenwald MSS, University of Chicago, Box 34, folder 6.
53. Louise de Koven Bowen, *Growing Up with a City* (New York: Macmillan Co., 1926), pp. 51–52.
54. Ibid., pp. 92–93.
55. Charles L. Hutchinson, "Art: Its Influence and Excellence in Modern Times" (lecture delivered before the Art Institute, reprinted in the *Saturday Evening Herald*, March 31, 1888).
56. Civic Music Association, "Objects," in *Financial Statement for Year Ending May 4, 1915*.
57. Letter, William H. Rehm to James B. Forgan, July 24, 1916, in Civic Music Association File, Incoming Materials, Horace S. Oakley MSS, Newberry Library.
58. *Success Magazine* 5 (November 1902): 643.
59. Nettie Fowler McCormick, *Daily Journal*, January 31, 1862, Nettie Fowler McCormick Papers, State Historical Society of Wisconsin, Madison.
60. Charles O. Burgess, *Nettie Fowler McCormick: Profile of an American Philanthropist* (Madison: State Historical Society of Wisconsin, 1962), p. 41. For a fuller discussion of "family images," see Robert D. Hess and Gerald Handel, *Family Worlds: A Psychological Approach to Family Life* (Chicago: University of Chicago Press, 1959).
61. "Notes by Nettie Fowler McCormick, 1899," in Anita McCormick Blaine MSS, State Historical Society of Wisconsin.
62. Anita McCormick Blaine to Harriot Hammond, February 28, 1888, quoted in William Bruce White, "The Philanthropies of Anita McCormick Blaine" (Master's thesis, University of Wisconsin, 1959), p. 9.
63. Blaine to Mrs. James G. Blaine, August 29, 1892, ibid., p. 13.
64. Note, dated November 22, 1892, Blaine MSS.
65. Anita McCormick Blaine, "A Dissertation on the Disadvantages of Being a School Girl," *Notebook* (May 21, 1881), ibid., p. 85.
66. Ibid., pp. 86–87.
67. Ibid., p. 83.
68. "Ten Ways of Showing Selfishness," ibid., November 28, 1882, pp. 128–29.
69. MSS, October 30, 1882, quoted in White, "Anita McCormick Blaine," pp. 24–25.
70. Colonel Francis Parker to Anita McCormick Blaine, June 29, 1898, Blaine MSS.
71. Anita McCormick Blaine, "The Ideals Which Led to the Founding of the School of Education," *Elementary School Teacher* 14 (October 10, 1913): 80.
72. Blaine to Emmons Blaine, Jr., September 20, 1911, Blaine MSS; interview with Gilbert Harrison, December 1, 1976. Mr. Harrison is Mrs. Blaine's grandson-in-law. For a more detailed account of Blaine's career, see Gilbert Harrison, *A Timeless Affair: The Life of Anita McCormick Blaine* (Chicago: University of Chicago Press, 1979).

73. Mary Prentice Lillie Barrows, *Moon Out of the Well: Reminiscences* (Privately printed, 1970), p. 113.
74. Lucy Sprague Mitchell, *Two Lives: The Story of Wesley Clair Mitchell and Myself* (New York: Simon & Schuster, 1953), p. 61.
75. Quoted in "The Multimillionaires of Chicago," *Chicago Tribune*, June 9, 1907.
76. Quoted in *Chicago Tribune*, December 29, 1907.
77. Ibid.
78. Richard Teller Crane to Charles R. Crane and Richard Teller Crane, Jr. Letter appended to Crane's Last Will and Testament, dated January 6, 1908, reprinted in Barrows, *Moon*, pp. 125–26. Crane died in 1912.
79. Mary Prentice Lillie Barrows, "Charles R. Crane (1858–1939)" (unpublished MS in Crane Family MSS, CHS), p. 20.
80. Mary Prentice Lillie Barrows, *Frances Crane Lillie (1869–1958): A Memoir* (Privately printed, n.d.), p. 5.
81. John B. Berryman, *An Old Man Looks Back* (Chicago: Privately printed, 1943), p. 45.
82. *Dictionary of American Biography* (New York: Charles Scribner's Sons, 1958), suppl. 2, p. 129. The entire Crane family is fascinating. One sister became a doctor, befriended Jane Addams and Ellen Gates Starr, was arrested for picketing during the International Ladies' Garment Workers' Strike in 1915, and was publicly denounced as a Socialist. Later, she married Frank Lillie, dean of biological sciences at the University of Chicago, and at the end of her life embraced Catholicism, much to her family's horror. Another sister embraced anarchism, while a third moved to Paris, befriended Gertrude Stein and Albert Einstein, and became a major contributor to Chicago's cultural institutions. Charles's daughter married the son of Thomas Masaryk, the president of Czechoslovakia, and his son, a former Hull-House resident who funded W. Lloyd Warner's *Yankee City* studies, served as the first United States minister to Czechoslovakia.
83. One can only imagine what R. T.'s response to the Wood's Hole project would have been, since "the research fad" was one of his pet peeves, "the acme of all the great hobbies of the higher educators." Richard Teller Crane, *The Utility of All Kinds of Higher Schooling* (Chicago: Privately printed, 1909), p. 227.
84. Barrows, *Moon*, p. 123.
85. Harold Ickes, *The Autobiography of a Curmudgeon* (Chicago: Quadrangle Paperbacks, 1943), p. 122.
86. Edwin F. Hirsch, *Frank Billings* (Chicago: Edwin F. Hirsch, 1966), p. 101. Although Hirsch tells the anecdote about "Richard" Crane, my own research leads me to believe that Billings's story was about Charles Richard Crane, rather than Richard Teller Crane, Jr. Dick Crane, as he was known to his friends, was the most conservative member of the family, taking up the presidency of the family business after it was abandoned by his elder brother. As rigidly dedicated to the company as he was opposed to unionization and strikes, he was not given to fits of impulsive generosity, and such a gesture would probably have been out of character for him.

## Chapter 6

1. "Letter from the President of the United States Embodying the Conclusions of the Conference on the Care of Dependent Children (1909)," *Proceedings of the Con-*

*ference on the Care of Dependent Children* (Washington, D.C.: Government Printing Office, 1909), p. 9.

2. For a fuller discussion of the American family, see Arthur W. Calhoun, *A Social History of the American Family from Colonial Times to the Present*, 3 vols. (Cleveland: Arthur H. Clark Co., 1919); and David M. Kennedy, *Birth Control in America* (New Haven: Yale University Press, 1970), chapter 2.
3. Steven L. Schlossman, *Love and the American Delinquent: The Theory and Practice of "Progressive" Juvenile Justice, 1825–1920* (Chicago: University of Chicago Press, 1977), p. 190.
4. *The Child in the City: A Handbook of the Child Welfare Exhibit* (Chicago: Chicago School of Civics and Philanthropy, 1911), back cover.
5. "Help Save the Babies," Infant Welfare Society flyer (1914), in Infant Welfare Society MSS, CHS, Box 4.
6. Herbert Hoover, quoted in IWS pamphlet (ca. 1919), ibid.
7. United Charities, *Annual Report* (1910), p. 22.
8. Ibid., p. 24.
9. Elizabeth McCormick Memorial Fund, notes from meeting held February 1, 1912, pp. 4–5, Harriet Hammond McCormick MSS, State Historical Society of Wisconsin.
10. Infant Welfare Society, "Hold the Home Lines" (1918), p. 3.
11. Jane Addams, *Twenty Years at Hull-House* (New York: New American Library, 1960), p. 121.
12. Chicago Relief and Aid Society, *Forty-ninth Annual Report* (1906), p. 7.
13. United Charities, *Annual Report* (1910), pp. 10, 12, 13, 14.
14. Louise de Koven Bowen, *Growing Up with a City* (New York: Macmillan Co., 1926), p. 80.
15. United Charities, *Annual Report* (1915–16), p. 21.
16. Marian C. Putnam, "Friendly Visiting," National Conference of Charities and Correction, *Proceedings of the Fourteenth Annual Session* (Boston, 1887), p. 149.
17. Josephine Shaw Lowell, *Public Relief and Private Charity* (New York: G. P. Putnam's Sons, 1884), p. 100.
18. Bowen, *Growing Up*, pp. 69, 70. For an excellent discussion of participants and their motives, see Kenneth L. Kusmer, "The Functions of Organized Charity in the Progressive Era: Chicago as a Case Study," *Journal of American History* 60 (December 1973): 657–78.
19. Lowell, *Public Relief*, p. 94.
20. Sophonisba P. Breckenridge, "The Care of Needy Families in Their Homes," *Studies in Chicago Philanthropy* 1, no. 3 (n.d.): 3.
21. Bowen, *Growing Up*, p. 58.
22. Visiting Nurse Association (hereafter cited as VNA), *Third Annual Report* (1892), p. 7.
23. Edna L. Foley, "The Nurse's First Visit," *Public Health Nurse* (April 26, 1929), p. 5, in VNA MSS, Box 2, CHS.
24. VNA, *Fifteenth Annual Report* (1905), p. 17.
25. VNA, *Twenty-third Annual Report* (1912), p. 40.
26. VNA, *Sixth Annual Report* (1896), p. 19.
27. Harriet Fulmer, "The Work of the District or Visiting Nurse," National Conference of Charities and Correction (hereafter cited as NCCC), *Proceedings of the Twenty-ninth Annual Session* (Detroit, 1902), p. 201.
28. VNA, *Seventh Annual Report* (1897), p. 18.

29. VNA, *Third Annual Report* (1892), p. 13.
30. Child Welfare Exhibit, *Handbook* (Chicago, 1911), p. 57.
31. VNA, *Second Annual Report* (1891), p. 13.
32. Mary Aldis, "President's Report," VNA, *Twenty-third Annual Report* (1912), p. 11.
33. VNA, *Twenty-first Annual Report* (1910), p. 38.
34. Fulmer, "The Work of the . . . Visiting Nurse," p. 202.
35. Letter, Edna L. Foley to Mrs. Joseph M. Cudahy, March 14, 1925, VNA MSS, CHS, Box 2.
36. "The Affiliation of Training Schools with Public Health Nursing Organizations," p. 2 (May 9, 1924), VNA MSS, Box 2.
37. National Association of Social Workers, *Executive Committee Minutes* (March 18, 1929), p. 2. National Association of Social Workers MSS, Box 20, CHS.
38. United Charities, *Annual Report* (1913), p. 33.
39. Chicago Institute of Social Science, untitled pamphlet (1907), p. 5.
40. Chicago Council of Social Agencies Minutes, June 18, 1915, p. 3, Welfare Council of Metropolitan Chicago (WCMC) MSS, CHS, Box 4.
41. Charter, April 7, 1919, ibid., Box 4.
42. Illinois General Assembly, *Report of the Illinois General Assembly Joint Committee on Home-Finding* (Springfield, 1915), p. 113.
43. Hastings Hart, *Preventive Treatment of Neglected Children* (New York: Russell Sage Foundation, 1910), p. 237.
44. Roy Lubove, *The Professional Altruist: The Emergence of Social Work as a Career, 1880–1930* (Cambridge: Harvard University Press, 1965).
45. Julius Rosenwald, "The Burden of Wealth," *Saturday Evening Post* 201 (January 5, 1929): 13.
46. R. R. Reeder, "Institutionalism," *Charities* 11 (July 4, 1903): 7.
47. Judge Pinkney, quoted in Illinois General Assembly, *Report*, p. 26.
48. Minnie Low, quoted in the *Chicago Tribune*, January 22, 1905.
49. Illinois General Assembly, *Report*, p. 71.
50. Reeder, "Institutionalism," p. 8.
51. Chicago Orphan Asylum president, Mrs. Bennett Botsford, quoted in Clare L. McCausland, *Children of Circumstance: A History of the First 125 Years (1849–1974) of the Chicago Child Care Society* (Chicago: R. R. Donnelley & Sons Co., 1976), p. 96.
52. Mrs. W. B. Burr, quoted in Ruth Orton Camp, "The Chicago Orphan Asylum, 1849–1949" (unpublished MS, CHS), p. 118.
53. Chicago Orphan Asylum, *Seventy-ninth Annual Report* (1928), p. 10. See also, McCausland, *Children of Circumstance*, pp. 121–22; and Charolette Ashley Crawley, "Dependent Negro Children in Chicago in 1926" (Master's thesis, University of Chicago, 1927).
54. Chicago Orphan Asylum, *Eighty-second Annual Report* (1931), p. 15.
55. CHFF, *Forty-sixth Annual Report* (1904), p. 24.
56. CHFF, *Forty-first Annual Report* (1899), p. 23.
57. CHFF, *Forty-fifth Annual Report* (1903), p. 14.
58. Letter from boy sent to South Dakota farm in 1896, dated August 11, 1902, quoted in Ruth Ann Sayre, "A Study of the Changes in Structure and Function of the Board of Managers of the Chicago Home for the Friendless, 1858–1933" (Master's thesis, University of Chicago, 1945), p. 88.
59. Ibid., p. 114.

60. CHFF, *Seventy-first Annual Report* (1929), p. 14.
61. CHFF, *Seventy-fourth Annual Report* (1932), p. 25.
62. CHFF, *Seventy-third Annual Report* (1931), p. 10.
63. "A Plan for the Re-organization of the Service of the Chicago Home for the Friendless," March 10, 1930, p. 2, Welfare Council of Metropolitan Chicago MSS, CHS, Box 281.
64. CHFF, *Seventy-third Annual Report* (1931), p. 25.
65. Isabel M. Devine, "Report of Study of the Chicago Nursery and Half-Orphan Asylum," November 1, 1935, "Recommendations," p. 4, Welfare Council of Metropolitan Chicago MSS, CHS, Box 259.
66. Clarence King, *Social Agency Boards and How to Make them Effective* (New York: Harper & Bros., 1938), p. 21.
67. Ibid., p. 12.
68. CHFF, *Seventy-eighth Annual Report* (1936), p. 6.
69. CHFF, *Minutes*, January 21, 1935, p. 237, Child and Family Services, Chicago.
70. Ibid., January 13, 1936, p. 254.
71. Homer Folks, "Prevention Succeeds," presidential address, National Conference of Social Work, *Proceedings of the Fiftieth Annual Session* (Washington, D.C., 1923), p. 5.

## Chapter 7

1. Henry Blake Fuller, *With the Procession* (New York: Harper & Bros., 1895), p. 114.
2. Algernon Tassin, "The Craftsmanship of Begging Letter Writing," *Bookman* 36 (November–December 1912): 247; "The Gentle Art of Giving," *Current Literature* 34 (February 1903): 131; "The Benefactions of the Year," *World's Work* 12 (August 1906): 7816; "Billions for Practical Piety," *Literary Digest* 100 (January 26, 1929): 28.
3. Tabulations in Chicago Community Trust MSS, CHS, Box 5.
4. The figures in this and the ensuing paragraphs were compiled from a wide variety of charitable and cultural organizations using annual reports, MSS collections, histories, biographies, and additional information culled from the Community Trust papers. All donors of $5,000 or more were included. Although citywide nonsectarian agencies like the YMCA were included, churches and theological seminaries were not. Because the number of organizations varied from year to year, depending on the availability of their records, some gifts may have been overlooked. These figures, therefore, merely represent the *minimum* donated in each category.
5. Walter L. Newberry died in 1868, but due to contingencies in his will the money did not become available until after the deaths of his daughters, in 1874 and 1876, and his wife in 1885.
6. The number of donors listed in individual groupings may not add up to the totals, since some gave in more than one category.
7. These figures do not include donations to religious or ethnic organizations.
8. Julius Rosenwald's gifts are listed three times—in culture, education, and under foundations.
9. Dedicatory speech (1896), quoted in Thomas Wakefield Goodspeed, *The University of Chicago Biographical Sketches* (Chicago: University of Chicago Press, 1925), 2:97.
10. Quoted in Charles H. Dennis, *Victor Lawson: His Time and His Work* (Chicago: University of Chicago Press, 1935), p. 67.

11. Edward E. Ayer, "The Museum's First Million," Field Museum of Natural History *Bulletin* 41, no. 8 (August 1970): 13. Added to this, of course, was the attractive prospect of being permanently immortalized in brick and stone. As Ayer was quick to point out, "You can sell dry goods until Hell freezes over" and still be forgotten within a generation (p. 14).
12. Henry Justin Smith, "Chicago: Her Plans and Growing Pains," *Century Magazine* 113 (March 1927): 612.
13. Louise de Koven Bowen to Anita McCormick Blaine, November 21, 1922, Anita McCormick Blaine MSS, State Historical Society of Wisconsin.
14. Ibid., October 6, 1922.
15. Julius Rosenwald, "Speech before the Advertising Association of Chicago (concerning) United Charities," October 30, 1913, p. 1, Julius Rosenwald MSS, University of Chicago, Box 34, folder 6.
16. Mrs. Cornelius Stevenson, "The Training of Curators," American Association of Museums, *Proceedings* 3 (1909): 118–19.
17. Laurence Vail Coleman, *The Museum in America: A Critical Study* (Washington, D.C.: American Association of Museums, 1939), 2:391.
18. Undated MS, p. 6, Edward E. Ayer MSS, Newberry Library, Box 3, folder 1.
19. Thomas Wakefield Goodspeed, *A History of the University of Chicago: The First Quarter-Century* (Chicago: University of Chicago Press, 1972), p. 69 (originally published 1916).
20. Frederick Taylor Gates, *Chapters in My Life* (New York: Free Press, 1977), p. 114.
21. Frederick Taylor Gates, "Rules of Procedure" in Correspondence of the Founder, University of Chicago MSS, cited in James Howell Smith, "Honorable Beggars: The Middlemen of American Philanthropy" (Ph.D. diss., University of Wisconsin, 1968), pp. 256 ff.
22. Goodspeed, *University of Chicago*, p. 72.
23. [Edgar J. Goodspeed], "Suggestions for a Plan of Finance Campaign, 1924," p. 1, in Harold Swift MSS, University of Chicago, Box 73. For an excellent history of the professionalization of fund raising, see Scott M. Cutlip, *Fund Raising in the United States: Its Role in America's Philanthropy* (New Brunswick, N.J.: Rutgers University Press, 1965).
24. John Price Jones, "Program of Publicity" (August 28, 1925), p. 4, in Harold Swift MSS, University of Chicago, Box 73.
25. John Price Jones, "A Survey and Fund Raising Plan for the University of Chicago" (March 8, 1924), p. 97, Swift MSS, University of Chicago, Box 73.
26. Jones, "Program of Publicity," p. 18.
27. John Price Jones to Harold Swift, January 27, 1925, Swift MSS, University of Chicago, Box 73.
28. H. A. Overstreet, "A Quarter-Century of Psychology," *Century Magazine* 113 (March 1927): 526.
29. Lucille C. Birnbaum, "Behaviorism in the 1920's," *American Quarterly* 7 (Spring 1955): 15–30; Stuart Ewen, *Captains of Consciousness: Advertising and the Social Roots of Consumer Culture* (New York: McGraw-Hill Book Co., 1976).
30. R. F. Duncan, "Special Gifts Procedure," December 11, 1924, Swift MSS, Box 75.
31. Undated, untitled memo, Swift MSS, Box 102.
32. Undated letter, Harold Swift to President Max Mason, Swift MSS, Box 102.
33. "Appendix to a Memorandum for the Information of the Trustees of the University" (July 1924), prepared by Kixmiller and Baar (tax attorneys), Swift MSS, Box 112.

34. Jones, "Survey," p. 6.
35. Otto L. Schmidt to President Ernest D. Burton, April 15, 1924, Swift MSS, Box 112.
36. Jones, "Survey," p. 48.
37. Ibid., p. 65.
38. Harold Swift to James H. Tufts, January 25, 1924, Swift MSS, Box 74.
39. Abraham Flexner, *An Autobiography*, rev. ed. (New York: Simon & Schuster, 1960), p. 175.
40. William Rainey Harper, quoted in Howard S. Miller, *Dollars for Research: Science and Its Patrons in Nineteenth-Century America* (Seattle: University of Washington Press, 1970), p. 184.
41. Harriet Fulmer, "The Work of the District or Visiting Nurse," National Conference of Charities and Correction, *Proceedings of the Twenty-ninth Annual Session* (Detroit, 1902), p. 203.
42. Silas Bent, "If I Had All That Money," *Century Magazine* 114 (September 1927): 548.
43. Quoted in Edward F. Williams, *The Life of Dr. D. K. Pearsons: The Friend of the Small College and of Missions* (Chicago: Pilgrim Press, 1911), p. 82.
44. Ibid., p. 302.
45. Lucy Sprague Mitchell, *Two Lives: The Story of Wesley Clair Mitchell and Myself* (New York: Simon & Schuster, 1953), p. 72.
46. Quoted in M. R. Werner, *Julius Rosenwald: The Life of a Practical Humanitarian* (New York: Harper & Bros., 1939), p. 333.
47. Julius Rosenwald, "The Burden of Wealth," *Saturday Evening Post* 201 (January 5, 1929): 13.
48. Louise de Koven Bowen, *Growing Up with a City* (New York: Macmillan Co., 1926), pp. 87–88.
49. Jane Addams, "The Subtle Problems of Charity," *Atlantic Monthly* 83 (February 1899): 163.
50. United Charities, *Annual Report* (1911), p. 19.
51. Frank D. Watson, *The Charity Organization Movement in the United States: A Study in American Philanthropy* (New York: Macmillan Co., 1922), p. 339.
52. Clarence Elmer Glick, "Winnetka: A Study of a Residential Suburban Community" (Master's thesis, University of Chicago, 1928), p. 210.
53. Ibid.
54. Ibid., p. 209.
55. Arthur Meeker, *Chicago with Love* (New York: Alfred A. Knopf, 1955), pp. 65, 66.
56. FBO Pictures, 1928.
57. Carlos Productions, 1925.
58. Astor Pictures, 1925.
59. Hunt Stromberg Productions, 1921.
60. Harvey W. Zorbaugh, *The Gold Coast and the Slum: A Sociological Study of Chicago's Near North Side* (Chicago: University of Chicago Press, 1929).
61. "Solidarity," p. 4. Harvey Zorbaugh Files, Ernest W. Burgess MSS, University of Chicago, Box 139, folder 7.
62. Ibid., p. 7.
63. "The Gold Coast Woman," p. 4, Zorbaugh Files, Burgess MSS, Box 140, folder 1.
64. Cyrus H. McCormick, Jr., to Katharine Ludington, March 10, 1936, quoted in James Harold Stuckey, "The Philanthropy of Cyrus Hall McCormick, II" (Master's thesis, University of Wisconsin, 1955), p. 104.

## Chapter 8

1. Allan Herrick, *You Don't Have to Be Rich* (New York: D. Appleton-Century Co., 1940), pp. 201–2.
2. Samuel Insull, "Civic Leadership Development and Responsibility" (St. Louis: Privately printed, 1927), pp. 3–4.
3. Edward L. Ryerson, *A Businessman's Concept of Citizenship* (Privately printed, 1960), n.p.

# SELECTED BIBLIOGRAPHY

## Primary Sources


Addams, Jane. "Child Labor and Pauperism." *Charities* 11 (October 3, 1903): 300–304.

———. *Democracy and Social Ethics.* New York: Macmillan Co., 1902.

———. "The Subtle Problems of Charity." *Atlantic Monthly* 83 (February 1899): 163–78.

———. *Twenty Years at Hull-House.* New York: New American Library, Inc., 1960. Orginally published in 1910.

———. MSS. Archives. Hull-House.

Alcott, Dr. William A. *The Gift Book for Young Ladies.* Buffalo: George H. Derby & Co., 1852.

Alger, G. W. "Generosity and Corruption." *Atlantic Monthly* 95 (June 1905): 781–84.

Allen, William H. "Efficiency in Making Requests." *Atlantic Monthly* 99 (March 1907): 328–35.

Anderson, Mrs. Galusha. *The Story of Aunt Lizzie Aiken.* Chicago: Jensen, McClurg & Co., 1880.

Andreas, A. T. *History of Chicago.* 3 vols. Chicago: A. T. Andreas Co., 1885.

Armour Institute of Technology MSS. John Crerar Library, Illinois Institute of Technology.

Arnold, Isaac N. "Address Delivered at the Annual Meeting of the Chicago Historical Society." Chicago: Fergus Printing Co., 1877.

———. "William B. Ogden and Early Days in Chicago." Paper read at the Chicago Historical Society, December 20, 1881. Chicago: Fergus Printing Co., 1882.

Art Institute of Chicago. *Annual Reports.*

———. *Bulletins.*

———. Scrapbooks. Ryerson Library, Art Institute of Chicago.

Atwater, Mrs. Elizabeth E., comp. "Scrapbook of Clippings from the Centennial." Chicago Historical Society.

Ayer, Edward E. MSS, Newberry Library.

———. "The Museum's First Million." Field Museum of Natural History. *Bulletin* 41, no. 8 (August 1970): 13–15.

Barrows, Mary Prentice Lillie. "Charles R. Crane (1858–1939)." Crane Family MSS, Chicago Historical Society.

———. *Frances Crane Lillie (1869–1958): A Memoir.* Privately printed.

———. *Moon Out of the Well: Reminiscences.* Privately printed, 1970.
Bartlett, Mary K. "The Philanthropic Work of the Chicago Women's Club." *Outlook* 49 (May 12, 1894): 827–28.
Beecher, Catharine. *A Treatise on Domestic Economy.* New York: Marsh, Capen, Lyon & Webb, 1841.
Beecher, Henry Ward. *Lectures to Young Men.* New York: J. B. Ford & Co., 1873.
"The Benefactions of the Year." *World's Work* 12 (August 1906): 7816–17.
Bent, Silas. "If I Had All That Money." *Century Magazine* 114 (September 1927): 549–55.
Berryman, John B. *An Old Man Looks Back.* Chicago: Privately printed, 1943.
Bethune, Joanna. *The Power of Faith, Exemplified in the Life and Writings of the Late Mrs. Isabella M. Graham.* New York: American Tract Society, 1843.
"Billions for Practical Piety." *Literary Digest* 100 (January 26, 1929): 28.
*Biographical Sketches of the Leading Men of Chicago.* Chicago: Wilson & St. Clair, 1868.
Blaine, Anita McCormick. "The Ideals Which Led to the Founding of the School of Education." *Elementary School Teacher* 14 (September–October 1913): 11–19, 73–81.
———. MSS. State Historical Society of Wisconsin, Madison.
Blanc, Madame. *The Condition of Women in the United States.* Boston: Roberts Bros., 1895.
Blatchford, Eliphalet W. MSS. Archives. Newberry Library.
*Blockade.* FBO Pictures, 1928.
Bowen, Louise de Koven. *Growing Up with a City.* New York: Macmillan Co., 1926.
———. *Scrapbooks.* 4 vols. Chicago Historical Society.
Breckenridge, Sophonisba P. "The Care of Needy Families in Their Homes." *Studies in Chicago Philanthropy* 1, no. 3 (n.d.): 3.
Brooks, John G. "The Future Problem of Charity and the Unemployed." *Annals of the American Academy of Political and Social Science* 5 (June 1894): 1–27.
Burgess, Ernest W. MSS. Archives. University of Chicago.
Calhoun, Arthur W. *A Social History of the American Family from Colonial Times to the Present.* Vols. 2 and 3. Cleveland: Arthur H. Clark Co., 1918–1919.
Camp, Ruth Orton. "The Chicago Orphan Asylum, 1849–1949." MS. Chicago Historical Society.
Carnegie, Andrew. *The Gospel of Wealth and Other Timely Essays.* Edited by Edward C. Kirkland. Cambridge: Harvard University Press, Belknap Press, 1962.
———. "Wealth." *North American Review* 148 (June 1889): 653–64, and 149 (December 1889): 682–98.
"Catalogue of Paintings, Statuary, Etc. in the Art Department of the Great Northwestern Sanitary Fair." Chicago, June 1865.
Census Report. 1850 Census Population Schedules, Illinois.
———. Eighth Census, 1860. City of Chicago.
———. Ninth Census, 1870. City of Chicago.
———. Tenth Census, 1880. City of Chicago.
Central Relief Association. *Annual Reports.*
Charity Organization Society of Chicago. *Annual Reports.*
Chatfield-Taylor, Hobart. *Cities of Many Men.* Boston: Houghton Mifflin Co., 1925.
Chicago Academy of Sciences. "Historical Sketch, Act of Incorporation, Constitution and By-Laws, Officers and Members." Chicago, 1877.

Chicago Atheneum. *Annual Reports.*
Chicago Bible Society. *Annual Reports.*
———. Minutes. Archives. Chicago Historical Society.
Chicago Bureau of Charities. *Annual Reports.*
Chicago Eye and Ear Infirmary. *Annual Reports.*
Chicago Commons. MSS. Archives. Chicago Historical Society.
Chicago Community Trust. MSS. Archives. Chicago Historical Society.
———. Scrapbook. Vol. 1. Chicago Historical Society.
Chicago Exhibition of the Fine Arts. *Catalog.* Chicago: Press & Tribune Co., 1859.
Chicago Foundling's Home. *Annual Reports.*
Chicago Historical Society. MSS. Archives. Chicago Historical Society.
Chicago Home for the Friendless. *Annual Reports.*
———. Minutes. Child and Family Services. Chicago.
Chicago Home for Incurables. *Annual Reports.*
Chicago Hospital for Women and Children. *Annual Reports.*
Chicago Manual Training School. "Fifth Annual Catalog." Chicago, 1887–1888.
———. "Souvenir." Chicago, 1893.
Chicago Nursery and Half Orphan Asylum. *Annual Reports.*
———. MSS. Chapin Hall Collection. Chicago Historical Society.
Chicago Orphan Asylum. *Annual Reports.*
Chicago Public School Art Society. *Annual Reports.*
Chicago Reform School. *Annual Reports.*
Chicago Relief and Aid Society. *Annual Reports.*
———. MSS. Archives. Chicago Historical Society.
———. *Report of the Chicago Relief and Aid Society of the Disbursement of Contributions for the Sufferers by the Chicago Fire.* Chicago, 1874.
Chicago Relief Society. "Constitution and Directory of the Chicago Relief Society." Chicago, 1851.
Chicago Society of Decorative Art. *Annual Reports.*
———. MSS. Archives. Chicago Historical Society.
———. Miscellaneous pamphlets. Chicago Historical Society.
———. Scrapbook. Chicago Historical Society.
Chicago Society of the Home for Aged and Indigent Females. "Constitution and By-Laws." Chicago, 1862.
Chicago Woman's Club. Board Minutes, 1876–91. Archives. Chicago Historical Society.
———. "Columbian Souvenir Edition." Chicago, 1893.
*Child in the City: A Handbook of the Child Welfare Exhibit.* Chicago: Chicago School of Civics and Philanthropy, 1911.
Child Welfare Exhibit. *Handbook.* Chicago, 1911.
Citizen's Association of Chicago. "Report of the Committee on Education." Chicago, 1881.
City of Chicago. Assessment Roll for Real Estate in North Division, 1850. Archives. Chicago Historical Society.
———. Assessment Roll for Real Estate in South Division, 1850. Archives. Chicago Historical Society.
———. Assessment Roll for Real Estate in West Division, 1849. Archives. Chicago Historical Society.
———. Real Estate Assessment List, 1899. Municipal Reference Library. Chicago.
Civic Music Association. Financial Statement for Year Ending May 4, 1915.

Colbert, Elias, and Chamberlin, Everett. *Chicago and the Great Conflagration.* New York: C. F. Vent, 1871.
Community Trust (Chicago). MSS. Archives. Chicago Historical Society.
Crane, Richard Teller. *The Autobiography of Richard Teller Crane.* Chicago: Crane Co., 1927.
———. *The Utility of All Kinds of Higher Schooling.* Chicago: Privately printed, 1909.
De Tocqueville, Alexis. *Democracy in America.* Translated by Henry Reeve. 1st rev. ed. New York: Colonial Press, 1889.
Devine, Edward T. *The Family and Social Work.* New York: Association Press Inc., 1912.
Donnelly, Ignatius. *Caesar's Column: A Story of the Twentieth Century.* Cambridge: Harvard University Press, Belknap Press, 1960. Originally published 1890.
Elizabeth McCormick Memorial Fund. MSS. Archives. University of Illinois at Chicago Circle.
Emerson, Ralph Waldo. *Essays and English Traits.* New York: P. F. Collier & Sons Corp., 1937.
———. "Self Reliance." In *The Literature of the United States,* pt. I:400–17. Edited by Walter Blair. Glenview, Ill.: Scott, Foresman & Co., 1969.
Erring Woman's Refuge of Chicago. *Annual Reports.* (Later renamed the Chicago Home for Girls.)
Everts, W. W. *Christian Womanhood: Life of Mrs. M. K. Everts.* Chicago: Church & Goodman, 1867.
"Failure of Philanthropy." *Living Age* 209 (April 25, 1896): 230–36.
Ferry, Abbe Farwell. *Reminiscences of John V. Farwell by His Elder Daughter.* 2 vols. Chicago: Ralph Fletcher Seymour, 1928.
Field, Marshall. *Elements of Success.* Chicago: Lakeside Press, 1896.
Field Museum of Natural History. *Annual Reports.*
Fitzgerald, F. Scott. *The Great Gatsby.* New York: Charles Scribner's Sons, 1925.
Flexner, Abraham. *Abraham Flexner: An Autobiography.* Rev. ed. New York: Simon & Schuster, 1960.
Flower, Mrs. J. N. "The Illinois Training School for Nurses." *Reporter of Organized Charity* (November 1887), p. 54.
———. Scrapbooks. Archives. Chicago Historical Society.
Folks, Homer. *The Care of Destitute, Neglected and Delinquent Children.* New York: Macmillan Co., 1907.
———. "Prevention Succeeds." Presidential Address, National Conference of Social Work. *Proceedings of the Fiftieth Annual Session.* Washington, D.C., 1923. Pp. 3–9.
*The Foolish Age.* Hunt Stromberg Production, 1921.
Frank, Harriette Greenbaum, and Jerome, Amalie Hofer. *Annals of the Chicago Woman's Club, 1876–1916.* Chicago: Chicago Woman's Club, 1916.
Fuller, Henry Blake. *With the Procession.* New York: Harper & Bros., 1895.
Fulmer, Harriet. "The Work of the District or Visiting Nurse." National Conference of Charities and Correction. *Proceedings of the Twenty-ninth Annual Session.* Detroit, 1902. Pp. 200–212.
Gates, Frederic Taylor. *Chapters in My Life.* New York: Free Press, 1977.
"Gentle Art of Giving." *Current Literature* 34 (February 1903): 131.
Gladden, Washington. "Christianity and Wealth." *Century* 6 (188): 903–11.
———. "Tainted Money." *Outlook* 52 (November 30, 1895): 866–67.

*Godey's Lady's Book.* 1840–75.
Goodspeed, Thomas Wakefield. *A History of the University of Chicago: The First Quarter-Century.* Chicago: University of Chicago Press, 1972. Originally published 1916.
———. *The University of Chicago Biographical Sketches.* 2 vols. Chicago: University of Chicago Press, 1925.
Gregory, Addie Hibbard. *Reminiscences of Lydia Beekman Hibbard, by Her Eldest Daughter.* Chicago: Privately printed, 1929.
Hall, Bolton. "Giving and Getting." *Forum* 42 (November 1909): 453–60.
Ham, Charles H. "Manual Training." *Harper's Magazine* 72 (February 1886): 404–12.
———. *Manual Training: The Solution of Social and Industrial Problems.* New York: Harper & Bros., 1886.
Harpel, Charles, comp. Scrapbooks. Chicago Historical Society.
Harris, Martha Emmaline. *Norman Wait Harris: A Tribute of Love by His Sister.* San Francisco: Privately printed, n.d.
Hart, Hastings. *Preventive Treatment of Neglected Children.* New York: Russell Sage Foundation, 1910.
Henderson, Charles R. "Public Outdoor Relief." National Conference of Charities and Correction. *Proceedings of the Eighteenth Annual Session.* Indianapolis, 1891.
———. *The Social Spirit in America.* New York: Chatauqua Century Press, 1897.
Henshaw, Mrs. Sarah Edwards. *Our Branch and Its Tributaries: Being a History of the Work of the Northwestern Sanitary Commission and Its Auxiliaries During the War of Rebellion.* Chicago: Alfred A. Sewell, 1868.
Herrick, Allan. *You Don't Have to Be Rich.* New York: D. Appleton-Century Co., 1940.
Higinbotham, Harlow N. *The Making of a Merchant.* Chicago: Forbes & Co., 1906.
Hirsch, Emil G. "The Place of the Individual in Organized Charity." *First National Conference of Jewish Charities.* Chicago, 1900. Pp. 145–65.
*Hoge, Jane C.: In Memoriam.* Privately printed, 1890.
Hull-House. Minutes, 1889–1919, and Account Books, 1893–1915. Archives. Hull-House.
Hunt, Freeman. *Lives of American Merchants.* Vol. 1. New York: Hunt's Merchants' Magazine, 1856.
———. *Worth and Wealth: A Collection of Maxims, Morals, and Miscellanies for Merchants and Men of Business.* New York: Stringer & Townsend, 1856.
Hutchinson, Charles L. MSS. Archives. Newberry Library.
———. "Chicago as an Art Center." *World To-Day* 13 (September 1907): 912–14.
Hyde, James Nevins. *Early Medical Chicago.* Chicago: Fergus Printing Co., 1879.
Ickes, Harold L. *The Autobiography of a Curmudgeon.* Chicago: Quadrangle Paperbacks, 1943.
Illinois General Assembly. Joint Committee on Home-Finding Societies. *Report.* Springfield, 1915.
Illinois Training School for Nurses. *Annual Reports.*
———. MSS. Archives. Chicago Historical Society.
———. Scrapbook. Chicago Historical Society.
———. "Woman Physicians and Training Schools for Nurses in Illinois." Chicago, 1893.
Infant Welfare Society. *Annual Reports.*
———. "Hold the Home Lines." Chicago, 1918.

———. MSS. Archives. Chicago Historical Society.
Ingraham, Mrs. Sarah R. *Walks of Usefulness, or Reminiscences of Mrs. Margaret Prior.* New York: American Female Moral Reform Society, 1844.
Insull, Samuel. "Civic Leadership Development and Responsibility." St. Louis: Privately printed, 1927.
Jefferson, Thomas. *Papers.* Edited by Julia Boyd. Princeton: Princeton University Press, 1950.
Johnson, W. Alexander. *Adventures in Social Welfare Being Reminiscences of Things, Thoughts and Folks during Forty Years of Social Work.* Fort Wayne, 1923.
———. "Methods and Machinery of the Organization of Charity." Chicago: Charity Organization Society, 1887.
"The Justification of Wealth." *Nation* 70 (January 25, 1900): 66.
Kelley, Florence. "Socialism and Charity." *Charities* 18 (July 6, 1907): 394–98.
King, Clarence. *Social Agency Boards and How to Make Them Effective.* New York: Harper & Bros., 1938.
Kingsley, Sherman C. "Program for the Promotion of Physical Welfare of Children and the Prevention of Tuberculosis Among Them." Chicago: American Medical Association, 1915.
———. "The Substitution of Family Care for Instructional Care for Children." *Charities* 10 (April 18, 1903): 387–92.
Lewis, Allen C. Will and Codicil. Chicago Historical Society.
Livermore, Mary A. *The Story of My Life.* Hartford, Conn.: A. D. Worthington & Co., 1899.
———. *My Story of the War.* Hartford, Conn.: A. D. Worthington & Co., 1889.
Loomis, Frank D. "History of the Coordination of Charities in Chicago." Typescript MSS. Chicago Historical Society.
Lowell, Josephine Shaw. "The True Aim of Charity Organization Societies." *Forum* 21 (June 1896): 494–500.
———. *Public Relief and Private Charity.* New York: G. P. Putnam's Sons, 1884.
Lunt, Cornelia. *Sketches of Childhood and Girlhood: Chicago, 1847–1864.* Evanston: Privately printed, 1925.
McCagg, Ezra B. "The Charities of Chicago." *Proceedings of the Sixth Annual Conference of Charities.* Chicago, 1879. Pp. 145–52.
McCormick, Cyrus H., Jr. MSS. Archives. State Historical Society of Wisconsin, Madison.
McCormick, Harold. MSS. Archives. Chicago Historical Society.
McCormick, Harriet Hammond. MSS. Archives. State Historical Society of Wisconsin, Madison.
McCormick, Nettie Fowler. MSS. Archives. State Historical Society of Wisconsin, Madison.
Macrae, David. *The Americans at Home: Pen-and-Ink Sketches of American Men, Manners, and Institutions.* Edinburgh: Edmonston & Douglas, 1870.
McGuffey, William H. *McGuffey's New Fifth Eclectic Reader.* New York: Wilson Hinkle & Co., 1857.
Martineau, Harriet. *Society in America.* 3 vols. New York: Saunders & Otley, 1837.
Mason, Amelia Gere. *Memories of a Friend.* Chicago: Laurence C. Woodworth, 1918.
Meeker, Arthur. *Chicago, with Love.* New York: Alfred A. Knopf, 1955.
Memorial Institute for Infectious Diseases. *Brief History and Description.* Chicago, 1915.

Merrill, Marie Georgetta. *The History of St. Luke's Hospital School of Nursing.* Privately printed, n.d.

Mitchell, Lucy Sprague. *Two Lives: The Story of Wesley Clair Mitchell and Myself.* New York: Simon & Schuster, 1953.

Monroe, Lucy B. "Art in Chicago." *New England Magazine*, n.s. 6 (June 1892), pp. 411–32.

National Association of Social Workers, Chicago Chapter. MSS. Archives. Chicago Historical Society.

New York Association for the Improvement of the Condition of the Poor. *Annual Reports.*

Nightingale, Florence. *Notes on Nursing: What It Is and What It Is Not.* London: Harrison & Sons, 1860.

North, Franklin H. "A New Profession for Women." *Century Magazine* 25, n.s. 3 (November 1882): 41.

Oakley, Horace S. MSS. Archives. Newberry Library.

Ogden, William Butler. MSS. Archives. Chicago Historical Society.

Old Ladies' Home (Chicago). *Annual Reports.* (Later renamed Old People's Home.)

Otis, Philo Adams. *The Chicago Symphony Orchestra: Organization, Growth and Development, 1891–1924.* Chicago: Faulkner-Ryan Co., 1924.

Overstreet, H. A. "A Quarter-Century of Psychology." *Century Magazine* 113 (March 1927): 526–35.

Palmer, Bertha Honoré. MSS. Archives, Chicago Historical Society.

Patterson, Charles Brodie. "Organized Charity." *Arena* 25 (March 1901): 281–86.

Peabody, Francis G. "How Should a City Care for Its Poor?" *Forum* 14 (December 1892): 474–91.

Peebles, James C. "A History of the Armour Institute of Technology, 1896–1940." Typescript MSS. Chicago Historical Society.

Poole, Ernest. "Art and Democracy: How the Chicago Art Institute Reaches the People." *Outlook* 85 (March 23, 1907): 665–74.

Presbyterian Hospital. *Annual Reports.*

*Prince of Pep.* Carlos Productions, 1925.

Pritchett, Henry S. "Gifts of Millionaires." *Outlook* 73 (January 31, 1903): 269–71.

*Proceedings of the Conference on the Care of Dependent Children.* Washington, D.C.: Government Printing Office, 1909.

Public Laws of the State of Illinois Passed at the Twenty-second Session of the General Assembly. "An Act to Protect Married Women in Their Separate Property." Chicago: D. B. Cooke & Co., 1861. P. 140.

Pullman, George. MSS. Archives. Chicago Historical Society.

Pullman, Harriet. "Scrapbook Dealing with the Pullman Family." Vol. 1. Chicago Historical Society.

Putnam, Marian C. "Friendly Visiting." National Conference of Charities and Correction. *Proceedings of the Fourteenth Annual Session.* Boston, 1887.

Reeder, R. R. "Institutionalism." *Charities* 11 (July 4, 1903): 7–8.

Reynolds, Laura Houghteling. "Reminiscences of the War of the Rebellion." Typescript MS (1890). Chicago Historical Society.

"Richard Teller Crane: A Real Friend of Education." *Value World* 8 (April 1912): 21.

Ridpath, John Clark. "The Cry of the Poor." *Arena* 18 (September 1897): 407–18.

Rosenwald, Julius. "The Burden of Wealth." *Saturday Evening Post* 201 (January 5, 1929): 12–17.

———. "Charity." *Harper's Weekly* 60 (May 29, 1915): 522.
———. "Principles of Public Giving." *Atlantic Monthly* 143 (May 1929): 559–606.
———. MSS. Archives. University of Chicago.
Ross, Edward Allsworth. "Philanthropy with Strings." *Atlantic Monthly* 114 (September 1914): 289–94.
Ryerson, Edward L. *A Businessman's Concept of Citizenship.* Privately printed, 1960.
St. Luke's Hospital (Chicago). *Annual Reports.*
Scammon, J. Y. "Address Delivered at the Chicago Historical Society, November 19, 1868." Chicago: Fergus Printing Co., 1877.
———. MSS. Archives. University of Chicago.
Scudder, Vida D. "Ill-Gotten Gifts to Colleges." *Atlantic Monthly* 86 (November 1900): 675–79.
Smith, Henry Justin. "Chicago: Her Plans and Growing Pains." *Century Magazine* 113 (March 1927): 607–12.
Snowden, Clifford L. "The Armour Institute of Technology." *New England Magazine,* n.s. 16 (May 1897), pp. 354–72.
Stead, William T. *If Christ Came to Chicago!* Chicago: Laird & Lee, 1894.
Stevenson, Mrs. Cornelius. "The Training of Curators." American Association of Museums. *Proceedings* 3 (1909): 115–19.
Sumner, William Graham. *What Social Classes Owe to Each Other.* New York: Harper & Bros., 1883.
Swift, Harold. MSS. Archives. University of Chicago.
"Tainted Money." *Independent* 58 (April 6, 1905): 789–90.
Tassin, Algernon. "The Craftsmanship of Begging Letter Writing." *Bookman* 36 (November–December 1912): 246–54.
Taylor, Graham. "Shall the Dollar's Pedigree Defeat Its Destiny?" *American Review of Reviews* 32 (October 1905): 471–72.
———. MSS. Archives. Newberry Library.
Trusdell, Rev. Charles G. "The History of Public and Private Outdoor Relief." National Conference of Charities and Correction. *Proceedings of the Twentieth Annual Session.* Chicago, 1893.
———. "Organized Charities." National Conference of Charities and Correction. *Proceedings of the Twelfth Annual Session.* Washington, D.C., 1885. Pp. 329–35.
Tuthill, Mrs. Louisa C. *The Young Lady's Home.* New Haven: S. Babcock, 1839.
United Charities. *Annual Reports.*
United Charities. *Sixty-six Years of Service.* Chicago: United Charities of Chicago, 1923.
———. MSS. Chicago Historical Society.
University of Chicago. Presidents' Reports. Archives. University of Chicago.
———. *Presidents' Reports.*
Visiting Nurse Association. MSS. Archives. Chicago Historical Society.
———. *Annual Reports.*
Vrooman, Rev. Harry C. "Charity, Old and New." *Arena* 11 (January 1895): 274–88.
Welfare Council of Metropolitan Chicago. MSS. Archives. Chicago Historical Society.
Welsh, William, ed. *Women Helpers in the Church: Their Sayings and Doings.* Philadelphia: J. B. Lippincott & Co., 1872.
Wheeler, Mrs. Charles Gilbert. *Annals of the Chicago Orphan Asylum from 1849 to 1892.* Chicago: Chicago Orphan Asylum, 1892.

Williams, Edward F. *The Life of Dr. D. K. Pearsons: Friend of the Small College and of Missions.* Chicago: Pilgrim Press, 1911.
Wisner, Benjamin B. *Memoirs of the Late Mrs. Susan Huntington.* Boston: Crocker & Brewster, 1826.
Woman's Medical School, Northwestern University. *The Institution and its Founders.* Chicago: H. G. Cutler, 1896.
*The Wrongdoers.* Astor Pictures, 1925.
Young, Alexander. *The Beneficient Woman: A Discourse Occasioned by the Death of Mrs. Catharine G. Prescott.* Boston: John Wilson & Son, 1852.
Young Men's Association. *Annual Reports.*
Young Men's Christian Association of Chicago. *Annual Reports.*
Zorbaugh, Harvey W. *The Gold Coast and the Slum: A Sociological Study of Chicago's Near North Side.* Chicago: University of Chicago Press, 1929.

## Theses and Dissertations

Coonley, Marjorie Helen. "Private Relief Societies in Chicago, 1871 to 1910." Master's thesis, University of Chicago, 1921.
Crawley, Charolette Ashby. "Dependent Negro Children in Chicago in 1926." Master's thesis, University of Chicago, 1927.
Davis, Mamie Ruth. "A History of Policies and Methods of Social Work in the Chicago Orphan Asylum." Master's thesis, University of Chicago, 1927.
Frankle, Barbara Stein. "The Genteel Family: High Victorian Conceptions of Domesticity and Good Behavior." Ph.D. dissertation, University of Wisconsin, 1967.
Glick, Clarence Elmer. "Winnetka: A Study of a Residential Suburban Community." Master's thesis, University of Chicago, 1928.
Goldstein, Leslie S. "Art in Chicago and the World's Columbian Exposition of 1893." Master's thesis, University of Iowa, 1970.
Haseltine, Helen Denton. "A History of the Chicago Home for Girls, Founded in 1863 as the Chicago Erring Woman's Refuge for Reform." Master's thesis, University of Chicago, 1934.
Hillman, William Arthur. "Urbanization and the Organization of Welfare Activities in the Metropolitan Community of Chicago." Ph.D. dissertation, University of Chicago, 1940.
Lyon, Helen Faye. "The History of Public Health Nursing in Chicago, 1883–1920." Master's thesis, University of Chicago, 1947.
Sayre, Ruth Ann. "A Study of the Changes in Structure and Function of the Board of Managers of the Chicago Home for the Friendless, 1858–1933." Master's thesis, University of Chicago, 1945.
Smith, James Howell. "Honorable Beggars: The Middlemen of American Philanthropy." Ph.D. dissertation, University of Wisconsin, 1968.
Smith, Marion Barnett. "History of the Chicago Home for the Friendless." Master's thesis, University of Chicago, 1930.
Stuckey, James Harold. "The Philanthropy of Cyrus Hall McCormick, II." Master's thesis, University of Wisconsin, 1955.
White, William Bruce. "The Philanthropies of Anita McCormick Blaine." Master's thesis, University of Wisconsin, 1959.
Whitridge, Eugenia Romelin. "Art in Chicago: The Structure of the Art World in a Metropolitan Community." Ph.D. dissertation, University of Chicago, 1946.

## Secondary Sources

Alexander, John K. "The City of Brotherly Fear: The Poor in Late-Eighteenth-Century Philadelphia." In *Cities in American History*, pp. 79–97. Edited by Kenneth T. Jackson and Stanley K. Schultz. New York: Alfred A. Knopf, 1972.

Andrews, Wayne. *Battle for Chicago*. New York: Harcourt, Brace & Co., 1946.

Angle, Paul M. *The Great Chicago Fire*. Chicago: Chicago Historical Society, 1971.

Arey, Leslie B. *Northwestern University Medical School, 1859–1959: A Pioneer in Educational Reform*. Evanston: Northwestern University, 1959.

Baltzell, E. Digby. *Philadelphia Gentlemen: The Making of a National Upper Class*. Glencoe, Ill.: Free Press, 1958.

Beadle, Muriel. *The Fortnightly of Chicago: The City and Its Women, 1873–1973*. Chicago: Henry Regnery Co., 1973.

Bennett, Charles A. *History of Manual and Industrial Education up to 1870*. Peoria: Manual Arts Press, 1926.

———. *History of Manual and Industrial Education, 1870 to 1917*. Peoria: Manual Arts Press, 1937.

Benson, Susan Porter. "Business Heads and Sympathizing Hearts: The Women of the Providence Employment Society." *Journal of Social History* 11 (Fall 1978): 302–13.

Berg, Barbara J. *The Remembered Gate: Origins of American Feminism: The Woman and the City, 1800–1860*. New York: Oxford University Press, 1978.

Birnbaum, Lucille C. "Behaviorism in the 1920's." *American Quarterly* 7 (Spring 1955): 15–30.

Bode, Carl. *The American Lyceum: Town Meeting of the Mind*. Carbondale: Southern Illinois University Press, 1956.

Bode, Carl, ed. *Midcentury America: Life in the 1850s*. Carbondale: Southern Illinois University Press, 1972.

Bonner, Thomas N. *Medicine in Chicago, 1850–1950: A Chapter in the Social and Scientific Development of a City*. Madison: American History Research Center, 1957.

Bremner, Robert H. *American Philanthropy*. Chicago: University of Chicago Press, 1960.

———. *From the Depths: The Discovery of Poverty in the United States*. New York: New York University Press, 1956.

Brown, James. *The History of Public Assistance in Chicago, 1833 to 1893*. Chicago: University of Chicago Press, 1941.

Bruce, Robert V. *1877: Year of Violence*. Chicago: Quadrangle Paperbacks, 1970.

Buder, Stanley. *Pullman: An Experiment in Industrial Order and Community Planning, 1880–1930*. New York: Oxford University Press, 1967.

Burgess, Charles O. *Nettie Fowler McCormick: Profile of An American Philanthropist*. Madison: State Historical Society of Wisconsin, 1962.

Burrow, James G. *AMA: Voice of American Medicine*. Baltimore: Johns Hopkins Press, 1963.

Calhoun, Daniel H. *Professional Lives in America: Structure and Aspiration, 1750–1850*. Cambridge: Harvard University Press, 1965.

Chandler, Alfred D., Jr. *Strategy and Structure: Chapters in the History of Industrial Enterprise*. Cambridge: MIT Press, 1962.

Chapin Hall: *One Hundred Years of Devotion to Children*. Chicago: Chapin Hall, 1960.

Clark, Herma. *The Elegant Eighties: When Chicago Was Young*. Chicago: A. C. McClurg & Co., 1941.

Coleman, Laurence Vail. *The Museum in America: A Critical Study*. Washington, D.C.: American Association of Museums, 1939.
Cott, Nancy F. *The Bonds of Womanhood: "Woman's Sphere" in New England, 1780–1835*. New Haven: Yale University Press, 1977.
Cutlip, Scott M. *Fund Raising in the United States: Its Role in America's Philanthropy*. New Brunswick, N.J.: Rutgers University Press, 1965.
Davies, Wallace Evan. *Patriotism on Parade: The Story of Veterans' and Hereditary Organizations in America, 1783–1900*. Cambridge: Harvard University Press, 1955.
Davis, Allen F. *American Heroine: The Life and Legend of Jane Addams*. New York: Oxford University Press, 1973.
———. *Spearheads for Reform: The Social Settlements and the Progressive Movement, 1890–1914*. New York: Oxford University Press, 1967.
Dennis, Charles H. *Victor Lawson: His Time and His Work*. Chicago: University of Chicago Press, 1935.
Diamond, Sigmund. *The Reputation of the American Businessman*. Cambridge: Harvard University Press, 1955.
*Dictionary of American Biography*. Edited by Allen Johnson and Dumas Malone. New York: Charles Scribner's Sons, 1929.
Ditzion, Sidney. *Arsenals of a Democratic Culture: A Social History of the American Public Library Movement in New England and the Middle States from 1850 to 1900*. Chicago: American Library Association, 1947.
Dock, Lavinia L., and Stewart, Isabel Maitland. *A Short History of Nursing from the Earliest Times to the Present Day*. New York: G. P. Putnam's Sons, 1920.
Douglas, Ann. *The Feminization of American Culture*. New York: Alfred A. Knopf, 1977.
Douglas, Paul H. *American Apprenticeship and Industrial Education*. New York: Columbia University Press, 1921.
Duis, Perry. *Chicago, Creating New Traditions*. Chicago: Chicago Historical Society, 1976.
Dulles, Foster Rhea. *The American Red Cross*. New York: Harper & Bros., 1950.
Earhart, Mary. *Frances Willard: From Prayers to Politics*. Chicago: University of Chicago Press, 1944.
Embree, Edwin R., and Waxman, Julia. *Investment in People: The Story of the Julius Rosenwald Fund*. New York: Harper & Row, 1949.
Ewen, Stuart. *Captains of Consciousness: Advertising and the Social Roots of Consumer Culture*. New York: McGraw-Hill Book Co., 1976.
Farrell, John C. *Beloved Lady: A History of Jane Addams' Ideas on Reform and Peace*. Baltimore: Johns Hopkins Press, 1967.
Fletcher, Robert Samuel. *A History of Oberlin College from Its Foundation through the Civil War*. Vol. 1. Oberlin, Ohio: Oberlin College, 1943.
Fox, Daniel M. *Engines of Culture: Philanthropy and Art Museums*. Madison: State Historical Society of Wisconsin, 1963.
Fredrickson, George M. *The Inner Civil War: Northern Intellectuals and the Crisis of the Union*. New York: Harper & Row, 1965.
Ginger, Ray. *Altgeld's America: The Lincoln Ideal versus Changing Realities*. Chicago: Quadrangle Paperbacks, 1958.
Goffman, Erving. "The Nature of Deference and Demeanor." *American Anthropologist* 58 (1956): 473–502.
Goodman, Paul. "Ethics and Enterprise: The Values of a Boston Elite, 1800–1860."

*American Quarterly* 18 (Fall 1966): 437–51.

Griffin, Clifford S. *Their Brothers' Keepers: Moral Stewardship in the United States, 1800–1865.* New York: H. Wolff, 1960.

Harrington, Michael. *The Other America: Poverty in the United States.* New York: Macmillan Co., 1962.

Harris, Neil. *The Artist in American Society: The Formative Years, 1790–1860.* New York: Simon & Schuster, 1966.

———. "Four Stages of Cultural Growth: The American City." *Indiana Historical Society Lectures, 1971–1972.* Indianapolis: Indiana Historical Society, 1972.

Harrison, Gilbert. *A Timeless Affair: The Life of Anita McCormick Blaine.* Chicago: University of Chicago Press, 1979.

Hayden, Dolores. *The Grand Domestic Revolution: A History of Feminist Designs for American Homes, Neighborhoods, and Cities.* Cambridge, Mass.: MIT Press, 1981.

Hess, Robert D., and Handel, Gerald. *Family Worlds: A Psychological Approach to Family Life.* Chicago: University of Chicago Press, 1959.

Hirsch, Edwin F. *Frank Billings.* Chicago: Edwin F. Hirsch, 1966.

Holli, Melvin G., and Jones, Peter D'A. *The Ethnic Frontier: Essays on the History of Group Survival in Chicago and the Midwest.* Grand Rapids, Mich.: William B. Eerdmans Publishing Co., 1977.

Horowitz, Helen Lefkowitz. *Culture and the City: Cultural Philanthropy in Chicago from the 1880s to 1917.* Lexington: University of Kentucky Press, 1976.

Huggins, Nathan I. *Protestants against Poverty: Boston's Charities, 1870–1900.* Westport, Conn.: Greenwood Publishing Co., 1971.

Irons, Ernest E. *The Presbyterian Hospital of the City of Chicago: Sixtieth Anniversary, 1883–1943.* Chicago: Presbyterian Hospital, 1943.

John Crerar Library. *The John Crerar Library, 1895–1944: An Historical Report.* Chicago: Board of Directors of the John Crerar Library, 1945.

Jones, John Finbar, and Herick, John. *Citizens in Service: Volunteers in Social Welfare During the Depression, 1924–1941.* East Lansing: Michigan State University Press, 1976.

Jordan, Wilbur K. *Philanthropy in England, 1480–1660: A Study of the Changing Pattern of English Social Aspirations.* London: George Allen & Unwin, Ltd., 1959.

Karl, Barry D. "Philanthropy, Policy-Planning, and the Bureaucratization of the Democratic Ideal." *Daedalus* 105, no. 4 (Fall 1976): 129–49.

Kennedy, David M. *Birth Control in America.* New Haven: Yale University Press, 1970.

Kett, Joseph. *The Formation of the American Medical Profession: The Role of Institutions, 1780–1860.* New Haven: Yale University Press, 1968.

Kusmer, Kenneth L. "The Functions of Organized Charity in the Progressive Era: Chicago as a Case Study." *Journal of American History* 60 (December 1973): 657–78.

Lasch, Christopher, ed. *The Social Thought of Jane Addams.* Indianapolis: Bobbs-Merrill Co., 1965.

Leech, Harper, and Carroll, John Charles. *Armour and His Times.* New York: D. Appleton-Century Co., 1938.

Lerner, Gerda. "The Lady and the Mill Girl: Changes in the Status of Women in the Age of Jackson." *Midcontinent American Studies Journal* 10 (Spring 1969): 5–15.

Lindsey, Almont. *The Pullman Strike.* Chicago: University of Chicago Press, 1942.

Linn, James Weber. *Jane Addams: A Biography.* New York: D. Appleton-Century Co., 1935.

Lockwood, Frank C. *The Life of Edward E. Ayer.* Chicago: A. C. McClurg & Co., 1929.

Lubove, Roy. *The Professional Altruist: The Emergence of Social Work as a Career, 1880–1930.* Cambridge: Harvard University Press, 1965.

———. *The Struggle for Social Security, 1900–1935.* Cambridge: Harvard University Press, 1968.

Lynes, Russell. *The Tastemakers.* New York: Harper & Bros., 1949.

McCallig, Patrick, and Solomon, Ramon. "A History of Michael Reese Hospital and Medical Center." Unpublished MS. Michael Reese Hospital.

McCausland, Clare L. *Children of Circumstance: A History of the First 125 Years (1849–1974) of the Chicago Child Care Society.* Chicago: R. R. Donnelley & Sons, 1976.

Mandelbaum, Seymour J. *Boss Tweed's New York.* New York: John Wiley & Sons, 1965.

Melder, Keith. *Beginnings of Sisterhood: The American Women's Rights Movement, 1800–1850.* New York: Schocken Books, 1977.

Miller, Howard S. *Dollars for Research: Science and Its Patrons in Nineteenth-Century America.* Seattle: University of Washington Press, 1970.

Miller, Perry. *The Life of the Mind in America.* New York: Harcourt, Brace & World, 1965.

Mohl, Raymond A. *Poverty in New York, 1783–1825.* New York: Oxford University Press, 1971.

Morgan, Edmund. *American Slavery, American Freedom: The Ordeal of Colonial Virginia.* New York: W. W. Norton & Co., 1975.

Naylor, Timothy J. "Responding to the Fire: The Work of the Chicago Relief and Aid Society." *Science and Society* 39, no. 4 (1975–1976): 450–64.

Nelson, Otto M. "The Chicago Relief and Aid Society, 1850–1874." *Journal of the Illinois State Historical Society* 59 (1966): 48–66.

Northrup, Flora L. *The Record of a Century, 1834–1934.* New York: American Female Guardian Society and Home for the Friendless, 1934.

O'Neill, William L. *Everyone Was Brave: A History of Feminism in America.* Chicago: Quadrangle Books, 1971.

Parker, Gail, ed. *The Oven Birds: American Women on Womanhood, 1820–1920.* New York: Doubleday & Co., 1972.

Pessen, Edward. *Riches, Class and Power before the Civil War.* Toronto: D. C. Heath & Co., 1973.

Pickett, Robert S. *House of Refuge: Origins of Juvenile Reform in New York State, 1815–1857.* Syracuse: Syracuse University Press, 1969.

Pierce, Bessie Louise. *A History of Chicago.* 3 vols. New York: Alfred A. Knopf, 1937–1957.

———. *As Others See Chicago: Impressions of Visitors, 1673–1933.* Chicago: University of Chicago Press, 1933.

Pocock, J. G. A. "Machiavelli, Harrington, and English Political Ideologies in the Eighteenth Century." *William and Mary Quarterly* 23, no. 4 (October 1965): 549–83.

Pred, Allan R. *Urban Growth and the Circulation of Information: The United States System of Cities, 1790–1840.* Cambridge: Harvard University Press, 1973.

Roberts, Mary M. *American Nursing: History and Interpretation.* New York: Macmillan Co., 1954.

Ross, Ishbel. *Silhouette in Diamonds: The Life of Mrs. Potter Palmer.* New York: Harper & Bros., 1960.
Rothman, David J. *The Discovery of the Asylum: Social Order and Disorder in the New Republic.* Boston: Little, Brown & Co., 1971.
Schlossman, Steven L. *Love and the American Delinquent: The Theory and Practice of "Progressive" Juvenile Justice, 1825–1920.* Chicago: University of Chicago Press, 1977.
Scott, Donald M. *From Office to Profession: The New England Ministry, 1750–1850.* Philadelphia: University of Pennsylvania Press, 1978.
Shryock, Richard H. *The Development of Modern Medicine: An Interpretation of the Social and Scientific Factors Involved.* Philadelphia: University of Pennsylvania Press, 1936.
———. "A Medical Perspective on the Civil War." *American Quarterly* 14 (Summer 1962): 161–72.
———. *Medicine and Society in America, 1660–1860.* New York: New York University Press, 1960.
Shryver, Grace Fay. *A History of the Illinois Training School for Nurses, 1880–1929.* Chicago: Board of Directors of the Illinois Training School for Nurses, 1930.
Sklar, Kathryn Kish. *Catharine Beecher: A Study in American Domesticity.* New Haven: Yale University Press, 1973.
Smith, Timothy L. *Revivalism and Social Reform in Mid-Nineteenth-Century America.* New York: Abingdon Press, 1957.
Smith-Rosenberg, Carroll. "Beauty, the Beast, and the Militant Woman: A Case Study in Sex Roles and Social Stress in Jacksonian America." *American Quarterly* 23 (1971): 562–84.
———. *Religion and the Rise of the American City: The New York Mission Movement, 1812–1870.* Ithaca: Cornell University Press, 1971.
Smuts, Robert W. *Women and Work in America.* New York: Schocken Books, 1971.
Taylor, George Rogers. *The Transportation Revolution: 1815–1860.* New York: Harper & Row, 1951.
Trattner, Walter I. *From Poor Law to Welfare State: A History of Social Welfare in America.* New York: Free Press, 1974.
Wade, Louise C. *Graham Taylor: Pioneer for Social Justice, 1851–1938.* Chicago: University of Chicago Press, 1964.
Wade, Richard C. *The Urban Frontier: Pioneer Life in Early Pittsburgh, Cincinnati, Lexington, Louisville, and St. Louis.* Chicago: University of Chicago Press, 1959.
Wall, Joseph Frazier. *Andrew Carnegie.* New York: Oxford University Press, 1970.
Warner, Sam Bass, Jr. *The Private City: Philadelphia in Three Periods of Its Growth.* Philadelphia: University of Pennsylvania Press, 1968.
Warner, W. Lloyd; Low, J. O.; Lunt, Paul S.; and Srole, Leo. *Yankee City.* New Haven: Yale University Press, 1963.
Watson, Frank D. *The Charity Organization Movement in the United States: A Study in American Philanthropy.* New York: Macmillan Co., 1922.
Welter, Barbara. "The Feminization of American Religion." In *Clio's Consciousness Raised: New Perspectives on the History of Women,* pp. 137–57. Edited by Mary S. Hartman and Lois Banner. New York: Harper & Row, 1974.
Werner, M. R. *Julius Rosenwald: The Life of a Practical Humanitarian.* New York: Harper & Row, 1939.

Whitaker, Ben. *The Foundations: An Anatomy of Philanthropy and Society.* London: Eyre Methuen, 1974.

Wilenski, Harold L., and Lebeaux, Charles N. *Industrial Society and Social Welfare.* New York: Russell Sage Foundation, 1958.

Williamson, William Landram. *William Frederick Poole and the Modern Library Movement.* New York: Columbia University Press, 1963.

Wilson, Howard E. *Mary McDowell, Neighbor.* Chicago: University of Chicago Press, 1928.

Wood, Ann Douglas. "The War Within a War: Women Nurses in the Union Army." *Civil War History* 18, no. 3 (September 1972): 197–212.

Wyllie, Irvin G. *The Self-Made Man in America: The Myth of Rags to Riches.* Glencoe, Ill.: Free Press, 1954.

# INDEX